I have something to say

say

Thoughts along the way

Volume 4

Paul W. Murphey (signature)

Paul W. Murphey

Create Space

2017

I Have Something to Say

ISBN 13: 978-1545209318

ISBN 10: 1545209316

Create Space, North Charleston, SC

© Paul W. Murphey, 2017

Since this was first published I have made minor stylistic, formatting, and typographical corrections. No substantive changes were made with one exception: I removed "Old Language in a New Age". It is therefore a reissue rather than a revised edition. (October 2017)

Table of Contents

Preface to the series: *Thoughts along the way*   v

Introduction to the series: *Thoughts along the way*   ix

Preface to *I have something to say*   xi

Introduction to *I have something to say*   xiii

I. Public speaking   1

    A. Reflections on public speaking   1

    B. Speaking from the heart and mind   6

        1. "Campus and Church in Common Commitment"   6

        2. Two presentations to a District Meeting   12

           a. "A Christian's Responsibility for a New Morality"   12

           b. "What in Hell is the Church doing?"   15

        3. "Getting it all Together"   21

        4. Some shorter presentations   28

           a. "All kinds of love"   28

           b. "A Prayer for Veterans Day"   31

           c. "Veterans Day, 2012"   32

           d. "PTA devotion"   34

           e.. "Ombudsmen Council devotion"   36

           f. A tribute to Dr. Bob Rozendal on his retirement   36

    C. Having something to say and listeners who want to hear it   38

        1. "The Limits of Christian Ethics in a Pluralistic Society"   38

        2. "The Biblical Concept of the Covenant"   57

        3. "The Christian Ministry and the Literary Arts Today"   68

        4. "When doing the right thing isn't easy"   72

    D. Radio broadcasts, Far East Network (FEN Radio), Morning Meditations   75

1. First series, 1977	77
2. Second series, 1986	83
3. Third series, 1988	91
4. Fourth series, 1989	97
E. Television broadcasts, KMID-TV, USS MIDWAY (CV41)	103
1. February 1991	103
2. March 1991	105
II. Writing	107
A. Writing isn't easy	107
B. The discipline of writing	108
C. A look at some of what I have written	112
1. Books	112
2. Articles	114
a. Articles on teaching and learning	115
b. Articles for a college Newspaper	125
c. An unpublished journal article	134
d. A series of articles on Business Ethics	152
3. Papers	167
a. *Death is not dead yet, a bibliographic essay*	168
b. *The College Connection*	185
c. *Baldrige Quality Award*	193
d. *Steinway & Sons*	200
e. *Goodyear, the Gault years, 1991-1996*	206
f. *Weyerhaeuser Company: a strategic management research project*	215
4. Book reviews	224
a. *What Christians Believe*	224
b. *The Church in the racially changing community*	224
c. *Strangers and Exiles: A history of Religious Refugees*	225
d. *The Literature of Theology: a guide for Students and Pastors*	227

e. A single review of three books on
Business ethics   229

e. *Destiny in the Pacific*   233

f. *Ready Sea-Power, a History of the*
U.S. Seventh Fleet   235

g. *At the Center*   237

5. Correspondence   239

6. Poems   242

III. What might have been – a flight into fancy   245

Conclusion   251

Appendices: 253

I. Biographical listings and treatments   253

II. Bibliography   257

III. Speaking engagements   267

IV. What might have been   271

Books by the Author   273

Preface to the Series
Thoughts along the way

If you are expecting this series of books to be an autobiography you will be disappointed. I did not have the courage to lay bare my weaknesses, failures, faults, flaws, imperfections, bad decisions and actions, much less my sins. To have done so would have disillusioned my children and other relatives, former students, and colleagues.

Nor will you find this book to be a memoir in the traditional sense. I have not lived so exceptional a life as to dignify what I write with the term Memoir. That should be reserved for someone who has had an extraordinary impact in one or more disciplines of life such as in philosophy or education, politics or government, military or public service, the arts including music and architecture, spiritual or religious leadership or devotion. However, current usage makes memoir apply to any telling of one's personal experiences.

What you will find is a bringing together of some of the major themes of my life. The volumes in this series are distinct but related dimensions of my life, each with its primary focus. Each begins with some observations and follows with examples of that theme.

I did not expect to live this long. My mother was 65 when she died. My father died when he was 69. None of my grandparents reached the age of 80. I have, much to my surprise, reached 85.

A few years ago I had quadruple by-pass surgery. The surgeon said afterwards, "We have given you another five to ten years to live." I have now passed the 13th year. Each day is truly a much appreciated gift from God. When I asked my doctor why the heart problems became so severe he said it was largely genetic. Even though I had a different life style including diet and exercise than my parents I could not escape the effects of what they had passed on to me. This extra time has enabled me to write a few books which in David Hume's famous words, "fell still-born from the press."

Now I have the opportunity to bring together some of my thoughts along the way to pass along to my children, grandchildren, and great grandchildren. These books are written to provide information for them which they may, or may not, find of interest. I doubt that anyone else with the possible exception of a few former students and colleagues or someone who once heard me preach, give an address, or offer a prayer will ever find and read the books.

These *Thoughts along the Way* will not duplicate, with a few exceptions, material included in my three volume set (four if you include the Index volume) titled *Sacred Moments: Prayers of a Navy Chaplain at Sea and Ashore*. Those books provide a spiritual log to that important phase of my life.

In an interview I did for a local newspaper I told the reporter my life was like a drama in three acts.

The first act was from childhood in Augusta, Georgia, through college at Texas Christian University, my marriage to Marilyn Miller Shipp, seminary and graduate school at Vanderbilt University, the birth of our children (Margaret Lucretia who died in infancy, Paul Andrew, Frank Warren, John Vinson Evans, and Marilyn Amelia), college teaching at Eureka College and Transylvania University.

The second act was my active duty naval career which I embarked on at age 44 after leaving Transylvania where I was a tenured full professor, my divorce from Marilyn after 27 years, some incredible naval assignments, my marriage to Namiko Yabuki Kawai, who was a perfect Navy wife, and our retirement in Bremerton, Washington. I then resumed college teaching as an adjunct professor in both undergraduate and graduate programs. After Namiko developed Alzheimer's disease and returned to Japan to live with her family we ended our 29 years of marriage. She died in Japan December 13, 2014.

The third act has been the retirement years. I continued college teaching part-time and married Blossom Tibbits whom I had known for many years. We eventually moved from her lovely home on Liberty Bay, Poulsbo, Washington which had a fantastic view of the Olympic Mountains with spectacular sunsets, to a retirement community, Country Meadows, in Silverdale, Washington. We have lived happily here for a number of years

Far too many people have played a vital role in my journey to include all of them by name. Though many of them are not included I still owe a deep debt of gratitude to them -- parents and relatives, school teachers, and youth counselors, preachers, professors, friends, mentors, colleagues, students, neighbors – are all truly cherished though most of them are not mentioned by name.

Introduction to the Series
Thoughts along the way

These thoughts along the way started out as a single manuscript but kept getting longer and longer. I can't imagine anyone picking up a 1000 page book and enjoying it. So I decided to divide the work into four parts each of which is a way of characterizing what I have done and to a certain degree who I am. These smaller volumes are a bit more digestible or at least readable.

To be a Preacher, volume 1, focuses on the prominent role preaching has played in my life. It gathers together thoughts about preaching and its place in the culture into which I was born and the wider communities of faith in which I was involved as I grew.

The reader will see definite changes as I moved from my first sermon as a high school senior at the age of 16 to sermons from the vantage point of maturity in retirement. A chronological list of sermons preached is included as an appendix to the first volume. There is also a selective chronology, a list of church affiliations, and "a model sermon" by the Reverend Susie Beil, my Pastor.

Ministry is Caring, volume 2, focuses on caring starting with the widest dimension of our caring for one another simply because we are human beings. It then moves to more specialized caring of pastoring and praying known as ministering. Here readers will find observations on human caring and expressions of my own involvement in caring/ministering for and with others including offering prayers on public occasions, baptisms, weddings, funerals and memorials. There is a section on ordination to ministry including treatment of my own ordination as well as ordinations in which I have participated. There are appendices for clubs, organizations, and associations to which I have belonged, and a listing of work experiences. There is also a copy of my Ordination Service and Certificate of Ordination, as well as a copy of the Ordination sermon preached by Dr. Nels F.S. Ferre. There are appendices listing baptisms, weddings, funerals and memorial services I have performed.

To teach is to learn, volume 3, focuses on my true vocational passion under-girding my foundational belief that learning/teaching is a life-long adventure. It explores the stimulation to learning from the earliest years up to my present advanced age. The reader will find here observations on the significance of engaging in life-long learning and teaching and the contexts in which teaching has expressed itself in my life. The outlines of several courses are given. This volume contains appendices listing academic preparation, institutions where I taught and academic positions held, both full-time and part-time, college courses taught as a full time professor, and courses taught as an adjunct professor, number of students, non-academic teaching engagements, and evaluations by students.

I have something to say, volume 4, focuses on the privilege of public speaking and the exhilaration when speaker and hearers connect with one another. It also sets the sometimes laborious process of writing in the context of intended readers and the relevance of the message to them. Here the reader will find the most succinct and insightful glimpse into my thoughts along the way particularly in a series of radio messages which are included. Since preaching is a special form of public address and was covered in volume 1 of the series no sermons are included in this fourth volume. This volume also contains appendices including a list of biographical treatments in various publications, a bibliography of my writings, and a list of some of my speaking engagements.

I have tried to make these volumes flow from one to the next without imposing an artificial structure. Though I have written them in sequence they may, of course, be read in whatever order the reader chooses. Needless-to-say, a careful reader will find some overlap in the four volumes. Taken together I believe they have provided me a venue for expressing some thoughts along the way which have helped give meaning, purpose, and form to my life and which I wish to share with my family and anyone else who may consider reading them worth their time.

Preface to
I have something to say

One of the most anticipated human events is a baby's first words. In the development of a normal child there is a lot of communication before the first words are spoken. From the time proud parents hold their infant son or daughter in their arms words of awe and wonder gush forth. What joy when the child responds with a broad smile or captivating grin. A life-time of communicating with others has begun. In fact, there are those who believe that even while the baby is still inside the mother much is being communicated to it.

For a few years while I was teaching at Transylvania University, Lexington, Kentucky I was deeply involved with the Lexington Talent Education Association. John and Amelia my two youngest children were students in the program. I served as its President among other involvements. We had five instructors and about 125 students. One of the basic philosophies of that approach was that the developing baby would respond inside his or her mother to the soothing and enriching sounds of classical music. It would have a calming effect on both mother and child. I mention this to say that communication does not start at birth though that is where we are able to observe and perceive the forms it takes.

We are eager for those first "mama" and "dada" to delight us. Other species have systems of communication which are both quite remarkable and effective. However, none of these compares with the intricacies of human communication. Communication is such a complex area of attention that I have decided not to focus on the complexities but simply on two of its most vital aspects: speaking and writing.

My concern here is to see the roles speaking and writing play in our human growth and particularly in my own human and professional life.

Introduction to
I have something to say

We communicate in so many ways including non-verbal communication but our primary modes are speaking and writing.

As a child, I was so excited to learn to read and write. Little did I know how important both of those abilities would be the rest of my life. Good reading is another side of good writing. I have not set aside a section of this book devoted to Reading though it would be easy to justify doing so. There I could list some of the books that influenced me along the way. First and foremost would be a used copy of A *Tale of Two Cities* given to me by my 5th grade teacher, Miss Skinner. She had guided me and encouraged me, as had all my teachers, both at school and in Sunday school. At the end of the school year in Miss Skinner's class I broke my arm quite severely. After another doctor had misdiagnosed it, Miss Skinner persuaded my mother to take me to see her brother who was the leading orthopedic doctor in Augusta at the University of Georgia Medical College. After about 50 x-rays he decided to operate but offered little hope of restoring use of the arm and grimly noted that it might have to be amputated above the elbow.

Let me digress here to tell about how I broke my right arm in three places – the wrist, mid-forearm and crushed elbow. It was 1942 and paratroopers jumping from planes over Europe was very much in the news. My sister, Switzer, and I had rigged up a long door frame using garden hose over a tall iron swing frame my Dad had built. We would stand on the frame and swing back and forth. At the right moment we would jump out of the "plane". I had a doll's blanket over my shoulders and was holding it in front with my right hand. I jumped from the "plane" and hit the ground elbow first before pulling the rip cord. The pain was excruciating. When my Dad came home from work he and Mom took me to her first cousin who was a local doctor who had received his medical education in Russia. In spite of swelling and displacement of bones he shrugged it off as a serious sprain and ordered the usual Epsom salts soaking. About five days later when the arm was black and blue Miss Skinner felt called upon to intervene. Thank God she did since that probably saved my arm. After the surgery I had to lie in bed for all three months of the summer vacation with the arm in a cast hanging from a hook on the wall. I loved being read to and reading to myself when I could. What a way for a 10 year old to spend the summer. How fortuitous that Miss Skinner gave me a book that began: "It was the best of times; it was the worst of times." My ability to write was affected. For several months I tried writing with my left hand. In time I went back to writing with my right hand but was never too good at penmanship after that.

Since this is the fourth volume in the series, the first of which concentrated on preaching it is necessary to distinguish public speaking from preaching.

Public speaking, like preaching is both an art and a skill. It is different than preaching which is centered on the Word and seeks to engage listeners in an encounter with God. Preaching depends not only on the abilities of the preacher but on the receptiveness of the hearers. That unity between Preacher and Hearer is a gift of the Holy Spirit. One may truly prepare and have all the right intentions and approaches and the message may still fail to ignite the waiting minds and hearts of those for whom it has been prepared. Speaking is a more generalized form of oral communication in which speaker and hearers engage in communicating something each considers worthwhile.

Writing is the other main form of communication. Anyone who has learned another language than the one they grew up with will quickly affirm a marked difference between being able to converse effectively in the new language and the ability to express oneself accurately in writing. Over the course of my teaching experience I had opportunity to work with many students for whom English was their second or third language. Many of them had a pretty good grasp of the fundamentals of written English but found it difficult to express themselves comfortably and idiomatically orally and in writing. It is a common place observation that the earlier we begin to speak or write another language than our native one the more proficient we will be.

Dudley Strain said it well, "There is a vast difference between having to say something and having something to say" (*Measure of a Minister*, Bethany Press, 1964). This applies as much to writing as to speaking. I hope the presentations in this volume measure up to that goal.

This final volume also gives me a chance to engage in a flight of fancy by looking at "What might have been."

The appendices include a biographical listings and treatments, bibliography of my writings and a listing of those speaking engagements of which I have a record and concludes with some aspects of what might have been.

I. Public Speaking

A. Reflections on Public Speaking

Writing this takes me back to my freshman year at TCU when Don Brewer, my friend from Waycross, Georgia and I enrolled in an introductory speech class with Dr. Fallis, who was past his prime. As it turned out Don and I were the only two students in the class. That didn't deter Dr. Fallis from putting us rigorously through our paces. He was convinced that good speech began with control of the diaphragm and had us do exercises holding our mid-section while jumping on one foot then the other while loudly proclaiming, "BaBaLaBa" ad nauseam. I think he was right to concentrate on speaking from deep within oneself if one wants to project his voice to a large audience or those at some distance from the speaker.

Those lessons have stood me in good stead over the years as a public speaker. I developed a reputation for clarity and projection.

Rarely, if ever, do I recall anyone saying I couldn't hear you. Of course the size of the venue and the technical equipment to amplify the voice were critical elements for successful speaking as well.

For a few years I taught managerial communication for City University of Seattle and had the opportunity to work with some dedicated MBA students. There are, of course, many techniques of public speaking and I will not go into many of those here. It may be helpful to point out, however, that public speaking may be one directional, like a person shooting an arrow at a target. That is fine for conveying information or giving instructions. If one seeks to stimulate thought and encourage questioning of the issues or topics which are being presented by the speaker then it is best to see speaking as a kind of loop experience. The speaker presents what he or she has to say as clearly as possible all the while being attuned to the responses, primarily in eye contact or body movements to get some indication of how effective the presentation is at any given point. No matter how eloquent the speaker he or she cannot eliminate the noise which surrounds the presentation. Not the physical noise but the interference of such things as the listeners' background, experience, or interest in the subject. The best speeches are those which are presented with clarity and fulfill to the best of the speaker's ability the intent and purpose of the speech.

Something, perhaps a great deal, is lost when an oral presentation is reduced to words on a page. It takes a reader's willingness to image the words being spoken rather than written for him or her to gain some of the impact of the presentation. It is always easier for someone to read an address of someone they have heard speak and imagine him or her delivering the address he or she is reading. But even if one has never heard the person speak it is highly recommended that the reader seek to put him or herself in the context of the presentation and try to receive it as if he or she were hearing it delivered rather than reading it.

As in any other area of public communication public speaking has certain basic elements. There are many good books and resources available for someone wishing to develop expertize as a public speaker.

The two major categories are extemporaneous and carefully planned. Some people think well on their feet and have little difficulty expressing themselves clearly and often eloquently even with the shortest notice. Clear speaking is dependent on clear thinking. The better one is able to grasp knowledge of the area which he or she is addressing the better the verbal communication of that will be. Think of extemporaneous speaking as an opportunity to share accrued knowledge and insight and perhaps even wisdom one has gathered up to that point in life.

Toastmasters, though I was never a member, has a proven track record of helping men and women become proficient at this art and craft.

My approach in this volume is in the cultural context of civility and courtesy. Alas this seems to be a fading dimension of our public life. Haranguing and vilifying is also a form of public speaking. Its intent is to stir up the emotions of like-minded believers so that they will commit themselves to a common cause. It is not done with the intent of laying out a coherent plan or program. It is an "in your face" form of public speaking excluding any attempt at dialogue or reaching common ground with those whose views differ from the speaker.

But, that aside, public speaking is a chance to convey information, provoke critical thinking, and raise appropriate questions which stimulate intellectual growth. It often also has the purpose of stimulating the emotions of the hearers.

It has often been repeated that second only to the fear of dying is the fear of public speaking. Even the most experienced speakers sometimes acknowledge their initial fear before the speech begins. Paul Tillich, one of the 20th century's most renowned theologians who spoke often made it clear that he rarely approached a podium to deliver an address without "fear and trembling." He was quick to go on saying that once he had made eye contact with the audience and had a feeling that they were sharing in a mutually beneficial purpose the butterflies flew away.

So while the common place observation is true up to a point that the more one practices his or her art or craft the more confident they become in performance there are still times when it is not ideal and one realizes there is never a perfected form but one which is always in process.

As I noted above there are so many good resources available to help us with the process and performance of public speaking, let me simply put a very few elements I consider essential for anyone at whatever the stage in the process: I will limit them to three:

1) "Know thyself". The ancient Greeks and the New Testament Christians both were convinced that unless one really knew who he was he could not know others. As we are all aware this is not as easy as it seems. We all come to a

knowledge of ourselves through the myriad experiences which have brought us to where we are. We know we have a basic make-up formed by our genetic structure. But, many of us see this as a predisposition not a determinant. One may have the God given talent to be a world class musician but without the studied, persistent, painstaking discipline of regular practice under expert instruction this talent will not manifest itself on its own.

We know ourselves in quiet reflection and meditation on who we are, where we have been, and where we want to go. We know ourselves through interaction with others, both positive and negative. Human beings are meant to live in community, Aristotle was right about that. "You can't be human alone" is more than a catchy book or song title; it is an essential fact of life. Can a person speak, perhaps to thousands and move them in his direction without knowing himself? There is no question about it – he can. But, I am talking about public speaking with integrity at its core and knowing oneself is the center of that integrity.

2) "Know your audience". Every great speech, from Pericles funeral oration through Lincoln's Gettysburg Address and Winston Churchill's blood, sweat and toil speech the speaker has directed his or her remarks to a specific audience. He was not content to simply broadcast his views like fireworks exploding. Rather he or she concentrates on where the audience is intellectually and emotionally as well as physically.

Many effective speakers give this bit of advice. As you begin your speech, find one or more responsive faces whose eyes are telling you they are with you and draw encouragement from them to open your heart and mind freely anticipating that you will be heard and understood. It is commonplace to acknowledge that the very words chosen if one is speaking to a group of disgruntled workers is quite different than those one chooses when addressing the board of directors. A person delivering a paper to a learned society has no alternative than to use the jargon and technical terms of that society though he or she should seek as much clarity as possible in the judicious use of those terms.

The emotional mood of the occasion is an inescapable element of the presentation. To misread quietness as sadness or joviality as acceptance is to set up obstacles to understanding. It is like the once popular TV commercial, "Can you hear me now?" The question is not only is what I am saying audible, but can you hear what I am intending to convey in the words and phrases I am using? Every prescient speaker will be asking himself that question and trying his or her best to read the answer in the "body language" of the audience.

3) "Know your material". In most cases, it is all too evident when the speaker is "faking it." There are a lot of expressions for this, e.g. "blowing smoke," "full of hot air", "bs", "obfuscation," "wool gathering" and so on. Let's assume you do not want any of these applied to what you have to say. The only way around it is to make certain you know what you are talking about and can express it in a way that the audience grasps it, maybe not immediately, but as the speech unfolds.

It would be the height of folly to agree to present a speech on a topic about which one knows little or nothing. There is an interesting joke that made the rounds about a local physician who was asked to speak to a Ladies Club. He did not want to tell his wife what he had been asked to talk about so he told her they had asked him to talk about sailing. The day after the presentation his wife met one of the ladies who had been there who was effusive in her praise. The wife hrumpfed, "I don't know what made him an expert on that since he has only tried it twice and he fell off both times." Unbeknownst to her he had been asked to speak on "Sex for the middle aged woman." Make sure you know what you are being asked to speak about and that you are qualified to do so.

B. Speaking from the heart and mind

Now let us turn from these brief and incomplete reflections on public speaking to my practice of the art and craft remembering that effective public speaking is a happy blending of intellect and emotion, indeed a matter of heart and mind united to convey something the speaker and hopefully the audience considers worthwhile.

1. "Campus and Church in Common Commitment"

I was invited to deliver an address to the Georgia Convention of Christian Churches (Disciples of Christ) in Athens, Georgia, November 7, 1964. I had received my Ph.D. degree in the spring of that year and was in my fifth year as Chaplain at Eureka College. The address was well received and I was able to have it published in *Liberal Education*, October 1966. I am including it here as I delivered it though the printed article follows it quite closely. . It will be helpful if you will imagine hearing these words spoken rather than receiving them as written. The context is a church convention in a university town. It is not a sermon but an address on a topic of concern to both the church and the university.

"Campus and Church in Common Commitment: rethinking the campus ministry to today's students,"

Campus and church belong to one another. The life of either without the other would be not only impoverished but distorted. Until the time of the American Revolution, almost without exception the college was the child of the church. Early American colleges were founded not merely to provide a fitly trained clergy but a properly educated Christian citizenry.

Americans moving westward had more desire for founding colleges than means for supporting them; one out of eight survived. Land-grant colleges in the mid-nineteenth century were expressive of the belief in every man's right to a college education. Their growth embarrassed church-related institutions to the point where they were ashamed of being a valid expression of the church's concerns. Campus and church alike questioned whether religion and higher education could be mutually beneficial. But this mood has subsided and once more intelligent and committed men affirm the need of church and college for one another in order to conserve and criticize basic human values.

The campus is at once the arena for conservation as well as deliberate criticism of society's knowledge and values. The transmission of conserved resources is a valid purpose of higher education. But it is not an exclusive purpose, for the college must assist men to see such contributions as directives for thought rather than settled answers to unsettling questions. Consequently, the campus is a critic of the past whose greatness it seeks to conserve. It is called to vigilant protection against smallness of perspective of prejudiced and closed minds. As a critic of society the campus is charged with examining, exploring and exposing the claims of the new while reminding men of the achievements and failures of the past.

The church, because of its ultimate commitment, can and must insist that the campus be left free to discover and pursue truth. In this the church receives from the campus a greater appreciation of the past as together they seek a fuller understanding of the demands of the present and the destiny of the future. Charles McCoy has phrased it well: "...the campus is a place where the past is being reshaped and appropriated for the present, where the meaning by which society lives is being transmitted and transformed." (*Humanity*, 1964) Transformation in terms of moving from idea to action in the lives of college students is often not readily or easily accepted by either church or campus.

We can no longer refer to this student generation as uncommitted and apathetic as we did but a decade ago. The commitment from the campus to the crises of a tumultuous society has reawakened the church to its commitment in the Spirit of the Christ to the world. Commitment and faith in the conflicts of society have issued in a renewed pursuit of learning sufficient for commitment to such causes.

Clear voices sometimes come from unexpected sources as when an instructor in floriculture marketing research at Michigan State University speaks to church and campus of the interdependence of faith and learning and commitment:

So we see that the learned, the committed and the faithful each

7

have their own ways of effecting change in the world. But it is clear that the learned without faith are a menace; the learned without commitment are useless. The committed without learning are fanatic; the   committed without faith tempt God with their idolatry.

Hear what L.J. Tolle has to say about this:

The faithful without commitment have lost their faith; the faithful without learning, though dearly loved by God, are a little out of date.

Here, then, is the crucial service of the church to the university; to be at the crossroads of learning and faith, and amongst them to define and structure a community of commitment.

The general objective of a modern fulfilling ministry to the university is to challenge, to expose, to claim and to engage the community of learning and with God's help, to synthesize and unify, under Christ, a vigorously committed community of faith amongst the learned. (L. J.Tolle, Jr. *Faith, Learning and Commitment*)

Indeed, church and campus belong essentially to one another in the contemporary world.

Consideration must be given to actual means whereby this relationship is being and might yet be expressed. The most general is the recognition of the inter-relatedness of church and campus so that the church becomes informed about the present state of affairs and the promise of the campus for its ministry. There can come about a realization that the campus ministry is a valid expression of the church's mission in the world. Apologies no longer need be made for one who sees his vocation as a minister on the campus rather than in the pastorate of a resident congregation. This is no intermediate stage between seminary and pastorate, between graduate school and professorial rank. It is a legitimate form of ministry characterized by flexibility, fluidity and experimentation.

The church must leave its campus ministers free to make responsible decisions as to the relevant expressions of ministry in the particular academic community in which the ministry is carried on. College campuses are so diverse that no one pattern or set of patterns is to be accepted as the right ministry for the campus. The unified humanitarian/Christian witness and fellowship of a small semi-rural campus may be an utter impossibility for the urban university where specialized ministries are the only viable and accepted entry to the segments which comprise the whole. Freedom to explore unconventional and unfamiliar ministries is an imperative not to be ignored. Consequently, the campus ministry is more urgently interdenominational and ecumenical than most local congregations.

It is necessary for the church to remember always that the most authentic and effective ministry of the campus is fulfilled by the citizens of that educational society – the faculty, students and staff. Communication of one's faith and commitment, as well as of his learning, on the part of one member to and with others is an expression of the educational process itself. In their learning together they are better able to give evidence of what life together in society might become.

Church and campus alike must reiterate the fact that learning is for life, both for the better living one seeks and the duration of one's existence. True learning is enhanced by collegiate experiences, but is neither begun nor concluded in the span from orientation to commencement. While the campus has every right to press upon the church the demand of making its faith relevant, the church has an equal claim against the campus that its learning be of benefit to men in society. Both campus and church have a responsibility to impress upon the student the seriousness of his intellectual quest as an equipping for judicious discernment in responsible and mature involvement in a free society. Persons committed to the honest pursuit of learning and the deliberate realization of faith cannot afford the ashen luxury of encouraging the extension of adolescence into the college years. The campus is a community of people thinking things through and acting upon what they think and believe. There is no room for the swinger just along for the ride.

We have become immensely skillful at ascertaining a student's potential and probable success yet we are still baffled by the illusive quality which actualizes this. Motivation is so intensely personal that it defies reduction to statistical prediction. But it is, at least in some degree, a conviction that one has the mental equipment essential for the satisfactory attainment of goals worthy enough of his best effort. Socrates' observation that the unexamined life is not worth living has lost no truth with the passing of centuries. The campus becomes the very theater of the exhilarating examination of one's life in terms of commitment and faith.

Commitment and faith on the part of the church are seen through the support of church-related colleges and college-town churches. The most effective Christian preachers should be in the pulpits of college town churches. Men are needed in these crucial situations whose unexcelled ability to preach is matched by a warm and receptive spirit. Men eager to learn as well as to teach, to listen as readily as to talk, are required. College-town congregations need to exercise creativity in developing appropriate forms for worship and service. They must be continually reminding themselves that they are ministering to persons whose learning seeks expression in faith and whose commitment brings them there to worship and work. These are not intruders into the established order but persons whose needs are human and whose gifts are usually seeking adequate expression.

Church-related colleges must be urged and equipped to fulfill their primary task of providing for excellence in education with the freedom given to the Christian in Christ. The church-related college often stands as mediator between the demands of the world and the crucial involvement of the church in God's meaningful purposes in the world. Her faculties and facilities should not be made second-rate by superficial utilization in program building which exhausts their energies and dulls their scholarly incentive. Nor should these be ignored when church and campus think about the concerns of the church in the world. Rather, they should be expected to render the service of which they are capable, by their own commitment and education, of thinking things through as best they can at a given time.

It is time the church as well as the campus tangibly encouraged its most competent youth to pursue the vocation of Christian scholarship and teaching. If it is as Elton Trueblood has contended, "The best school is the school with the best teachers. It is that simple." ("Deciding for the Difficult," in *Education for Decision*, Frank E. Gaebelein, ed. Seabury Press, 1963. Page 32) then we have no higher priority than the preparation, conservation and stimulation of excellence in teaching. The primacy of classroom teaching must be recaptured. The good teacher may or may not be a good writer or research scholar. He must be, however, one who is able to communicate with others in such a way that they themselves assume personally the responsibility for learning. Empirical scholarship in publication should come from the campus but not as its major product. The good teacher will no doubt wish to extend his teaching beyond those whom he sees face to face, but this will not be the compelling motivation of his vocation. The church-related college can never afford the false economy of inadequate or incompetent teachers and it ought to be able to afford some among its faculty who by their expertness in research and writing bring honor and encouragement not invidious rivalry, to the whole campus.

The church, through its denominational agencies, has a decided stake in the campus. One concrete expression of its concern could come through well-planned and executed exchange programs for faculty and students around the world. It can at least serve as a clearing house of information about "non-religious" opportunities for such exchange and beyond this as an introductory channel of communication to those whose services may be rendered in other places than their homes and for limited periods.

This advice from Ralph McGill is appropriate:

We must somehow find the faith, the compassion, the commitment to causes, the joy in values, that will give us the strength to find a personal view of life and self – to see to it that the great ideas of our age have a chance to triumph over the irrational evil and errors of it …. ("Notes to a Freshman Class," *Orientation*, 1964. Page 5)

Such a quest for personal integrity and social values is the legitimate meeting ground of campus and church in common commitment. #

11

2. Two presentations to a District meeting

On September 15, 1968 I spoke twice to the Greater St. Louis Council of Christian Churches meeting at Hamilton Christian Church, Missouri. Again, these were not sermons but oral presentations though in a religious context. The first presentation (a) was as a panel member on contemporary Christian ethics. The second address (b) was the featured address of the conference. Once again I urge you to take seriously that these were spoken to a live audience ranging from youth to old age at a specific time in history – the late 1960s. If you put yourself in their place I think you will find what is being said at least disturbing if not shocking at times. If it were a written presentation it would be a private event. As it was, it was a public event conveyed by voice to ears which could ponder it, be challenged or enlightened by it. Though I expect there were some turned off by it I dare to say few simply ignored it.

a. "A Christian's Responsibility for a New Morality."

When as a student at Texas Christian University I took a course in logic we used a textbook which had as one of its examples the dance hall sign: "Clean and decent dancing every night except Sunday."

The reaction to the new morality is much like that of persons to that sign. Some rubbed their hands together lustfully drooling as they sneered, "Oh Boy, come Sunday." Others wrung their hands in pious desperation exclaiming, "What is the world coming to?" Both say in essence of the new morality that the church has turned morality over to the unclean and indecent letting loose a license for anything to go.

Neither the expectations of the one nor the fears of the other is the case. We are like the beginning student of logic confusing our own outlook with the message. Obviously, the information was that the proprietor maintained a clean premise but closed it entirely on Sunday.

New morality says that creative and responsible human freedom expressing love is the crucial issue in man's ethical existence.

New morality is unfortunately almost synonymous with sex. Not that sex isn't a good topic, but it is just a bit narrow for a Christian ethic. New morality is applicable to the other dimensions of our ethical life also. However, the make-up of our panel leaves me to focus on this prime concern. New Morality is a way of doing ethics which faces such issues as war and peace, politics, and economics, race and the urban crisis.

Since these have been dealt with by the other panel members let us look together for a few minutes at what we are talking about when we refer to a new morality, why the issue is so much discussed today, and what might come of a new morality.

We are concerned here with a new morality, not with a new ethic. What's the difference? Basically this: morality is the action of human beings with one another that contributes to the growth or development of a person or belittles, denies, or destroys him as a person. Ethics is the thought, reason, or rationale which underlies a person's morality. Morality is the action: ethics is the reason for the action. The ethic we are committed to has not changed. It is still a Christian ethic. The morality has and must change. Anything that lives grows and changes. A living morality changes to express the basic values in a specific time. What a new morality is after all is aiding us in being Christian in the late 20th century.

Simply put, a new morality says something negative and something positive. It says that a meaningful morality cannot come from learning and making rules, commandments, or codes the basis for moral action. This too quickly leads to arrogance, pride, and moral deception. Take sex: a code morality says "thou shalt not commit adultery or make-out before or outside marriage." The rigidity of this position can lead to the cult of technical virginity. Sex ethics is then approached with questions like: how heavy should petting be, is French kissing a moral sin, can I look but not touch, or are hands o.k. but other parts of the anatomy off-limits? You get the picture.

Now, positively new morality says human freedom and responsibility are to be taken seriously. When it comes down to it sex is a matter that looks like it is just between two people. But, is it? Those two people in their actions reflect not only their own experiences but the values of all those who have aided their values. Two people alone physically are not alone emotionally and spiritually. They are free to use or reject some of the emotional resources and spiritual values they have received. They are people who have a past and look forward to a future

13

and whose actions are affected by both. Yet, it is they who bear the responsibility of their free act.

Secondly in a positive manner, new morality puts love at the center of moral action. No action, with the exception of rape or molesting a child is an immoral action. One of the maturest developments of a positive new morality I have found is in an unlikely spot – a book carrying a Roman Catholic imprimatur. It is not written as an essay on new morality for the Roman church officially takes a dim view of the whole subject. It is a book written for husbands and wives by a husband and wife. It is *The Freedom of Sexual Love* by Joseph and Lois Bird (Doubleday, 1967). It sees such a freedom in sexual love that the variations on sexual themes are almost limitless. It is bold to say that love is most intense in sexual intercourse and that Christian husbands and wives know Christ in this act of mutual orgasm. Love is at the center and love acts in responsible freedom for the other person.

Why did a new morality make such a splash? Again, in oversimplified terms, there are three reasons:

1. The morality taught to us in the church was too rigid for our humanity. We asked for the bread of life and were given a couple of stone tablets to munch on. Rules and commandments were considered more significant than the relationships between persons which these rules were designed to provide for and make possible. Not that rules aren't needed. Let's get that clear – they are. But, you can't enjoy the game if all you know is the rule book; whether the game is golf, tennis, football, or sex.

2. The morality of the church was hypocritical. It was an open secret that good people were doing those naughty things they were told not to. There was a credibility gap between practice and preaching. Along came a generation of youth who screamed, "phony" and like the child they said that we stood naked in our imperial moral clothes. New morality doesn't say forget the preaching; it does say take a hard look at it to determine whether it expresses a Christian ethic.

3. The morality of the church was impotent. A technological revolution was occurring and things will never be the same. The automobile made every teenager a lover fit for the wide screen and the pill

made the world safe not for democracy but for sexual intercourse. The church was still selling a morality of sex based on fear of discovery, or pregnancy, or disease and youth and young adults weren't buying it. Surely, the Gospel had something to say in such an age as this.

So when the wringing of hands has stopped and the tears are dried away and we get to the serious business of thinking about a new morality for a Christian ethic we see two focal points: Jesus and contemporary man.

Jesus was a new morality man. He honored the law and heritage of his ancestors enough to see where its limits were for his own life. He pushed himself beyond the rules to the relationships and looked for God in the midst of the loving act. He said in effect don't stomp on the rules but remember rules are made for man not the other way around.

Modern man lives so much of his life by the rules. Else how could we have driven to this place this afternoon?. But the rules didn't drive the car. You did. You are responsible for what happens when you are driving. The actions are yours and the consequences too.

New morality sees us as free responsible persons growing toward maturity and growing most in our creative actions. Each of us is to act for himself though not by himself. Nowhere is this better brought to focus than in relation of two people – a man and a woman – with one another.
#

b. "What in Hell is the Church doing?"

"What in hell is the church doing?" This is the outcry today!!!

Lest we be offended at the non-theological use of a theological concept I hasten to remind us that this is a legitimate voice of our time. The emphasis is on action – doing. The question is not what is the church thinking or believing or even preaching or teaching. The question is the direct reflection of an action-oriented age which justifies anything by its usefulness or measures its value by what it can do. "Form follows function" is more than a principle of architecture. It is the working design of the times.

When the question "what in hell is the church doing" is raised it is an honest query of an age which holds as its basic fact the constant role of change.

We have learned how to do remarkable things. Your magnificent Gateway Arch is but a present reminder of the ingenuity of men who know how to bring about in tangible form what their minds can conceive. It is a symbol of the splendor of an age of technological proficiency that makes obsolescence a built-in consideration. Change occurs so constantly, so insistently, so rapidly that we have lost the sense of wonder. People who have never known life without automobiles, television, or jet air travel fail to see the tremendous breakthroughs that created such a world. People whose way of life is such as to live in a dozen states and do a half-dozen different jobs are not excited about the thoughts of men and women whose birthplace and cemetery plot are but a holler apart. Movement, change, innovation, invention are the marks of a time sometimes turbulent, sometimes evolutionary, sometimes revolutionary and even sometimes taken for granted. When a people come to believe that the new is unquestionably better than the old, that this year's model is superior to last year's, that today's product antiquates yesterday's it is little wonder that they see no reason to stop with technology in their way of thinking.

Every discipline seems embarrassed to be late in declaring a new, vastly improved brand. Thus, there is not only the new math as most of us now ignorant parents know, but there is a new sociology, new economics, new politics, new theology, new morality. The list is endless.

The church lives then in an age intent on making all things new. She should not be at all surprised when her critics cry out to her, if she lives her old life and preaches her old message in the same old way and she is met with the deflating, "so what else is new?" She should not rise up with presumption or indignation when the taunt is tossed, "what in hell is the church doing?"

In the question is the voice of suspicion, doubt, mistrust, ridicule from critics outside who see the church as part of the establishment, an institution obstructing change, marked too often by bitterness and

16

bickering, envy, jealousy, and pettiness among her members or her branches. They are too busy feuding over the trivia of the time and place of the next potluck dinner, or the color of the paint for the nursery, or whether to buy new or used pianos to be concerned with the ocean currents of change that cry "archaic", "obscurant", "irrelevant", "indifferent" about her very existence in the world.

What is rather surprising or astounding is that the critics' voices are not all outside. In fact, from within the sharpest shots are fired about comfortable pews and frozen people. From within the church is accused of pride in her own failures, insensitivity to human life, appeals to partial and perverted loyalties, regrettable ability to wrap herself up in her own pursuit of self-preservation.

The glorious day of the supremacy of the church in society is gone. Once her buildings stood at the city square or the town common. Once her minister was the parson – the person whose education and erudition made him the professional center of the town. Once her message was the focal point of community life by which all else was measured. That day was not so long ago.

But today she still has her beautiful buildings, her ministers are professionally trained and her message uses every available medium. Yet, her force or impact has declined. It does not take a genius to assert that her role of priority is not likely to return into a world so rapidly changing.

A recent writer has remarked: "Without being prophets we can today predict that the established churches will decrease in numbers. The influence of the institutionalized churches will become weaker. We still talk too much and do too little .... The number of non-Christians who try to help themselves and to improve the conditions of the world with moral goodness and respectable intelligence will increase. The Church will learn that she is not permitted to waste her energies by working for her own self-preservation." (Dietrich Ritschl, *Memory and Hope*, page 228)

It is in the light of this disturbing context that we ask again the question, "What in hell is the church doing today?" This time we make the question the answer and use it theologically. That's just it – she is

17

doing something in hell, though maybe not enough and maybe even sometimes doing the wrong things. But, <u>she is doing.</u>

We have been so sickened by the twisted minds that have made hell a fiery furnace turning men into firewood and making man of less value than natural gas that we have felt it better to leave it alone than to be identified with such distortions. We who believe the heart of the Gospel is the love of God have felt unclean and indecent in the very word hell. Our age demands us to pick it up and make it new.

The church is doing something in hell – in hell where men are separated from one another before God, where anguish and agony is the miserable lot of the damned of dead existences, where hopelessness produces strife and frustration, breeds riots, where isolation of youth reared by an electrical nurse that gave them no chance to talk back lost the art of talking things through.

Christians hesitantly and painfully have come to see ourselves for what we are, a minority in a world that for far too many is but the arena of hell. We have come to see that for far too many of those whom God loves human existence is hell.

Honesty demands we not overplay it.

The church has always been concerned to preach hell, judgment, and salvation. But hell was at the end of the line. It was the equalizer that acted as a social safety valve for oppressed peoples. They could be kept in line by the threats of hell or they could piously believe their subservient life would save them for heaven while dooming the rebellious and wicked to hell. The church too often sided with those who had the upper hand and used hell to stand on the underdog.

We are not talking about the Middle Ages when serfdom was maintained by the church who gave the majority of men only the respite of a few Holy Days rather than the freedom of a holy community. More recent was the American experience of the Puritan virtues and the Protestant ethic using hell as a way of fashioning the world. The poor and sick were not only lazy, shiftless, no good, and ignorant. They were sinful. The church plainly preached that hard work, abstinence, thrift, and charity were rewarded by God in this life with wealth and power and in the life to come by heaven.

That ancient good has become uncouth and more than uncouth – immoral and irreligious. It made God irresponsive to human need and man irresponsible for human community.

God is in the world and if the world is a hell of a place then the church takes its cue from early Christianity in declaring again that Christ descended into hell.

Christ is made real by those who see and do something about the separation of husbands and wives and dependent children, or about the torment of tenement dwellers tortured by grasping landlords (many of whom are respectable church members) as well as by their own ignorance of the use and power of money, by the hopelessness of youth who want all they see to make life better but don't see where to turn for the hope of a better life.

So the church despite the consternation of some and the fears of others has been doing something in the hell of the political arena seeking ways of peace in a war weary world. Her tactics have varied and she has found her plea carried to dramatic extremes. The healing of the nations which she has sought has often opened wounds in her own community of faith.

The church has been doing something in the hell of the economic arena as she has walked the way of the poverty stricken and watched the wave of automation. Her front guard in migrant ministry and community organization has embarrassed her rear guard which does not yet see the impersonal dimension of economic systems that can't be made better by Christmas baskets or boxes given to the Salvation Army.

The church has been doing something in the hell of the social arena where racial injustice keeps us tottering on the fiery brink of anarchy and where urbanization shakes up our nostalgia for the good old days of close neighbors and closed neighborhoods. Her children and youth have often shamed her adult members by such disarming questions as "what's the color of his skin got to do with it?" or "Daddy, why do

Negroes always live in crummy houses?" or "Why are most garbage men black?"

The church has been doing something in the hell of the personal arena of sex and love where a marriage license is believed to be more than legalized sex. It has been trying to recall a biblical truth of the goodness of sexual life and its potential for human fulfillment while recognizing its potential for distortion and human slavery of the spirit.

In the hell of the here and now the church is struggling for her soul. She is trying to take seriously Jesus' contention that whoever would find his life must lose it. Sometimes she has become confused about the life she finds when she loses the familiar one she has known. She has experienced too often the loss of her life without the rebirth to a new life in Christ.

The hell of the world in which she works has led some to cry there is no hope for the church. They have shouted, "Let the church go to hell." They have not meant that she should go as Christ to bring release to the captives but that she should die in her hopeless, helpless desire for her own purity and perfection. She who is to make men aware of God in her midst has too often been dumb because she could not recognize Him there. She has often seen only crucifixion in the things which she sought to put to death and not the resurrected Lord who makes all things new.

Another question should therefore be asked before we are through. "What in heaven's name is going on in the church?"

If she is doing her thing only in hell she has lost her life but not yet found her way out as her Lord had done. Jesus has left us a program, a platform which you have read before. Read it again in Luke chapter 4. Jesus had taken the prophetic tradition of his past and made it new for his time. Into the hell of the everyday he brought the heaven of the forever. Release, deliverance, hope, community were opened up to men bound by fears, shut up in failure, hopeless with frustration and isolated by lack of love, either for and from others or genuinely for themselves. He brought to men a blinding awakening to their divine origin and destiny. He reminded them what they found too incredible to believe that they were sons of God and belonged to one another. He lived, as he taught, the sacred responsibility of being human.

The church's forms will change. They must. It is not a question of whether we will change. We will. It is a question of how and for what purpose. Her structures will always need restructuring and her theology will always need rewriting just as her programs must ever be reworked.

A community of people who recognize the sacred responsibility of being human and who live in love for one another and in openness to the age in which they live and the urgent voices of their time will always be the instrument of God. If the church defaults in being such a community, in doing God's will He will not be thwarted. Men are born to love and be loved and God who causes this to be will be present wherever this is realized and this will be in action as in actuality the church.

What in hell is the church doing needs to be answered with the question, "what in heaven's name is going on in the church?"

What is going on in your congregation is the crucial issue. Is there a community broad enough for tolerance of divergent beliefs and lives, deep enough for commitment to many causes and dreams, aware enough for involvement which challenges the resources of people who see things differently, faithful enough for patience in the midst of turbulent change and generous enough for love in the spirit of Christ.

Is it a people like Jonah shut off from God's presence because it doesn't want to be where the action is? Or is it a people like Christ who came and are alive that men might know and have life abundant and eternal? #

3. "Getting it all Together,"

My most memorable public address was the Commencement Address at Transylvania University, June 13, 1971. Transylvania has a rich history of Commencement Speakers including President Dwight D. Eisenhower. The Commencement Committee at Transylvania selects the Commencement Speaker. In 1970/71 the budget was severely limited and the Student Body was given the opportunity to select someone as the Speaker. They might choose anyone so long as she or he knew there would be no honorarium. They stayed close to home and I was selected.

21

Among those receiving honorary degrees that day was Colonel Harland Sanders of Kentucky Fried Chicken fame. My wife, Marilyn and I, along with the other platform guests and dignitaries had lunch at the Lexington Country Club with him. He was as resplendent in his signature white suit as any picture you have ever seen of him. Here is the address given later in the afternoon.

"Getting it All Together,"

It was not long ago, a decade or so, that commencement speakers were observing, "Everything not nailed down is coming loose." In doing so they were echoing the clamors of society whether the sedate confession of the learned as they remarked bemused, "I don't understand the erosion of order and the violent upheavals of our time," or the more direct exclamation of the non-academic, "what the hell is going on?"

They spoke of gaps widening to chasms polarizing society and threatening to swallow up institutions in the earthquake of radical change.

There was a generation gap and parents were warned that those who could not get with it, enter the currents of times a-changing, would be drowned in their own stubbornness or inability to comprehend what was happening. Willie Loman was a fading American tragic figure, not just because he could not face himself, but more pathetically because he could not open himself to the searching of his sons for a life based on something more than productivity and its monetary rewards. It was more than hair, whether the length or the sound, that separated fathers and sons.

There was a credibility gap which baffled those whose childhood had prepared them to trust those in authority, whether parent, principal, policeman, or president and made them impatient with those who refused to believe that what a man says officially does not have to correspond too closely with what he is talking about or the professed convictions of his private life. For parents who fought to make the world safe for democracy or for the freedom of men from fascist tyranny, it was hard to believe that official pronouncements could cover ulterior economic motives in pursuit of mineral rights and trade agreements for American corporations in far-off places whose political future became our present dominant national interest. What those who had lived through World War II could understandably believe was in the interest of national security, or the containment of "godless communism" or at least was a matter of political expediency, their sons and daughters blatantly called "lies". Men began publicly to ask what they had trembled to wonder at privately: "What can you believe?" "Who can you trust?" "Where is the truth?"

There was a communications gap: a yawning, menacing hole as electronic media multiplied the voices, sights, sounds, images, pictures, concepts not just for the traveler jetting from city to city, but for the folks back home on farm or in factory. We had grown up with the wonder of radio which left us with fertile imaginations or with the stable impressions of a printed page to which we could return if the meaning was unclear. Now there was not only the engulfing captivation of television alternately diverting us from the inequities and injustices of life and bombarding and brutalizing us on the other with the entertainment of mass murder at My Lai, or riots in Watts, Detroit, or Buffalo, or poverty and ghetto existence in Mississippi or Missouri, Chicago or Cleveland. Added to this was the incredible swiftness with which computer technology began to affect our ways of living and fill us with fears of automation, invasion of privacy, and further dehumanization.

We grew uncomfortable, uneasy, insecure as protests rose from non-violent to violent, or demonstrations moved from persuasion to coercion, from civil rights to higher education. We who had been brought up on the reasonableness of man and his ability to reform society in an orderly manner; we who had believed the competitive struggle was so essential to success that it could be kept within bounds; we who had acquired the credentials for dealing with problems by way of classifying men and separating them so as to allow some to make it and perpetuate the system moved quickly from fear and insecurity to the horrible possibility that we might not be able to control it much longer. Our slogans and clichés slid from our clutching minds as protest multiplied in social, political, environmental, ecological, economic, educational, moral and religious arenas we had been able to avoid or evade. New slogans vied for ascendancy so fast we couldn't assimilate them to our neatly arranged

23

conviction that there was a place for everything and everybody should stay in his place.

But was this so unusual? Who in human history has been able to discern the significance of what he is living through without the conviction that the certain present built upon the cumulative past is preferable to the unexperienced future?

Yet, some things we can see with clarity.

Some of us too eagerly and some too reluctantly, but all of us to some degree, have come to realize the permanence of change. There will be no return to a simpler, quieter life. We have with our industrial and technological revolution set loose forces which while they may be directed and given different meanings will not be stopped except in global destruction. There will be no return to the age before electronic amplification or mechanized elaboration. We are inescapably in the midst of an historical situation which in numberless and numbing ways produces what Alvin Toffler has termed "future shock".

This permanence of change may be seen even in language which throughout history has been notably conservative. Words are coined and replaced with dizzying pace. We find out to our embarrassment when we try to use faddish terms that what was hot has become cool, or tough, or deep, or heavy. Words we once saw gasping for breath have been blown upon and man has soul.

This only illustrates a dialectical tension which will increasingly overcome the polarities of life by which many of us have lived. The haves were set against the have-nots, man against the machine, the human against the technological, the self against society, the child against the parent, the student against the teacher, the philosopher against the plumber, the personal against the impersonal, I against you.

Somehow if we are to get it all together we must see in the accelerating change the drawing together and drawing upon one another, the self-fulfilled in community, the community enriched by the diversity of people doing not only different jobs and performing different roles, but actually coming to an awareness and an appreciation of their uniqueness discovered in relatedness with others.

The turbulence of the years you graduates have spent in college has shown us a second thing – the legitimacy of challenge, the creativeness of conflict, and the necessity of shaking up the staid and stagnant.

Perhaps the most profound effect of this recognition of the legitimacy of challenge will occur in education. Many non-Americans have wondered why children in so permissive a system would rise in protest. Was it because they saw through the perversion of education by those who sold the American people a bill of goods by convincing them that a college education, the same kind of education resulting in the same kind of degrees, was the answer to life's problems – national or individual. Too many of us encouraged the lie that a college diploma was the ticket to success and prosperity. Our educational system became a slick machine indoctrinating the young with the idea that college degrees multiplied the cash value of human life. We tried to become efficient in administering programs for a better product and the distance grew between those who built and ran the education machine and those being assembled smoothly by it. The teacher was viewed as a transmitter of the status quo. Unfortunately, this succeeded all too often. We convinced ourselves that this was the most educated generation in history and in characteristic American fashion equated most with best. Then something happened. Students said in no uncertain terms, we are not parts to be pressed, molded, and stamped. We are not grades in a book or factors in financial solvency. We are people, persons, individuals who expect an education to help us discover our humanity.

Colleges and universities are indeed having a difficult time today. It isn't only the small or inadequately endowed, but the prestigious also are paring budgets, reducing faculties, and curtailing programs. The crisis of the classroom will not be solved by money, though money, lots of money is needed in seeking appropriate solutions. Whatever forms the solutions take will come partly when we rediscover what education is, when we affirm with our lives the joy of teaching and learning, when there is greater openness to the future coupled with a wise assimilation and appreciation of the past and a constructive encounter with the present.

Solutions will be found when people are freed from the regimentation of curricula everywhere the same, when schools on all levels from kindergarten through graduate school find the courage to believe in the special value of what they are doing and have the humility to admit they cannot do all things equally well for everybody, when administrators, curators, parents and faculty can work together with students and alumni to find ways of knowing which set them free for a life-time of learning, when we can admit that vocational and technical skills are better taught elsewhere, when we quit insisting that everyone from the gas station attendant to the oil company board chairman have a college diploma. We will be moving toward a solution when we as parents and as a society can get over the stigma of our sons and daughters not going to college immediately from high school or staying there without interruption, when we can realize the wisdom of people coming and going with freedom as they find how college fits into their life-goals.

We come now to a third consideration: the humanizing of systems. Bureaucracy and technocracy have become obscenities. "The establishment", "the system", "them, they, and those" have been assailed. Some have seen this challenge to change as a desire to rid themselves of any entanglement, responsibility, or obligation. Others were more near the truth who say it is a cry for organizations more fit for humans than for replaceable parts.

The Vietnam War became a focal point for questioning the distance between the people who make the decisions and those who have to carry them out. Somehow there is a yearning in so complex an age for new ways of responsible involvement allowing those who say what is to be done and those who have to do it to come together. There is a seeking for means of admitting that systems are the creation of men so that when men's values, hopes, and dreams change their institutions change also. Our institutions have too often been used to inculcate a belief in power as the means of solving problems so that our heroes have usually been the lords of industry or battle.

Some of today's youth having encountered the incredible difficulty of humanizing systems have dropped-out, copped-out, or popped-out.

But, many more of them believe that such humanization is mandatory and they want to be a part of it. Law and medical school applicants, as well as civil service applicants, are at an all-time high. This is not for the same reasons my generation would have given – status, wealth, or security. There is a new breed of law and medical student and civil servant on the rise. He or she is one who is trying to get it all together, to work within the system to make it work for the people for whom it is created.

There is one other area I would like to mention: moral responsibility and mutual involvement.

Some of us have awakened to the schizophrenia of our ideals and our actualities. When you graduates were high school students some of you were shocked at the phoniness, hypocrisy, and lip-service of life about you. You have changed the slogans but the message is pretty much the same. There is discord in singing America the Beautiful as you peer through the tears of the smog, or hold your nose at the bloated fish, or pick your way through paper plates and beer cans to picnic. The apathy of so many provokes the energies of some calling for scrutiny of individual and institutional priorities, values, and commitments. Poverty amidst plenty perplexes more than the poor. The present involvement may not be overwhelming in solving the problems of our time, but at least many refuse to rest comfortable and blind at the misery of others and the ominous threats to the quality of human life.

Every liberal arts student learns from Socrates, "the unexamined life is not worth living." Much of the collegiate experience is devoted to knowing oneself. Fortunately, some also know the other side of Socrates, or for that matter Jesus of Nazareth as well, that "the uncommitted life makes human life meaningless". The high possibilities of the human spirit are not restricted to the intellect. Man's ingeniousness may lead only to his annihilation.

The human spirit feeds on beauty, kindness, love, creativity, and commitment. Higher values are not mere words to impress the pious or please the tender-hearted. They are the essence of humanness. They are the realization of the unlimited needs and demands of the world and the awesome responsibilities of man, the awareness of the sacred dimensions

27

of life. They are the freedom of men and women who are freed from the illusion of being God and are convinced of the worthwhileness of being human, of doing what they can even when they realize they cannot do it all any more than they can know it all. They are the realization that I am somebody whose self is enhanced rather than destroyed by others and whose work and play are manifestations of who I am. They are the impetus to a commitment of mutual involvement seeking community with respect, dignity, and life for all people breaking the bond of provincialism in quest of intercultural relationships where peace makes possible living and learning from and with one another.

Getting it all together is a prospect, not a program. It has a reality. We have gotten much from you in these four years, hopefully you have gotten much from us. Neither of us will ever be the same because we have been with one another and at times have gotten it all together. As Charles Reich, in *The Greening of America*, would say characteristic of the new generation regardless of age, "Oh Wow!" #

The address ended and the students were immediately on their feet as the auditorium reverberated with thunderous applause, Soon parents and other guests joined the students with equal enthusiasm. Even the dignified platform party rose to its feet and offered heartfelt applause. It was indeed one of the most memorable days of my life.

4. Some shorter presentations

There were many other occasions for speaking from the heart and mind, though none ever as grand as the Commencement Address. So many presentations were much briefer such as these two at Silverdale Rotary:

a. "All Kinds of Love", a ten minute presentation to Silverdale Rotary on Valentine's Day, 2008.

Thanks for the overwhelmingly impossible opportunity Mary Gerry Taylor and Elayne Burton have given me to make this presentation today.

When I googled the word LOVE I found 2,040,000,000 hits. There were 5,850,000 hits for Kinds of Love and 5,620,000 for All Kinds of Love. Under this last entry the first item was *All Kinds of Love: the Hospice Experience* by Carolyn Jaffee and Carol Ehrlich.

Today, I speak as a philosopher, a lover of wisdom, not out of my own personal experience as a lover. One of Plato's most often read dialogues is the *Symposium,* an account of an all-night drinking party in which Socrates and seven of his friends talk about Love (Eros).

The Greeks have four words for LOVE. We have only the one word which has to carry all kinds of freight. C.S. Lewis has a book on *Four Kinds of Love* and Robert Solomon a well-respected contemporary philosopher has one titled *About Love: Reinventing Romance for our Times.*

These four terms are not mutually exclusive and relate to one another. First there is **Storge**, then **Philea**, then **Eros**, and the fourth is **Agape**. Each is directional – reaching around, reaching between, reaching up, and reaching down.

1. **Storge** is the affection a parent has for a child and is essential to becoming a fully human being. It is seen in the bond of parent and child at birth such as we have seen in Jason and Heather when Amelia was born. Or Bob and Christy when they talk about Justin, Or John and Jane when they tell us about all their children.

This observation bears repeating: "If he were not my son I wouldn't even like him, but I am his Mother so I love him."

That raises the question whether we can love someone whom we don't like. We answer yes, since love is wanting the very best someone else is capable of becoming. I think of the urgent longing of a young sailor who came to my stateroom when we were in port Subic Bay, the Philippines and asked if I could marry him the next day. I explained that was not possible. Under the Status of Forces agreement it would take several months to complete the paperwork. I knew this young man well for he had visited my office often and told me he had been in 23 foster homes growing up and could not recall any one of those foster parents holding him and telling him they loved him. So he was indeed starved for affection. Little wonder that when the cute little bar girl sat on his lap and whispered in his ear "I love you, no shit," he was in paradise.

Love is essential for growth as much as good food, clean air and water. It is a love which reaches around or surrounds us.

2. We are more familiar with the second expression of the term – **Philea**. It is brotherly love as we are familiar with in Philadelphia, the city of brotherly love. It is a beautiful thing. We see it here in our Club with such friendships as that between Bud and Ron. It is this kind of love Jesus is talking about when he says, "Greater love has no man than this than that he lay down his life for his friend." Time and space don't diminish this. I think of my special friend David with whom I have been friends for over fifty years. When friends such as this are absent from one another they are able to pick up where they left off immediately once they are together again. This love spans the distance between two persons.

3. The third expression is **Eros**. It is the search for completeness/wholeness, it is based on desire and is the impetus for romance. The erotic stimulates and excites. It is symbolized by warmth, heat, and fire. It is the word for desire, lust, need.

In Tennis the term for no score is Love. It is the concept of love which causes the poet to say, "it is better to have loved and lost than never to have loved at all."

We may see it also as a passion expressing itself in ways appropriate for the time, the person, the place, and the relationship. It is the symbol of incompleteness and the desire to find fulfillment in another. That is why we refer to it as reaching up – it is always wanting more than it has.

4. The fourth and highest form of love is **Agape** – love which overflows and for no reason at all except that it is the very nature of the Lover to love. Because it is a love from the overflow or superfluity it is directionally seen as moving down to fill the emptiness of the recipient.

It is this expression of Love which enables us to speak meaningfully of an epistemology of love. In other words, when someone says "I don't see what she sees in him," they have spoken the truth because they do not know the other person in the same way the one who loves him or her does.

This is the kind of love Elizabeth Barrett Browning has in mind when she asks the oft repeated question, "How do I love thee?" It is spiritual, religious, eternal rather than temporal or bodily. The book of Hosea focuses on this when the prophet graphically talks about the love which will not let go of the beloved no matter what she does and sees this as the analogy of God's love for Israel.

The Apostle Paul, after recounting numerous desirable gifts says, that love is the greatest gift of all and that we should put love first. The Gospel of John and the Letters of John center on God as Love. Indeed the hymn has it right when it exclaims, "Oh love that will not let me go."

It is time I close as I began as a philosopher. The biggest question we ask is "what is the meaning of life?" I found the simplest, and still the best, answer as a college freshman so many decades ago in the writing of a man named Joseph Fort Newton. He answers his question, "when is life worth living," with this reply. "Life is worth living when I have a self fit to live with, a work fit to live for, someone to love and be loved by."

Thank you all for loving me and letting me love you. Happy Valentine's Day! #

b. "A prayer for Veterans Day, 2011"

Here is a prayer, without preceding presentation, offered at Rotary. Though it is in the form of a prayer, it may well be seen as a carefully thought out oral presentation addressed to God but for the thoughtful reception and reflection of those who heard it.

Eternal God, we pause at the beginning of our Rotary meeting aware that tomorrow is Veterans Day and today is the 236th birthday of the Marine Corps. We are grateful for the contributions of men and women in all our armed forces to the cause of freedom and the pursuit of peace. Our admiration for them does not blind us to the services of others such as police and firefighters, medical personnel, educators, public service workers, and all the others whose work is necessary for a functioning society. By honoring those whose military service contributes so directly to our freedom, we do not wish to glorify war with its destruction, disruption, mutilation, and corruption. That is done to excess in movies and video games. Rather, we extol the values we learned in our

31

military involvement – the value of performing at our highest level for the sake of others whose lives depend on us, the value of teamwork and cooperation, of integrity and courage, of persistence and faithfulness, of vigilance and strength, of greater love of both family and nation.

As we pray for those men and women in uniform near at hand and around the globe, we pray also for a much smaller and less identifiable group of men and women engaged in Rotary peace studies learning how to become involved in the no less difficult and often dangerous attempts at conflict resolution and negotiation to prevent hostilities or to bring them to a humane cessation.

Help us as citizens and especially as Rotarians in these tumultuous times to use our power and our resources for creating a society where no artificial barriers, no greed, no self-centeredness will keep any among us from reaching their noblest, highest, and most realistic expectations. We pray by the power or your Holy Spirit. Amen. #

c. Veteran's Day, 2012:

On another occasion at the Silverdale Rotary I made the following presentation.

It was the eleventh hour of the eleventh day of the eleventh month – it was Armistice Day 1938. The church bells began to ring, the siren at the firehouse pierced the air, the whistles at the laundry plant and the cotton mills blasted as I, a six year old, stood beside my desk as did my classmates. The silence was pervasive. Then the teacher said simply, Amen before she read to us In Flanders Field, a well-known poem by John McCrae:

> In Flanders Fields the poppies blow,
> Between the crosses row on row,
> That mark our place; and in the sky
> The larks, still bravely singing, fly
> Scarce heard amid the guns below.
> We are the Dead. Short days ago we
> Lived, felt dawn, saw sunset glow
> Loved and were loved, and now we lie in Flanders fields.
> Take up our quarrel with the foe:

To you from failing hands we throw
The Torch; be yours to hold it high.
If ye break faith with us who die
We shall not sleep, though poppies grow in Flanders Field.

Armistice Day was first proclaimed by President Woodrow Wilson in 1919 when he said, "To us in America, the reflections of Armistice Day will be filled with solemn pride in the heroism of those who died in the country's service and with gratitude for the victory, both because of the thing from which it has freed us and because of the opportunity it has given America to show her sympathy with peace and justice in the councils of the nations."

It celebrated the end of The Great War, "the war to end all wars." Little did we know in our childhood innocence that a greater even more horrendous war was fast approaching both in Europe and Asia.

At the end of that war in 1945 it was proposed that we honor the dead of all wars and a few years later, in 1954 President Dwight D. Eisenhower, formerly Supreme Allied Commander in the European Theater of Operations signed into law the congressional bill replacing Armistice Day with Veterans Day.

I can think of no better words for us to hear on this Veterans Day, 2012 than these from President Lincoln as he addressed the assembled crowd at Gettysburg a century earlier on November 19, 1863:

Four score and seven years ago our fathers brought forth on this continent, a new nation, conceived in Liberty, and dedicated to the proposition that all men are created equal.

Now we are engaged in a great civil war, testing whether that nation, or any nation so conceived and dedicated, can long endure. We are met on a great battlefield of that war. We have come to dedicate a portion of that field, as a final resting place for those who here gave their lives that that nation might live. It is altogether fitting and proper that we should do this.

But, in a larger sense, we cannot dedicate – we cannot consecrate – we cannot hallow – this ground. The brave men, living and dead, who struggled here, have consecrated it, far above our poor power to add or detract. The world will little note, nor long remember what we say here, but it can never forget what they did here. It is for us the living, rather, to be dedicated here to the unfinished work which they who fought here have thus far so nobly advanced. It is rather for us to be here dedicated to the great task remaining before us – that from these honored dead we take increased devotion to that cause for which they gave the last full measure of devotion – that we here highly resolve that these dead shall not have died in vain – that his nation, under God, shall have a new birth of freedom --- and that government of the people, by the people, for the people, shall not perish from the earth.

Only two days ago that resolve was tested again – though there was vitriol, and lying, and incivility, and mendacity and bitterness aplenty, not a shot was fired nor was the President's residence stormed nor were gangs fighting in the street. This imperfect democracy purchased and continually paid for by its valiant heroes and committed citizens took the opportunity to continue to seek to forge a more perfect union through the electoral process.

So to all those Veterans past and present for whom courage and loyalty and strength and devotion were not mere words but the very fabric of their endeavor we are grateful.

Gracious God we thank you for these very special sailors and marines here with us at Rotary today who represent the finest virtues of military service in whatever branch and who have distinguished themselves by their personal excellence and their exceptional contributions to the common good. We commend to your care and keeping those far from home and especially those in harm's way and their loving anxious families who pay so high a sacrifice for their service. May we all, military and civilians alike, use our abilities to find ways of peace and justice in this turbulent world. Amen #

d. "PTA Devotion"

Often I was called upon to present a "meditation", usually at the beginning of an event. This is a briefer form of speaking usually seeking to focus the group's attention on some particular issue or concern. When the following meditation was given it was a very different age than the one

34

we now live in. For instance, in the 1960s I was often asked to open Parent Teacher Association meetings with a devotion. Here is one of those given at Southern Junior High School, Lexington, Kentucky.

At least a part of the purposes of public school education is to transmit the essential and minimal knowledge which a society holds to be of value to its continued existence and progress. A breadth of subjects contributes to knowledge of the various relationships which make up life. Youth learn of the natural world through the sciences, of the world of social relations through social studies, of the ways by which men understand one another through communication arts or languages, of the spiritual dimensions of human life through the arts, and of moral values of a community of people by the very ways by which they live together enjoying the delights and accepting the consequences of their decisions. Hopefully, out of this our sons and daughters are learning not only knowledge but wisdom --the ability to use well what they know or can learn.

About 2500 years ago a teacher began his instruction by stating his purposes: That men may know wisdom and instruction, understand words of insight, receive instruction in wise dealing, righteousness, justice and equity; that prudence may be given to the simple, knowledge and discretion to the youth – and the wise men may also hear and increase in learning, and the man of understanding acquire skill, to understand a proverb and a figure, the words of the wise and their riddles. The fear of the Lord is the beginning of knowledge; fools despise wisdom and instruction. (*Proverbs 1:2-7*) His counsel has relevance for us as we visit the classrooms and meet the teachers. Maybe such a time will help us to accept our mutual responsibility for avoiding foolish despising of wisdom by creating or reinforcing in us a sincere and obvious gratitude for the ways youth learn, for the persons with whom they learn, and an enthusiastic encouragement of such learning leading to wisdom.

Let us pray: God grant to us an openness to change and a willingness to learn. Enable us to appreciate the crucial role of public school teachers who must attempt to teach all who are made to come to them. Grant to us, as parents, a firm desire to communicate to our sons and daughters a high value for learning that will kindle some readiness and enthusiasm about how and what they learn. Give to us wisdom to accept the necessity of assisting youth in developing the ability for making discriminating choices and the awareness of the inseparability of moral decisions in the very process by which they come to know the importance of their places in so dynamic and exciting a world. Grant us joy in living, patience in learning, and responsibility in using wisely what we know. Amen. #

e. "Ombudsman Council devotion"

Here is a brief devotional for the Ombudsman Council, Naval Submarine Base, Bangor Washington, March 15, 1985.

"Come then my love; my darling, come with me. The winter is over; the rains have stopped; In the countryside the flowers are in bloom. This is the time for singing; the song of doves is heard in the fields." (*The Song of Songs*, 2:10-12)

Now, doesn't that make you want to pack a picnic lunch and head for the mountains? Spring awakens in us feelings we had forgotten were there. It is God's love-letter to us. As if the flowers and soft breezes were not enough, He says from within the Jewish tradition, I set you free in the springtime, pass over with me from that tied-up feeling of gloom to freedom and joy. And from within the community of the Christian faith comes the message: Beyond the shattering loneliness of suffering night, I have broken a new morning, a resurrection day when brightness and beauty and wonder are my love gifts to you. So get out there. Take off your shoes and run in the grass, chase butterflies, and listen to birds singing, for it is once again the time for singing of love – God's love for us and ours for one another. #

f. "A tribute to Dr. Bob Rozendal on his retirement" Silverdale, Washington, August 25, 2000.

Bob and I share many things which make it easy for me to admire, respect and honor him:

The spiritual basis of life,

The uniqueness and preciousness of each human life,

The sustaining power of a deep religious faith,

36

The belief that life is to be shared and the responsibility to give back some of what one receives,

A recognition of the sustaining power of family relationships,

An appreciation for beauty and the finer things of life,

An awareness of the essential role of grace,

A continuing love of learning and teaching,

A fascination with the questions and concerns of medical ethics,

A debt of gratitude for the contributions of the Navy to our growth both personally and professionally,

A commitment to living well and dying well.

So what are the things I am most appreciative of in Bob's life of service to the community?

His integrity, his humility, his generosity, his graciousness, his perspicacity.

Bob and Kay were instrumental in their church, Central Kitsap Presbyterian Church, forming and developing a Stephens Ministry.

Bob has served the wider community in a number of ways; I am most aware and grateful for his continuing service to Hospice of Kitsap County.

After a class in which we shared the joy of learning, Bob shared with me the Physician's Prayer attributed to Moses Maimonides. It is a prayer to be prayed each day before beginning one's service as a doctor and epitomizes quite well the heart of Bob Rozendal so I share an excerpt from it now:

"I am about to apply myself to the duties of my profession. Support me, Almighty God, in these great labors that they may benefit mankind, for without Thy help, not even the least thing will succeed. Inspire me with love for my art and for Thy creatures. Do not allow thirst for profit, ambition for renown and admiration, to interfere with my profession, for these are the enemies of truth and love for mankind and they can lead astray in the great task of attending to the welfare of Thy creatures. Preserve the strength of my body and of my soul that they ever be ready to cheerfully help and support rich and poor, good and bad, enemy as well as friend. In the sufferer let me see only the human being. Amen.

C. Having something to say and listeners who want to hear it

The previous section collected a few public speeches uniting heart and mind. In this section I have gathered presentations deliberately prepared for academic settings. It isn't that they do not express emotion as well as intellect. It is rather that their purpose was to present as clearly and accurately as I could my research and thought on the given topic. There was a presumed receptivity since I had been requested to address the given topics. They were each met with positive acceptance encouraging dialogue for further exploration. Once again, I ask you to imagine you are hearing me present these to a live audience rather than reading them from the page.

1. "The Limits of Christian Ethics in a Pluralistic Society."

On April 24, 1967 I delivered a presentation for the Faculty Seminar at Transylvania University based on an unpublished paper. Its title was "The Limits of Christian Ethics in a Pluralistic Society". This was in a time before we had become conscious of gender discrimination in language and man or men was used when it today would be either men and women or human beings.

Following the material which was presented orally I have included an abstract of the paper, an outline, and a bibliography.

Introduction: Presently, all things are new – new economics, new sociology, new theology, new morality, and so forth. Such polarization is unfortunate -- it drives advocates to defend one position against another and limits debate to such ground.

The interpretative task is never completed. There are always new problems with which the old has to deal and new dimensions of the old reality itself. More immediate problems and more urgent needs are approached with greater difficulty and suspicion. We lack a historical perspective but then life itself must be lived in the present by living men.

I. Ethical formulation a human necessity.

38

Man is an actor or agent as well as an actant. His actions have effect upon the fullness or emptiness, adequacy or inadequacy, achievement or failure of life – his own and others both directly and indirectly. He reflects on the meaning of his actions and orders them in some fashion that has significance, at least to him. He desires certain ends from his actions whether tangible or ethereal, explicit or implicit.

If he is to act societally with satisfaction there must be some shared acceptance and agreement on objectives though not necessarily on methods.

Ethics is a reflective, reasonable, and more often rational formulation of the course of human action and is to be distinguished from morality which is the human act itself to which such terms as good, right, honest, adequate, humane, etc. may be applied.

Man is moral then by virtue of his role as actor in society, regardless of the specific content of that action.

Man is ethical as a reflector upon or director of his actions.

Both as moral and ethical, his existence is ambiguous and multi-vocal.

Ethics because of its continuity may be the style of life which is predominate rather than the verbalized system which a man expresses.

Pure ethical thought is an abstraction as pure moral action is a delusion. No man acts completely oblivious of his own involvement especially in a complex society where his life is lived in several dimensions. No man reflects on his past action with absolute honesty or forward to his future action with absolute certainty. Consequently, the truth of an ethical position is not to be sought in its most rigorous and idealized lucid formulations or extreme demands but in its function and form in providing impetus toward, motivation in, validation for, and critique of moral action.

II. Historical/Societal Context of Ethics

Ethics presupposes a context with two foci – 1) historical, i.e. spatial -- having some place to stand, and temporal – seeing things in the present in relation to the past and the future and 2) societal – i.e. having shared events, accepted myths, corporate images, and common destiny.

As Gibson Winter says, "... historical in the profound sense; it grapples with the present meaning of the past.... It considers the moral possibilities of the future in terms of human fulfillment." (*Elements for a social ethic*, 219)

Ethics is radically <u>historical</u>. This is true whether our orientation or emphasis is personal or social. Any given man has a heritage and a destiny, so do all men.

But, man's <u>history</u> is never <u>univocal</u> – either in terms of our ability to define it in one exclusive purpose or to reduce it to one all-consuming goal. A man is a citizen, husband, son, lover, worker, dreamer, thinker, etc. This multiplicity of dimensions allows us to consider man's <u>history</u> itself as pluralistic. Human decisions must be made sometimes simultaneously, sometimes consequently, sometimes concurrently.

Ethics is concerned with man as pluralistic decision-maker. In terms of social ethics we may say with Winter, "Man as maker of history is integral to the notion of a responsible society; in such a society, decisions are made with awareness of the values to be realized and in accountability for the consequences of social policy." (*Elements for a social ethic*, p. 259)

A specific ethic does not exhaust the dimensions of man's decision-making, though it has a pervasiveness akin to religion which though sometimes only implicit and consciously ignored is nevertheless operative.

The ethic may become the more conspicuous dimension of religion. By religion we mean that configuration of experiences relative to the holy, divine, sacred, or ultimate. It may express itself at any given time, for any community, or in any action, or in the decision-making that accompanies it.

Not all ethics are deliberately, intentionally, or in fact religious. However, all ethics have some particular referent, norm, standard, origin, interpretive principle, or focal point.

To identify one's ethical stance in terms of his religious commitment is to raise the question of its exclusive demands as well as its inclusive motivations.

Therefore, to talk of Christian ethics is to accept the limitation of such a qualifier though one may contend this limitation is the most advantageous means to ethical freedom.

III. "Christian" as a qualifier of ethics

Christian Ethics accepts a biblical interpretive orientation as qualifier. This needs serious clarification against charges of obscurantism, irrelevancy, anarchism, etc. Among the contributory dimensions of that qualification are:

1) A sense of meaningful history,

2) A conviction of life's basic goodness and its celebration with joy. As Peter Berger says, "The central message of the Christian Faith is not a call to struggle but a call to joy." (*The Precarious Vision,* p. 218)

3) Openness for praise and gratitude,

4) Realization of man's theological orientation,

5) Commitment to meaningful human experience,

6) Belief in ethical seriousness,

7) Recognition of movement toward community,

8) A claim to creativity, love, and service as marks of genuine humanity.

9) Response to human guilt, brokenness, separation, and fragmentation,

10) Acknowledgment of the finiteness of man,

11) Realism toward evil, abuse, and exploitation,

12) A transcendent dimension of justice and righteousness, since God is holy, just, and righteous,

13) Ultimacy to love as the divine-human link expressed primarily in love of the neighbor,

Three options are offered in determining the particular stance within Christian Ethics:

1) Ethics defined or authorized by the Christian community, not necessarily institutionalized church bodies,

2) Ethics meeting certain prescribed demands, such as "to be more like Jesus", to adhere to specific biblical, usually New

Testament passages, or to fulfill stipulated commands of an accepted religious leader,

3) Ethics oriented toward life in the light of Jesus as the Christ – "The man for others", God's man in history, the one through whom the power and the presence of the divine became personally real in the human situation.

I have opted for the latter option in Christian Ethics as the most adequate for human fulfillment in the historical/societal context.

Christian Ethics then may be thought of as that reflective lived experience of a man which while standing appreciatively in his heritage, looks critically at it and lives its values so far as possible while responsibly challenging its disvalues. It is the assertion of one's integrity in time by standing with men so as to participate in God's love for them and free them to accept for themselves such a vocation.

Christian Ethics seeks adequacy, fulfillment, and community for the self or person. Christ was one who did not need to claim all for himself since life's fullness was to be found in relationship with the Divine which made meaningful every significant relationship even that of the self with itself as well as with other men.

IV. Christian Ethics and historical/human fulfillment

Christian Ethics is obviously but one constituent ethic in a pluralistic society. It cannot claim supremacy to the exclusion of others without violating the integrity of the pluralistic society. Plainly, it finds itself both akin to and differing from other ethical positions.

If it loses all distinctiveness it has no positive value in a pluralistic society. If it has no common ground it has a negative value in the pluralistic society.

I find Gibson Winter's term, "an ethical style which we call historical contextualism." (*Elements of a social ethic*, p. 244) helpful.

Peter Berger sees a humanistic ethics as one devoted to working its principles out in actions for the betterment of humankind. He then sees Christian Ethics as a humanistic ethic. (*The Precarious Vision*, p. 199)

Christian Ethics shares certain ethical convictions with many ethical perspectives, whether these are of religious or non-religious

42

orientation. These include concerns such as search for human betterment, desire for more humane approaches to problems, and positive benefits from conflict.

Christian Ethics shares certain ethical convictions with other religious ethics in that it believes the best human life is somehow related to the divine, that there is a self-transcendence which serves man as critic, restraint, and judge, that there is a desire for depth in community, and that there is meaningfulness to time which gives it qualitative dimensions which are called eternal or spiritual.

Again Winter opens this up for us: "… the task of special communities of faith is to evoke, nurture, and extend the reconciling power of man's relational being – not calling men to another history or another existence but deepening their humaneness in their historical situation." (*Elements of a social ethic*, p. 234)

Christian Ethics finds itself strangely perplexed by the query – what is its distinctiveness and therefore its value to a pluralistic society? This is, of course, exceedingly difficult and perhaps really impossible to answer. But an attempt must be made.

Christian Ethics sees its basic orientation to God relative to Jesus Christ. It believes that somehow he was in his historical context the man in whom the divine reality found human fulfillment. It believes that he was one who lived not only for but with others in such a style of life that life found freshness, freedom and openness. It sees the goal of humanity as community preserving personal integrity and living responsibly before God.

It believes corruption is a human problem having deep roots affecting the very patterns and structures of human action, valuation, and response.

It believes that integrity before God necessitates the daring assertion that biological life cannot be the highest value, consequently physical death cannot be the greatest evil.

It believes that this world is the arena of God's love expressed in human action.

When we have thus delineated the interior terrain we have not, of course, said these ethical values are not found in other ethics. We are willing, however, to say that if they are <u>not</u> found in a given ethic it is quite dubious that that ethic should be designated Christian.

V. The Pluralistic Society and historical/human fulfillment

Before we turn to an examination of the pluralistic society with particular concern to show 1) the positive value of such a society and 2) its religious and ethical vitality let us look at the pluralistic society in its historical/human fulfillment in America.

The story of America's struggle toward a pluralistic society is too familiar to be retold here, except to remind us of some pivotal points.

The pluralistic society emerged from a Protestant Anglo-Saxon people who left Europe behind them and began to fashion a new and "lively experiment" in this new land. They did not arrive at pluralism easily. Eleven of the thirteen colonies had established or state churches. Tolerance and freedom meant only freedom to believe and act as the community proscribed or leave the community altogether.

Perry Miller is not so sure that the development was linear and even observes that America stumbled into pluralism. (Cited in *Voluntary Associations*, p. 134)

Acceptance of other views and positions came grudgingly as churches, for example, vied for the exclusive rights to a pathway to heaven. Tolerance came slowly and the bias was toward Protestant Christianity.

Roman Catholicism provided more toleration at the time than other religions but soon found itself denied legal rights as Anglicanism became established in Maryland.

This disenfranchisement in attitude if not in legality stayed in America until late into the 19th century. Judaism only became an effective constituent of the pluralistic society after the 20th century. Andre Siegfried observed that as late as 1927 the Pluralistic Society was not a reality in America. (Cited in *Voluntary Associations*, p. 138)

The 19th century was, however, a great age of the birth of voluntary associations and organizations which played a significant role in the expansion of the frontier westward. In fact voluntary association has been a characteristic of American religion since early on. As Langdon Gilkey puts it, "Religion is not something that comes to a man from an objective institution that possesses and communicates grace; rather, the institution is formed by the voluntary association in fellowship of religious people." ("Social and Intellectual Sources of Contemporary Protestant Theology in America," p. 78). He goes on to say, "Religion is viewed as primarily a moral and social-communal matter, relevant to the enactment of good in the lives of men and the wider social community." (p. 80)

The pluralistic society as a free society for all was often threatened not by evil men but by some of the most pious. For instance, Charles G. Finney, the great evangelist saw it as a definite threat to Christianity and demanded conformity to his revivalist views. (Cited in *Voluntary Associations*, p. 136)

From its present state the pluralistic society sometimes sees its past as easily won with everybody sharing equally. It tends to see the future in much the same way. It often tends to assume that prosperity is its birthright and if no longer "under God" as the benefactor then Ford, motor company and foundation, General Motors, or even the Department of Health, Education, and Welfare now acts on His default.

Too often the pluralistic society fails to appreciate the dynamics of its own situation as this could contribute to world community. Members and interpreters of the pluralistic society sometimes romanticize it by assuming that truth and justice for the socially and culturally disadvantaged will win out in time just as they have for religion and politics. Sometimes it naturalizes it by affirming that the course of nature is moving inevitably forward and such problems as pollution, poverty, and urbanization will by a homeostasis of the body politic soon bring health and wholeness. Sometimes it neutralizes it by saying that after all principles are higher than practices and not dependent on popular sentiment, moral consensus, or vigorous political life. Sometimes it dramatizes it by caricaturing it as locked in mortal combat with frost-breathing bears or fire-breathing dragons.

VI. Positive values of a pluralistic society

The pluralistic society's most positive value lives in the maximal possibilities it provides for historical/human fulfillment combining the idealism of human community with the realism of human indifference, separation, and conflict. Karl Hertz observes, "Pluralism implies the freedom of the individual to change his mind, his decisions, and his memberships." ("The nature of voluntary associations," p. 32)

It allows for fluidity of structures to some degree even in its bureaucracy by tolerating and encouraging voices of dissent, though perhaps when voices become actions this becomes another matter. Again Hertz, "The American protest is against unilateral structural control of one sphere of life by another, against totalitarianism of the right or the left. The maintenance of structured independence of conditioned freedom; the maintenance of vital relationships is equally a condition of meaningful freedom." ("the nature of voluntary associations," p. 33)

It seeks to be cognizant of the whole community even when its success is with meeting certain segment's needs more than of others.

The pluralistic society asks itself the disturbing question of the truth of social forms – how can we advocate the positive values of that which has proven of value, though obviously not perfectly, for us without denying other men the right to arrive at an appropriate form for them?

The pluralistic society functions positively in the richness of its diversity around a common national character.

Franklin Littell maintains, "The genius of our way of life is the dialogue, the practice of reaching decisions by open-faced discussion among those who share a common responsibility and a common destiny." ("A new pattern of community," p. 269)

It is in a position to offer hope to other peoples. Just as the constituents whether religious, political, social or whatever were not violated as they joined or were joined by others but were thereby made more healthily self-conscious, so in a world community such a pluralistic society might be an appropriate model.

In other words, the pluralistic society ideal helps to keep us from nebulous utopianism where all is harmonious tranquility on the one hand

and chauvinistic pessimism where all is belligerent antagonism on the other.

The pluralistic society is a recognition of the relativities of human history without succumbing to a relativism without valid discriminative principles and practices.

VII. The Religious and Ethical Vitality of the Pluralistic Society

At this point let us note three expressions of the vitality of the pluralistic society.

A. American pluralistic society grew out of a people expressing a Puritan Ethic. Though this Puritan Ethic had by the time of the American Revolution lost most of its direct religious contact with the religious tradition from which it had come it nevertheless functioned effectively in molding the national character. This is the thesis of Edmund S. Morgan, Yale Historian, who states, "Revolution was affected, not to say guided by a set of values... [which he denotes the Puritan Ethic] inherited from the Age of Puritanism." ("The Puritan Ethic and the American Revolution," p. 3) The Puritan Ethic emphasized such values as simplicity, industry, frugality, and a sense of the calling to serve God by serving oneself and society productively.

Americans believed freedom was inseparable from virtue so that the closer the colonies moved to a War of Independence the more vocal spokesmen became about American virtues and British vices. In 1775 Thomas Jefferson wrote Lord North, "We do not mean that our people shall be burthened with oppressive taxes to provide sinecures for the idle or the wicked." ("The Puritan Ethic and the American Revolution," p. 18)

Following the War Americans were jubilant over their success and took it as further validation of the rightness of the Puritan Ethic. The struggle itself had made better men of them and the very success became a cause for admonishing faithfulness. Many doubted the possibility of any real overcoming of provincialism and though the struggle was not finally settled even by constitutional convention Americans surprised themselves with the value for union of their pluralistic approach.

Perhaps as Morgan contends pluralism could work effectively because the differences of parties were not radical or ultimately different.

"Our political disputes are peaceful, because both parties espouse similar principles and objectives and neither feels itself severely threatened by the other. ("The Puritan Ethic and the American Revolution," p. 24) Their very diversity, however, was strength for a people seeking some common destiny. Back of the separate parties was the moral consensus of the Puritan Ethic.

As it expressed itself politically so it emerged in economic thought and practice. Boycotts, demonstrations, and protest marches were on the scene early. In 1764/65 Americans were boycotting British goods and students were doing their part by refusing to drink imported beer.

Though the merchant was suspect until well after the War because of his lack of tangible productivity, a sin against the Puritan Ethic, manufacturing saw a rapid rise blessed by the Puritan Ethic.

During the War and its aftermath voices were indignantly raised against those profiteering public officials who served themselves from the public Till. Henry Laurens, 5th president of the Continental Congress denounced the "sacrilegious robberies of public money by congressmen and military officers carrying on private trade in army supplies." ("The Puritan Ethic and the American Revolution," p. 29)

After the War "Americans were caught up in an orgy of buying". ("The Puritan Ethic and the American Revolution, p. 36) but depression soon followed. Once more in 1787 Americans were called upon to return to the Puritan Ethic in their economic life: "America will never feel her importance and dignity until she alters her present system of trade, so ruinous to the interests, to the morals, and to the reputation of her citizens." ("The Puritan Ethic and the American Revolution", p. 37) Some observers even went so far as to see demonic activity in trade with Great Britain who by her practices of overextending credit and flooding American markets with luxury goods was destroying the moral fiber of a people whom she had not been able to defeat militarily. The cry arose to buy American goods though they may cost more and be of inferior quality. This justification was moral, the private preference must be subordinated to the public interest and this was from the Puritan Ethic. The pluralistic society thus had the benefit of the Puritan Ethic.

Morgan points out, "The Puritan Ethic did not die with the 18th century. Throughout our history it has been there, though it has continued to be in the process of expiring." ("The Puritan Ethic and the American Revolution, p. 42.) He carries this forward into the 2oth century by observing, "The most popular analysis of American society after the Second World War was a lament for the loss of inner-directedness (read simplicity, industry, frugality) which had been replaced by other-directedness (read luxury, extravagance)". ("The Puritan Ethic and the American Revolution," p. 43)

B. The pluralistic society became the fullest expression of the secularistic ethos.

God is not absent from the pluralistic society but His presence is not dependent upon vocalization of His name by governmental decree. Even when religious constituents are vigorous the pluralistic society is a secular rather than a sacral society. The sacred society cannot tolerate the diversity of the pluralistic society for it is convinced that not only the theology or ideology by which it lives but the very forms of government which exist at its pleasure are divinely and unalterably ordained, for example in colonial America or Medieval Europe.

These points are made clear by a number of current authors. We look more closely at Langdon Gilkey's analysis in "Secularism's Impact on Contemporary Theology," an article appearing in *Christianity and Crisis*, April, 1965.

Gilkey sees secularism as "the pre-rational basis of all potent contemporary philosophies" ("Secularism's impact on contemporary theology," p. 128) and not as a competitive constituent of the pluralistic society. Secularism emphasizes, "the here and now, the tangible, the manipulatable, the sensible, the relative, and the this-worldly." ("Secularism's impact on contemporary theology," p. 128)

Current analyzes of secularism have led to a conclusion of the impossibility of meaningful language about God and the baleful cry has gone up of a fight to the death between godless secularism and godly religion. We fail to appreciate the fact that the present state of religious and political freedom could hardly be possible in any but a secular society where men are indeed responsible for their historic destiny.

Gilkey sees secularism playing a positive role in religious language, thus discourse. "A more valid analysis, probably of a phenomenological sort, of those realms of ordinary experience that we call secular will reveal dimensions for which only language about God is sufficient and thus will manifest the meaningfulness of that language." ("Secularism's impact on contemporary theology," p. 132)

Max Lerner finds secularization as a new kind of religious expression: "… instead of finding their democratic faith in supernatural religion, Americans have tended to find their religious faith in various forms of belief about their own existence." (*America as a Civilization*," p. 715)

As Franklin Littell says, "Non-sacral government is as important to religious liberty as free churches" (*The Churches and the Body Politic*, p. 28). Or again "secular government is the partner of religious freedom." (*The Churches and the Body Politic*, p. 31)

It is precisely the positive secularism of the pluralistic society which has kept America from becoming post-Christian. Such a society refuses to see this position as antithetical to religious pluralism. Martin Marty expresses it succinctly, "Americans have consciously, deliberately, and consistently regarded the 'secular', technological, problem solving, pluralist life as liberating and life-enhancing."

C. The positive secularity of the pluralistic society while no longer depending on the Puritan Ethic nevertheless finds its consensus in civil religion.

The pluralistic society has its religious consensus in a civil religion which takes its symbols from the Judeo-Christian tradition but is not to be identified with any of the religious constituents of the pluralistic society. This point is made by Robert Bellah, Harvard Sociologist, in his seminal article, "Civil Religion in America," *Daedalus,* Winter, 1965. According to Bellah American civil religion has three main focal points – the Revolution, the Civil War, and the present.

Almost from the beginning America was seen as the New Israel, God's Promised Land, even the New Jerusalem. Both Thomas Jefferson and Benjamin Franklin suggested symbols from the biblical story of the exodus for the great seal of America. Jefferson chose a scene of wilderness wandering led by cloud and pillar of fire. Franklin chose Moses and the parting of the Red Sea.

The American Revolution came to be regarded as the time of the exodus and the covenant. These were basic symbols of national beginnings even as they had been for the ancient Hebrews. This is a major point in H. Richard Niebuhr's influential *Kingdom of God in America.*

The second historic trial added symbols of sacrifice, death, and rebirth. A new savior appeared in Abraham Lincoln: "the noblest and loveliest character since Jesus Christ", said his law partner W. Henry Herndon. Lincoln's Gettysburg Address became the Lincolnian New Testament among civil scriptures. ("Civil Religion in America," page 10). Lincoln was too conscious of the moral ambiguity of "the almost chosen people" to share the self-righteousness of those who were not ready for this preparation for pluralism.

This civil religion was from the start headed in the direction of religious pluralism.

The third historic phase may be centered around the brief presidency and shocking assassination of John Fitzgerald Kennedy. The national reaction was religious and a new shared experience rehearsed the sacrificial motif. President Kennedy's New Frontier was a deliberate ritual expression of the American Israel.

Instead of the civil religion leading to isolation or arrogance it sets us free to face squarely the "problem of responsible action in a revolutionary world." ("Civil Religion in America", page 16) Since this American civil religion carries with it a transcendent dimension even with the secularization of symbols it frees the pluralistic society from worship of itself and thrusts it forward to a larger community for historical/human fulfillment.

As Bellah says, "Fortunately, since the American civil religion is not the worship of the American nation but an understanding of the

American experience in the light of ultimate and universal reality, the reorganization entailed by such a new situation need not disrupt the American civil religion's continuity. A world civil religion could be accepted as fulfillment and not denial of American civil religion. Indeed, such an outcome has been the eschatological hope of American civil religion from the beginning. To deny such an outcome would be to deny the meaning of America itself." ("Civil Religion in America," p. 18)

In the light of this one of the most vital functions of the Christian Ethic in a pluralistic society is the recognition of civil religion for what it is, that is, a means of national cohesion and character and a constant vigilance in proclaiming the transcendent realities which it relates to but must not become.

We are now ready to return to the major question of this paper.

VIII. What are the limits of Christian Ethics in a Pluralistic Society?

A. The limits of Christian Ethics:

1. Christian Ethics is limited because it is **Christian** Ethics which has a particular orientation, stance, or perspective.

2. Christian Ethics is limited because it commits itself to freedom and freedom is always meaningful contextually.

3. Christian Ethics is limited because it sees itself as existing before God and not as God, i.e. it is responsible for its freedom and dares not confuse its belief that God is at work in history with its own limited action in history.

4. Christian Ethics is limited by the fact that it is but one expression of man's humanity in a pluralistic society and common human decency may be in any given situation a more dominant motive than deliberate Christian action.

5, Christian Ethics is limited by the sobering awareness that decision-making is a complex phenomenon about which we have much yet to learn.

6. Christian Ethics is limited by the humbling experience that Christianity does not have ready-made answers to many problems and that the ethicist is but one voice in the problem of how a

pluralistic society goes about grappling with domestic and foreign issues.

7. Christian Ethics is limited in the pluralistic society by the abuse of religion which comes from those who see it as strictly private and those who see it as solely social.

8. Christian Ethics is limited by the confusion of its relationship with the church and traditional forms.

B. Positive expression within the limits

1. Expressions relative to the church

a. Prophetic criticism which assists in recognizing unethical practices within the church itself.

b. Assistance in stripping away the false sanctity from churchly institutions which conveys a moral superiority.

c. Refreshing the memory of its commitment to a Lord who lived and spoke of losing, giving, serving, suffering, finding, and dying.

d. Helping the church to accept graciously and with joy the ethical involvements of other social institutions in the pluralistic society both governmental and non-governmental as well.

e. Helping the church to preserve integrity of both religion and ethics by refusing to reduce either one to the other.

f. Challenging the church's demeaning demanding special privilege claims such as tax exemption, clergy rates, clerical exemption from national service, etc..

g. Reminding the church that the church is a cultural institution not tied to only a single form.

2. Expressions relative to the pluralistic society

a. Christian Ethics can offer to men a voluntary style of life which celebrates the goodness of creation, affirms life, and stands open to a historical destiny which makes it all the more poignantly aware of the baseness of human existence and the destructive possibilities of man. James Gustafson puts it this way, "In the complexity given us precisely by the voluntary character of the churches lies the vitality of American Christianity." ("The voluntary church: a moral appraisal," p. 315)

b. Christian Ethics can become better equipped in the social sciences and with the dynamics of decision-making so as to engage in intelligent dialogue.

c. Christian Ethics can seek out appropriate forms for historical/human fulfillment in such ways as helping to organize the powerless. John Bennett makes this clear: "... an important aspect of Christian social responsibility is the organization politically of the victims of social injustice so that they can use their power to change conditions." (*Christianity and Crisis*, March 22, 1965)

d. Christian Ethics can encourage men to accept the moral ambiguity of the historical situation without this leading to moral paralysis.

e. Christian Ethics can help men to realize that large segments of their lives are neither crises nor spectacular on the one hand nor meaningless on the other and face these appropriately..

f. Christian Ethics can urge upon men those pursuits of ever expanding human community which run risks of nastiness, as in the charged situation of racism and open housing, or confusion, branding anyone who seeks social betterment a communist.

g. Christian Ethics can help the pluralistic society redirect itself in this creative period of history away from provincialism to more adequate styles of community. Again Gustafson, "The parochialism or provincialism leads to a limited view of the world; the absence of diverse groups limits the contact with other sub-cultures." ("The voluntary church: a moral appraisal," p. 312)

h. Christian Ethics can help to keep the pluralistic society sensitive to the images by which it lives.

i. Christian Ethics can champion the right to dissent as a mark of health of the pluralistic society.

Conclusion: In conclusion let me say simply that Christian Ethics is still a viable, vital, and effective element in a pluralistic society when its limits are recognized and its forces employed appropriately in aiding both the individual and the society in finding a better way to live. #

Abstract: It is the purpose of this paper to indicate the limits of Christian Ethics in a Pluralistic Society and to maintain these limits have a salutary effect on both Christian Ethics and American society. The nature of Christian Ethics is stated so as to facilitate an understanding of its relation to ethics in general, to Christianity, to the church as an institution, and to the pluralistic society. The secularized pluralistic society is seen as a more appropriate arena for Christian Ethics than a sacrally sovereign society.

Outline:

I. Ethical Formulation is a human necessity

II. Historical/Societal context of ethics

III. "Christian" as a qualifier of ethics

IV. Christian Ethics and historical/human fulfillment

V. The Pluralistic Society and historical/human fulfillment

VI. Religious and ethical vitality of a pluralistic society

VII. The limits of Christian Ethics in a Pluralistic Society

    A. Stating the limits

    B. Positive expressions within the limits

        1. relative to the church

        2. relative to society

Bibliography: (some less central entries are not listed)

Beck, Bernard, "Welfare as a Moral Category," *Social Problems,* vol. 14, no. 3, Winter, 1967, pp. 258-277.

Bellah, Robert, "Civil Religion in America," *Daedalus,* Winter, 1965.

Berger, Peter L., *The Precarious Vision: a Sociologist Looks at Social Fictions and Christian Faith.* Doubleday, 1961.

Cowan, Wayne H., ed. *Witness to a Generation: Significant Writings from Christianity and Crisis (1941-1966),* Bobbs-Merrill, 1966.

Cox, Harvey. *The Secular City: Secularization and Urbanization in Theological Perspective.* Macmillan, 1965.

Gilkey, Langdon. "Secularism's impact on Contemporary Theology," *Christianity and Crisis,* April, 1965.

Gilkey, Langdon, "Social and Intellectual Sources of Contemporary Protestant Theology in America," *Daedalus,* Winter, 1967. pp. 69-98.

Granbard, Stephen R., ed. "Religion in America," *Daedalus*, Winter 1967.

Gustafson, James M., "The voluntary church: a moral appraisal," *Voluntary Associations, a study of groups in free societies,* edited by D.B. Robertson. John Knox Press, 1966.

Herberg, Will. *Protestant, Catholic, Jew.* Doubleday, 1955.

Hertz, Karl, "The nature of voluntary associations," *Voluntary Associations, a study of groups in free societies,* edited by D.B. Robertson. John Knox Press, 1966.

Lerner, Max. *America as a Civilization,* Simon and Schuster, 1957.

Littell, Franklin H., "A new pattern of community," *Voluntary Associations, a study of groups in free societies,* edited by D.B. Robertson. John Knox Press, 1966.

Littell, Franklin H., *The Church and the Body Politic,* Seabury, 1969.

Martindale, Don, ed., "National Character in the Perspective of the Social Sciences," *The Annals of the American Association of Political and Social Sciences.* March 1967.

Morgan, Edmund S., "The Puritan Ethic and the American Revolution," *William & Mary Quarterly,* vol. xxiv, no. 1, January 1967, pp. 3-43.

Niebuhr, H. Richard. *The Kingdom of God in America.* Harper and Row, 1959.

Robertson, D.B., ed. *Voluntary Associations: a Study of Groups in Free Societies,* John Knox Press, 1966.

Schneider, Louis, ed. *Religion, Culture, and Society: a Reader in the Sociology of Religion.* John Wiley, 1964.

Sellers, James. *Theological Ethics.* Macmillan, 1966.

Winter, Gibson. *Elements for a Social Ethic: Scientific and Ethical Perspectives on Social Process.* Macmillan, 1966. #

2. "The Biblical Concept of the Covenant"

On August 31, September 1, and September 2, 1967 I made three presentations on to the Southeastern Regional Conference for students and faculty, sponsored by churches participating in United Campus Christian Fellowship and United Ministries in Higher Education at Montreat, North Carolina.

A. "A Covenant with the Past"

Introduction: May I first express my gratitude to you for the gracious invitation to participate in this conference. Sometimes playwrights use comic relief to relieve the tension of a very serious situation. I feel like the comic relief to Dr. John F. A. Taylor, esteemed Professor of Philosophy at Michigan State University. He is also an esteemed poet able to express himself artistically and eloquently. He is a scholar on the cutting edge of dealing with reflective problems in a systematic, precise, and decisive way. We will need to stretch ourselves as we seek to explore the concept and role of Covenant.

We may ask ourselves why we are engaging in Bible Study? I think one response is because of the extreme situation of the contemporary church. The church certainly is not dead but it appears all too often to have become oblivious of its mission. Renewal can come through meaningful study of the Scripture. In this attempt to revitalize the Christian faith in our ministries we need all the help we can get. A study of the Covenant is a crucial place to focus. It is indeed one of the most basic and central motifs of biblical studies. Walter Eichrodt sees the covenant as the hermeneutical principle for Old Testament theology, especially the Law and Hebrew culture. God is a covenant God who not only is Who He Is but expresses his being or nature in what He does. The covenant is the instrument through which Israel's leaders guide the exodus people through the wilderness to the Promised land. Breaking the covenant brings judgment. Fulfilling it brings consummation in community.

I see these three mornings together more as addresses rather than lectures. They should be taken as a whole though we will examine them in three dimensions. Each dimension gives us a perspective on the covenantal reality. Covenant gives us a place to stand in following the Humanities axiom that "where one stands determines what one sees." Covenant is recital of, and reflection on, the past. Covenant is anticipation of or projection into the future. Covenant is participation or engagement in the present.

Without cognizance of the past and belief in the future there is no meaningful present. Existentialism, valuable as it is, must lead to absurdity because of its lack of celebration of the past and real anticipation of the future. Without a proper temporal perspective we get caught up in a social urgency which leads to chaos rather than creative community.

i. The Covenant is recital or reflection.

Josiah was considered one of the few good kings who recognized the cruciality of covenant for Israel's survival.

David, Israel's greatest king recited the primacy of the Covenant in Psalm 105:5-11 and Psalm 89. God would not violate His Covenant.

Joshua in the memorable ceremony at Shechem (Joshua 24) recited before the people the mighty acts of Yahweh in the exodus and the conquest of Canaan. He continued the impact of that covenant by reading from the law, the Ten Commandments. And he demanded of the people a free choice of the god they would serve. Those who would continue in the covenant must serve Him with moral obedience which they were to reaffirm.

Kings and judges were reciting the mighty works of God to Moses and Abraham before them. (Exodus 20; 24:7-18; 32:11-14, 33:11-13; 34:27-28). J. Phillip Hyatt rightly points out, "From Sinai on the Israelites were a covenant people bound to worship Yahweh alone as their deity and obligated to serve Him with moral obedience" That moral obedience was to be found in following the ten commandments: "The Ten Commandments represent the religious and moral terms of the covenant which the Israelites freely agreed to observe." (J. Phillip Hyatt)

Even before Moses there was Abraham whom God called out of Ur of the Chaldees and entered into a covenant the limits of which Abraham could not possibly know. He could only accept the covenant in faith and trust that God would lead him as promised.

58

Israel was indeed a people with a heritage – a heritage defined by the covenant.

ii.. What then is the nature of covenant? As a process it provides life with a goal and history with a meaning. It has two basic meanings: 1) ceremonial agreement, and 2) relationship between two parties. John F.A. Taylor compares the Hebrew covenant to the Constitution of the American people. "It was to the Hebrews what the American Constitution is to Americans, the solemn original agreement by consent to which individuals and families of individuals otherwise dispersed in the face of nature gathered themselves into the moral alliance of one community under law." (p. 37) Covenant is a complex notion. George Mendenhall says it is "the formal act which binds the actor to fulfill his promise." Walter Eichrodt says it is a "characteristic description of a living relationship." (p. 3).

Four basic types of covenants may be discerned: 1) suzerainty between superior and inferior in which only the superior has freedom, 2) patron between a patron and a beneficiary and even sometimes a third party, 3) parity in which the participants are equal, and 4) promissory which seeks to anticipate and chart a course for the future.

The basic structure of a covenant is 1) preamble, 2) historical prologue, 3) basic stipulation, 4) particular conditions, 5) invocation of gods as witnesses, and 6) curses and blessings formulae.

iii. What is accomplished by a covenant, in other words what is its function?

It recognizes existent relationships and formalizes them, e.g. David and Jonathan expressing their love for one another and Jesus and his disciples in the Last Supper.

It establishes the conditions or possibilities of ordered society, e.g. Jacob and Laban who feared one another and sought protection from one another (Genesis 31:44-50).

George Ernest Wright points out, "In nomadic or patriarchal society covenants between men and groups were the legal agreements or treaties which made peaceful community relations a possibility."

Gottfried Quell sees the covenant between Jacob and Laban in this light: "Those who are in fact equal hardly need to enter into a covenant. What produces a covenant is the need to secure oneself against someone who threatens one's security or to grant security to someone who is well-disposed and from whom something may be expected."

Because of the unequal status between God and the people of the exodus the covenant enabled Israel to be a pe0ple, a point that cannot be emphasized too strongly. Because they were convinced they had a destiny under God according to the covenant they could form for themselves a worthy heritage.

"Covenant is no longer a legal compact between human beings, but a device for explaining the meaning and nature of Israel's election." (G.E. Wright) Wright goes on to say, "Covenant then involved an interpretation of the meaning and aim of Israel's existence.... Neither covenant nor law, however, were viewed primarily as a legal burden to be borne. They were founded in a Divine act of grace: they were God's gift of life."

Wright sees this expression of relationship as unique to Israel among ancient peoples. "The all-pervading sense of election and covenant, therefore, is the chief clue for understanding Israel's sense of destiny and of the meaning of existence. In other countries of the day, as far as we have knowledge, there was no comparable conception." As Eichrodt succinctly states this covenant relationship was, "Israel's most fundamental conviction, namely its sense of a unique relationship with God."

iv. The role or purpose of covenant.

Gerhard von Rad maintains, "The making of a covenant is intended to secure a state of intactness, orderliness, and rightness between two parties, in order to make possible on the basis of their legal foundation, a relationship in matters affecting their common life."

Quell puts it simply, "There is no firmer guarantee of legal security, peace, or personal loyalty than the covenant."

The covenant had to be Israel's primary reality as the link between God and His chosen people.

The Hebraic covenant is a divine-human agreement. It is a declaration that "we're in this together." Israel had several covenant mediators including Moses, Joshua, and David who willingly took responsibility of impressing upon the people the formative role of the covenant.

The covenant must be primary. Even national life had to be subordinated to its purposes as the prophets so often admonished Israel and Judah.

Covenant had room for the stranger and alien as Eichrodt notes, "It is striking that this association draws no clear line to exclude the stranger, but is continually absorbing outsiders into itself."

v. The perversion of the covenant

Almost immediately, at Sinai, there is a misconception or if you will a perversion of covenant. Exodus 32:11; 33:13. Some saw this relationship between God and His people as favoring them to such an extent that they would receive a land and become a people without any cost, in any case without human responsibility. For them the Law would become a shield, a dodge.

Because of this abuse, the 8th century prophets rarely deliberately used the term covenant. Yet, as B. Davie Napier says, "Almost every recorded utterance of the 8th century prophets (Amos, Hosea, Isaiah, Micah) takes its meaning and relevance from the concept of Covenant." Amos 5 and Hosea 2:21 declared "you are my people and I am your God."

In their attempt to bend the covenant to their own use fractionalization split it into parts, requiring a restoration of wholeness and return to its true role and nature, i.e. a covenant of the heart not of laws as Jeremiah so vehemently exhorted. #

B. A covenant with the future

Introduction: As we noted yesterday, social urgency leads to chaos rather than creative community when we turn to mere expediency and limp or jerk from one fitful program to another. But what are we to do since we must do something.

Man is indeed an actor as well as a thinker who must use the past and the future to help him navigate through the present.

Let me briefly summarize a few thoughts from yesterday: Covenant is a constitutional reality which recognizes the value of relationships and establishes conditions of an ordered society. As Quell so succinctly states it covenant, "means legitimate order as opposed to caprice, uncertainty and animosity."

In covenant, "Israel awoke to historical self-awareness" as Eichrodt phrases it.

Covenant leads to community in law and opens up meaningful interpretations of faith. Abraham, Moses, Joshua, David are all exemplars of the centrality of covenant in the Hebraic experience.

There is no covenant in perpetuity; it must be renewed over and over again with a sense of gratitude and obligation.

i. Covenant provided for liberty in law, obligation in commitment.

There was, "a definite connection of the moral precepts with the basic religious commands". (Eichrodt)

Covenant law provided for 1) a deepened moral sensibility, 2) abolition of gross brutality, 3) elevation of the value of human life, and 4) rejection of justice founded on class distinction. (Based on Eichrodt)

Covenant had begun in mutuality and reciprocity even while recognizing God's gracious holiness. It combined demand and promise: "in this way it provides life with a goal and history with a meaning." (Eichrodt)

The covenant is for the whole people not for isolated individuals. "The covenant, the law, is God's will for the covenant community in its totality. All members of the community are covenant persons, and no part of their activity – none whatsoever – is exempt from covenant obligation." (Napier) Napier goes on to say, "The essence of human being is an essence derived from the covenant." To be human is to assume responsibility for the authorities by which one lives.

Hear how strong a responsibility a human being has for voluntarily keeping the covenant. Taylor could not be clearer: "God's command is as little competent to bind me as yours or another unless I bind myself, unless, by my own act, I be party to the command, and make his will or yours my own. God may give to the Law its goodness; I alone can give to it its authority, so far as it governs me."

ii. The reconceiving of the covenant

Jeremiah conveys our most pivotal point. The true prophet is one who discerns the nature of the covenant as of the heart as contrasted with the sons of the prophets who see it resting in an institution. (Jeremiah 1:6-10)

Jeremiah is speaking in a time of historical crisis. (Jeremiah 31:31) He lays the covenant upon their hearts as they face the uncertain future. It must be an authentic relationship – no second hand religion will do. They must reconceive the covenant with their hearts so that God will be their God and they will be His people. Each would know God personally. Isaiah looked to "earth being full of the knowledge of the Lord." (Isaiah 11:9) As Hyatt says, "The new covenant promise is that all men will know Yahweh as the prophets had known him directly and intimately."

When they renewed the covenant God would remember their sins no more. The new covenant brought with it a vision of a restored Israel. (Isaiah 35:40). Even though Israel in its observance of the covenant God would yet renew the covenant. "I will give them one heart and one way." (Jeremiah 32:38-40) It will be an everlasting covenant.

This is also the message of Ezekiel. "I will give them one [new] heart and put a new spirit within them." (11:19) Repeatedly, it is a new heart, an inward relationship. As Napier says, "Man will find the fulfillment of his life and participation in true community when his only object of worship is God and when he and his fellows hold in mutual inviolable respect the totality of the neighbor's life."

iii.. The hope of covenant

The hope is for restoration through a new covenant. Jeremiah envisages farmers and herdsmen living peacefully together. He sees his prophetic role as building and planting and sets his hope on the purchase of a field in a time of imminent destruction.

Once more the choice is man's as Ezekiel puts it: "Why will you die, O House of Israel. I have no pleasure in the death of anyone so turn and live." (18:32) In the breakup of the old in both state and temple Ezekiel saw the God who makes a new covenant. He sees it also as a covenant of peace (37:26)

Isaiah too believed God was doing a new thing (43:19)

iv. The covenant as anticipation

Taylor, echoing Isaiah says, "Where there is no vision, the people perish. We are as a people even in our honeyed Canaan in process of perishing. For we have grown blind to the moral premises of our simplest and most quiet acts."

Dreams are indeed the stuff life is made of. As one of my favorite children's books puts it, "dreams are to look at the night and see things." (*A Hole is to dig*)

"God's supreme work of redemption for Israel, his self- disclosure to the community in a covenant, is something that will only unveil its ultimate meaning in a community relationship beyond any earthly horizon in an order where the depth of personal life, the strength of the national life, and the breadth of the life of the whole human race are each and all renewed by the divine presence and so fulfill the purpose of their creation." (Eichrodt, p. 63)

The covenant leads to the kingdom of God, to God's new age in which the world is ideally ordered as Taylor puts it.

This now brings us from the Old Testament to the New. If we have come to the New Testament seeking a Christian politics, a Christian society, a Christian theology, a Christian economics, a Christian solution to human problems we have come to the wrong place. The New Testament is rather a witness to the covenant, a record of early Christian communities' covenant. The term covenant appears 34 times in the New Testament – 17 times in Hebrews, 9 in the Pauline epistles, 5 in the Synoptic Gospels, twice in Acts, and once in Revelation.

Jesus lays the foundation when he says, "To whom much is given, from him much is required." He sets forth the hope of the new covenant when he avows, "I have come that they may live life abundantly." This eternal life manifests itself in a rich diversity of ways: "he who is not for us is against us"; "he who is not against us is for us"; "other sheep I have who are not of this fold." In a way everything seems so problematic. We can't be sure. Even the biblical witness leaves room for different interpretations of the same event: "some said it thundered, others said an angel spoke" (John 12:27-2)   We must read scripture not only from where they stood but from where we stand.#

C. A Covenant with the Present

Introduction: We have looked at the covenant and the past and the covenant and the future but are aware there is much about the covenant we are unaware of. In our own day W.A. Brown sees it as "a protest against arbitrariness and indiscriminate voluntarism."

As we observed yesterday, the prophets believed if there were to be a future at all it would be because there would be a covenant of the heart which would be so deep it would touch the heart of man and so extensive it would reach out to all men.

A new covenant would bring about a new spirit which would characterize a new humanity holding inviolable a "respect for the totality of the neighbor's life." (Napier)

The function of covenant proclaimers is to build and to plant as Jeremiah said. It is to act on hope, to venture, to risk, and perhaps to gain. Even amidst the breakup of established order was the hope of a still greater community.

Again Taylor is profoundly on center: covenant asserts "a world ideally ordered." Its goal is to reach beyond any present manifestation. "God's supreme work of redemption for Israel, his self-disclosure to the community in a covenant, is something that will only unveil its ultimate meaning in a community relationship beyond any earthly horizon in an order where the depth of personal life, the strength of national life, and the breadth of the life of the whole human race are each and all renewed by the divine presence and so fulfill the purpose of their creation." (Eichrodt)

i. The reconstructive power of covenant

We continue our New Testament focus by admitting that there is little, if anything, new in the teachings of Jesus. He is firmly rooted and grounded in his Jewish heritage. The newness was in his embodiment of those essential teachings.

We must not make a false dichotomy between new and old as for instance in Judaism and Christianity, Christianity and other religions, or the Old Testament (covenant) and the New Testament (covenant). As in all significant movements in history there is both continuity and discontinuity, permanence and change.

The writer of Hebrews 8:8-12 quotes Jeremiah 31 when speaking of a new covenant which is better because it promises a universal and personal knowledge of God.

We move from the initial covenant with Adam to the liberating covenant with Jesus the Christ.

In the 16th century Bullinger saw Christianity as older than Judaism because it went back to a covenant of grace with Abraham.

For the Apostle Paul "there are two covenants, but there is only one divine will which governs salvation history and which manifests itself definitively in Christ who is both the telos nomou (Romans10:4) and the fulfillment of every promise (II Corinthians 1:20). (Behm in *Theological Wordbook of the New Testament*).

Jesus conceived of his Messianic work, fulfilled in his death, from the standpoint of the fulfillment of the prophecy of an eschatological diatheiea [covenant] (TWNT, 133)

John saw the terrible temptation to hide behind the covenant when he faced this issue. (John 8:31-50)

ii. The informative power of covenant

Jesus informs his disciples of a covenant of man with God. In Matthew 26:28 he speaks of the blood of the covenant evoking images of blood sprinkled on the altar when a covenant was "cut". In our own times that covenant evokes images of blood spilled in the streets in the recent destructive clashes in the streets of Detroit and elsewhere.

In Mark 14:24 we see his blood on the cross as the mediating sign between God and man.

Hebrews 13:20 calls his hearers/readers back to "the blood of the eternal covenant." Jesus is the surety of a better covenant than the Mosaic one. (Hebrews 7:22). Christ's ministry is better than the ministry of priests at the altar since it is based on the better promise of life eternal God gives in Jesus the Christ.

Paul draws the image plainly for the church in the "words of institution of the Lord's Supper" when he says, "This is the new covenant in my blood." (I Corinthians 11:25) He goes on in his second letter to the church at Corinth to say, "Our sufficiency is from God, who has qualified us to be ministers of a new covenant ... in the Spirit." (II Corinthians 3:6)

In Luke 4:14-30 Jesus sets forth his programmatic sermon taking his text from Isaiah 61:1-2: "The Spirit of the Lord is upon me because he has anointed me to bring good news to the poor. He has sent me to proclaim release to the captives and recovery of sight to the blind, to let the oppressed go free, to proclaim the year of the Lord's favor." To his hearer's consternation he declares that the scripture he has read is now fulfilled in him. This is the most striking example of the informative power of the covenant.

iii. The formative power of covenant

We remind ourselves that Jesus is the mediator of a new covenant. This covenant sets us free to seek to grapple with the issues of faith in ourselves and in society. In the biblical sense we seek to find ways of salvation, or wholeness in human community.

Taylor points out how difficult it is to determine what it means for a society to be healthy. "The real problem for education is not in identifying society's ills, or even in assisting in the removal of them. The real problem is in determining, in society's interest and for its sake, in response to its dumb aspiration, what constitutes its health."

There is a great deal of anger and resentment in our society leading to loud cries of protest and actions stemming from those. It is easy to tear down but hard to build up. Living in covenant community means engaging appropriately in both. Again Taylor is insightful, "If you would know the value of a thing ask what it would cost to replace it; its value is equal to the cost of its replacement."

Jesus cautioned his followers that they were like sheep in the midst of wolves. (Matthew 10:16-23). But even more intently he told them they must lose their life if they were to find it. (Matthew 10:34-39). He sought to keep things in perspective when he cautioned them against gaining the whole world and losing their souls. (Matthew 16:24-26.)

As God's covenant people we must find the meaning of this for ourselves as Christians and as members of communities of faith intent not in simply preserving life in the world but living creatively and restoratively in it.

We live in the multidimensional reality of a pluralistic society in which we are engaged in many often overlapping communities. Taylor says it this way, "If man shall not live by bread alone, so neither shall he live by politics alone, or by religion, or by science, or by art alone. Each is a moral community; no one of them is a sufficient community."

Conclusion: Briefly let us acknowledge that we live in God's new age in which life as covenant people enables us to accept the ever changing processes of history and culture and seek to live and work creatively in bringing to fruition communities fit for God's own people.

We are sometimes offended by Jesus' question to the paralytic at the pool of Bethsaida: "do you want to be healed?" (John 5:2-9). If our answer is "Yes Lord," then we will hear him saying, "love God by loving the neighbor" (I John 4:1-21) That is the heart of the covenant – so easy to say; so hard to do. "Love one another as I have loved you." (John 15:12-17) #

3. "The Christian Ministry and the Literary Arts Today"

On March 12, 1973 I spoke to the Central Kentucky Christian Ministers Association meeting at Lexington Theological Seminary.

Introduction: The local parish is the real firing line of ministry where both preaching and pastoral care must be held in balance. In preaching, especially, the minister must use and explore symbols which hopefully will enable persons to change and grow, symbols that convey the presence of God as the ultimate source of power for life.

1. Changes in cultural context: There was a time when it was easy to identify the literary arts as poetry, novels, biography, and essays. Now the concept has broadened to include television, movies, newspapers,

especially *the New York Times* and *the Christian Science Monitor,* and magazines, especially *the Christian Century* and *Christianity Today, the Saturday Review, the Atlantic* and weekly news magazines such as *Time* and *Newsweek.* For some the forms also include graffiti.

Goethe labored 60 years on *Faust.* We must deal with art produced in a moment. Art and symbols are rapidly produced and even more rapidly change.

There was a time when rituals and symbols of life were given, a part of the common agreed upon experience of all in the community. Now the artist, including the creator of the sermon must work in a world in which symbols are uncertain and rituals are not constant. He must attempt the impossible, the creation of symbols that actually bridge the gap between persons and between ideas and emotions. The categories for expression must be created. Samuel Beckett in *Waiting for Godot,* for example, assumes no context. The artist must face the fact that there is little or no commonality in the use of literary references. The desired contact with other persons cannot be assumed or assured.

2. Form and content: The artist, in our case, the preacher or writer today must face the questions about form and content. Does form influence content? Our times seek desperately to break away from old forms. The artist faces the questions of style and theme. Augustine was so fascinated by the style of Ambrose that he began to inquire more deeply into the theme or content of the message. We must think through Marshall McLuhan's, *The Medium is the Message.*

3. Faddishness: In the press of rapid change we are faced with the hazards of faddishness as illustrated in pop and rock music. It is impossible to keep up even in a narrow field today, hence the need for frank and honest facing of the temptation to pretense regarding volume of reading. We must avoid the superficiality of reports and learn to pull out the heart of a literary work, the pregnant scene that moves people.

4. Pastoral care: In pastoral care as well as in preaching and writing there is a point after thoughtful listening to share and to recommend the reading that can help reduce a person's isolation. At times

a poet or a novelist will be more helpful than the popular psychological approaches such as *I'm OK, You're OK.*

In counseling we need to keep in mind that it is a person-to-person process. However, the minister is not always able to give as much time to one person as perhaps they desire or he/she would like. But, by knowing the person and knowing some of the literary arts and their insights he may link the two together. They also may serve a valuable purpose in group therapy.

5. Preaching and teaching: The minister must set aside some time for reading, viewing, reflecting so that he or she can use the literary arts appropriately in ministry. In preaching, for example, they are illustrations not reports, insights not endorsements, reflectors not replacements for the major points of the sermon.

In teaching we need to keep in mind that our curriculum uses literature to point out the main points of the lesson, that the church school needs a library which includes these as well as biblical study material. Sometimes individual works, such as Alvin Tofler's *Future Shock,* are well worth study by Adult classes.

6. The literary arts in the personal life of the minister. In his or her personal life the minister needs to read to keep abreast of what is going on in our age, e.g. a. literary criticism – to keep a balanced and stable approach, b. the classics – for diversion, c. science fiction, -- for a sense of mystery, d. biography – to expand our acquaintance with other persons, and e. original works – Gerard Manley Hopkins (poetry), William Faulkner (novels), and so on in various fields of endeavor mean a great deal to me. .

The literary arts are so diverse as to allow no single interpretation and demand that we know what we are seeking when we come to them. We must make intelligent use of the literary arts in our preaching, teaching, and counseling by letting them replenish and renew us as persons.

Conclusion: This is but the barest glimpse of the topic but hopefully it is enough to stimulate us to renew our pursuit of expanding our knowledge of the literary arts and use them effectively in probing the issues and situations facing our parishioners today. #

I find it interesting to include this summarization or reflection on that presentation by Dr. Jack Sherley, Secretary, in the Minutes of that meeting:

Both preaching and pastoral care in the local parish (the real "firing line" in contrast to academia) continually involve the use and exploration of symbols that (hopefully) can enable persons to change and grow, symbols that convey the presence of God, the ultimate source of power for life.

There was a time when it was easy to identify "literary arts" in poetry, novel, biography, essay. Now the concept tends to broaden to include TV, movies, magazines broadly, newspapers, even graffiti. Goethe labored 60 years on Faust. We must cope with "art and symbols which are rapidly produced and even more rapidly change."

There was a time the rituals and symbols of life were given, a part of common and agreed experience. Now the artist, including the creator of the sermon must work in a world in which symbols are uncertain and rituals are changing. He must attempt the impossible, the creation of symbols that actually do bridge between person and between ideas and emotions. The categories must be created. Samuel Beckett in <u>Waiting for Godot</u>, for example assumes no context. The artist must face that there is little or no commonality. The touch between persons is severely limited.

The artist (preacher, writer) today must face the questions about form and content. Does form influence content? Our times seek to break the forms. The artist faces the questions of style and theme. Augustine was so fascinated by the <u>style</u> of Ambrose that he began to inquire more deeply about the <u>theme</u>. We must think through McLuhan's "The Medium [esp TV] is the message."

In the press of rapid change we are faced with the hazards of faddishness as illustrated in pop and rock music. It is impossible to "keep up" even in a narrow field, hence the need for frank and honest facing of the temptation to pretense regarding volume of reading. We must avoid the superficiality of "reports" and learn to pull out the heart of a literary work, the pregnant scene that can move people.

In pastoral care as well as preaching there is a point, after thoughtful listening to share and to recommend the reading that can help reduce a person's isolation. At times a poet or a novelist just may be more help than even Harris' I'm OK, You're OK.

5. "When doing the right thing isn't easy"

Presented to Leadership Forum on Ethics at Naval Hospital Bremerton, Washington, March 27, 2003.

Let's begin with the most difficult situation you ever found yourself in. What factors made it so hard? As you reflect on it, what insights are pertinent?

Here are several insights for us to consider:

1. It was not solely a rational decision.

2. It was a decision which had to be made by you but it would affect others as well as yourself.

3. It was a matter of great seriousness with far-reaching consequences.

4. It was a matter of urgency involving stress.

5. It was a matter which had viable options rather than one compelling solution.

6. It was not a clear-cut matter of what was unequivocally right.

7. It required putting your basic ethical values into play.

Decisions that matter most to us rarely are clear-cut, simple, single, and obvious. While each of us is ultimately responsible for her or his own decisions and actions, we do not make those decisions in isolation. We have a history – a past, a present, and a future which is part of the process. We are part of numerous groups or networks and are involved in diverse relationships which usually are harmonious but sometimes become difficult to reconcile with one another. In other words, we always have both personal and cultural/corporate values at work.

Rarely do we make those decisions on the basis of our expert or technical knowledge or expertise. Competence is required for success but competence alone will not guarantee success.

Somewhere in the midst of the crucial process of deciding what is the right thing and committing ourselves to doing it our most basic ethical values are at play and at stake.

While we acknowledge that ethical decision making involves other dimensions than reason alone, it is helpful to review some basic ethical theories. There are three major approaches to ethics in the western tradition: 1. Non-consequentialist, 2. Consequentialist, and 3. Virtue. Each has its strengths and weaknesses and none of them will answer all our moral questions or concerns. While there are several segments of each approach we have time to refer to only two in each perspective.

1. Non-consequentialist – doing the right thing intentionally
   a. Duty/obligation (Immanuel Kant and the good will)
   b. Prima facie (W.D. Ross (prioritizing overriding obligations
2. Consequentialist – achieving the right result
   a. Utilitarianism (John Stuart Mill advocating the greatest good for the greatest number)
   b. Pragmatism (William James concentrating on the difference a decision and action makes)
3. Virtue – living the right life
   a. Character (Aristotle for whom character is acquired by habitual practice)
   b. The Golden Rule (Jesus of Nazareth, but found in most major religions in one form or another: treating others as we want to be treated)

Think of these approaches as tools in an ethical tool kit, or musical pieces in a repertoire, or plays in a playbook. The tool will not do the job but it either makes doing the job possible or easier or better.

There are times when one of these ethical approaches is the right tool and other times when it is not. Therefore a pluralistic approach is more advantageous for doing the right thing when it isn't easy. In this

73

pluralistic approach a new category offers greater possibilities than restricting them to only two possibilities such as right or wrong, good or bad, good or evil. Appropriateness becomes a helpful paradigm because it takes seriously several contextual factors and is not limited only to rational considerations.

In a situation demanding an ethical decision and resulting action these questions become useful tools. Is the ethical decision and the ensuing action being done congruent? Here are five considerations: is the decision and ensuing action being made and done **1. By the right person, 2. For the right reason, 3 At the right time, 4. In the right way and 5. To the right extent.** Let's look at each of these more closely.

1. By the right person: am I the woman or man who must make the decision, do I have the authority and responsibility, and am I willing to fully accept the outcome of the decision and action without excuse or alibi?

2. For the right reason: am I making this decision out of a sense of desperation, a feeling of pressure because it would have adverse effects on my future, because I see no other way out, or because I believe it is the best, or right way considering all the factors and circumstances of which I am aware?.

3. At the right time: timing may not be everything but it requires the intuitive perception of the artist more than the rigorous persistence of the scientist, too soon or too late both can result in failure or even the best intentioned decisions and actions.

4. In the right way: while ends are primary for ethics, means are subject to even greater scrutiny. To act magnanimously, courageously, graciously, considerately, compassionately, justly, may not always be required but they set the moral act at a higher level.

5. To the right extent: every person has a line when it comes to ethics which says, "this far and no further." This is more easily seen in corporate moral situations where leaders have the responsibility to move the organization as far forward as it will go without losing the support of those who must live by the ethical principles or objectives advocated or

espoused but it is a matter for each individual as well to ask, "realistically, how far am I prepared to go in making this decision and living with it?

A few other suggestions are often made by ethicists when doing the right thing isn't easy.

1. Talk the matter over with a trusted friend (don't try to go it alone)

2. Gather as much relevant information about the situation as you have time for or desire to examine.

3. Ask yourself, "can I look myself in the mirror and say convincingly you did the right thing?"

4. Can I sleep well after doing it?

5. Put it to the public scrutiny test: what if someone you dearly love picked up the newspaper before you did and came running to you saying, "look there is your picture and a long story about what you have done."

6. Consider Grandma: even though you may be the dearest thing in her life and she would overlook all your faults, how would she react to seeing you after the decision became public?

This has been heavily theoretical and I apologize for not providing at least one real-life scenario or example in which the principles set forth are actually applied. At least for some of you we have made a beginning in exploring sound ethical theory or for others have refreshed your memory about your own ethical underpinning. There are expert ethical theorists but the real test comes when the theory is put into practice in our own moral decision making and action and only the person actually engaged in the process is the one who most matters. #

D. Radio broadcasts, Far East Network (FEN Radio), Morning Meditations

Speaking on the radio or television are two other distinct forms of public speaking. Even if the radio broadcast is performed before a live audience the vaster audience of hearers remain unseen.

I grew up in the age of radio, a time where what one was hearing with his or her ears created images to match the words and actions. Many a late afternoon found me stretched out on the living room floor listening to the exploits of *Jack Armstrong the All-American Boy, The Lone Ranger, Sky King* and so many other favorite programs. Though there were sound effects to match the action the driving force of the program was the speaker's/actor's voice. This was true for the evening programs as well such as *Inner Sanctum, or the Green Hornet* or even *Lux Radio Theater*. And what child of that era was not bewitched by the Saturday morning presentation of Nila Max's *Let's Pretend*. It was the voice that transported us to worlds we had to imagine but which were nevertheless real to us. Radio still holds a fascination not matched for me by all the later inventions such as television and electronic media.

When television became the dominant medium the hearer/viewer was no longer dependent on his or her imagination. Now the characters were real even if they were animations. Indeed something was lost while something else was gained. Though the actor/speaker could not see any of the audience except those gathered in the studio it was certainly easier to pin-point a target for one's speech.

I did a few radio and television broadcasts while at Woodmont Christian Church, Nashville, Tennessee and at Transylvania University, Lexington, Kentucky. I do not have the scripts of those so can only put here what I remember of them.

Woodmont's 11:00 am Sunday Morning service was broadcast for a while. I sat in a cloak room off the chancel and provided commentary on what was happening, especially during the Lord's Supper. That was well received. In fact more than one person commented "I would listen to you reading names from the phone book and be happy." Nice compliment but probably not deserved.

While at Transylvania I took part in a television broadcast on the Arab-Israeli conflict making a case for the Arab side while a local rabbi spoke on behalf of the Israelis. I do not remember other radio or television broadcasts prior to active duty in the Navy.

During my service as a Navy Chaplain I, along with many other chaplains of the Army and Air Force as well as the Navy, was invited to prepare and record Morning Meditations.

As I mentioned in the Introduction to the series *Thoughts along the Way* I believe the clearest and most succinct expression of my basic motifs, themes, beliefs and insights are to be found in these four series of Morning Meditations along with my favorite quotations and illustrative material.

Far East Network (FEN) programs were beamed to American Service men and women and their families stationed in the Far East, primarily Japan, Korea, and the Philippines. Many persons in those countries, particularly Japan, tuned in to FEN to improve their facility with English.

Four sets of five meditations are included here. The first was delivered while I was Chaplain to Destroyer Squadron 15, home-ported in Yokosuka, Japan. The second set was delivered while I was Command Chaplain on USS MIDWAY (CV41) home-ported in Yokosuka. The third and fourth sets were delivered while I was stationed at the Chapel of Hope, Commander Fleet Activities Yokosuka.

Each day's meditation in begins with "Good Morning, I'm Chaplain Paul Murphey of Destroyer Squadron Fifteen, Yokosuka" or appropriate duty station and ends with "This has been Navy Chaplain Paul Murphey for Morning Meditations."

1. First Series of Meditations, October 17- 21, 1977.
Meditation 1

I want to tell you about my love affair. My love is a mysterious lady. At times she is incredibly bright and beautiful, shimmering with serenity and reflective of remarkable calmness and peace, majestic and regal in her splendor. Then almost without warning she becomes violent and dangerous and her darkness challenges the hidden reserves of courage to quiet the fears that so easily arise. Her ravings often come unexpectedly and sometimes last for days. Then she can make me as sick as she at other times is able to relieve my cluttered heart.

My love affair was partly responsible for my becoming a Navy Chaplain. For sixteen years I was a college professor and during part of that time was a Naval Reserve Chaplain. Then by choice, a little help from my friends, and the grace of God, I was able to come on active duty and was assigned to Japan. It could not have been a more fortunate assignment for my love affair.

I am not her first lover and will surely not be her last. She has had many before me and will have many after I no longer enjoy her pleasures. For as long as men have had the courage to leave the snug comfort of their secure homes they have set out to sea. For most of them it has been a love affair and an oft times deeply moving religious experience. This is still the case even for men who would be embarrassed or ashamed to speak of going to sea either in romantic or religious terms. To be alone, even with a company of shipmates, in the midst of the constantly changing ocean is to come to an awareness that life is ultimately a religious experience. One whispers "thy sea is so vast and our boat is so small" and hears the echo of his own smallness in the vast universe.

Life, like the vast and changeable sea, is at once placid and serene and in a moment turbulent and destructive demanding resources deep within and far beyond our meager lives. To see the ocean's beauty, to feel its power, to know its peace is to become aware of the wonder of God's love which sustains us. We ask again with the Hebrew poet, "What are human beings by comparison with all this?" and hear within the assurance of an abiding faith: "God has made us a little less than himself – creative, free and loving." #

Meditation 2

Sometime, sooner or later, everybody gets around to asking, "What's it all about?" That seems to be the constant theme of movies or music, or literature or art. There are all kinds of answers. In fact, there are just about as many answers as the people who ask the question.

Years ago I ran across one man's answer that struck me as worthwhile at the time and has grown more meaningful as I have gotten older. Joseph Fort Newton asked, "When is life worth living?" and answered his question by saying, "life is worth living when I have a Self fit to live with, a work fit to live for, someone to love and be loved by." Those are pretty important ingredients.

The hardest person for any of us to live with is ourselves. Sometimes it is such a struggle to really know ourselves. We find all kinds of ways to deceive ourselves, to think either more or less of ourselves than we have a right to. So much of my ministry as a Navy Chaplain is with men who haven't settled the question of who they are. How fortunate we are when we can come to believe in ourselves, have confidence in our abilities, and really like ourselves.

A novelist [Christopher Morley] once used the title, *The Man who made Friends with Himself.* It's a rather simple truth that my attitude toward others and acceptance of them is largely dependent on what I think of myself. To see myself as a worthwhile, creative, caring person is to be open to the dignity, creativity, and significance of other people.

So many lives are crossed up by their work. It is hard for some people to see their work as fit to live for. Maybe a person's real work is being human – loving others, making life a bit better than we find it. Maybe our jobs are ways of expressing who we are. I have known people who were miserable in their work and made people around them miserable as a result. Maybe any job, from housework to military service, to tending bar, to business, or whatever is like an arena to act out our real work of being human. For some the job provides the opportunity to earn the resources to help themselves and others live a fuller human life.

Someone to love and be loved by may be what it is all about. Maybe life is a journey from love to love. Love is one of those rare qualities which increases rather than diminishes the more it is used. I have come to believe that the restless search of persons for someone with whom to spend the lonely hours is after all a search for someone to love. Fortunate indeed are we when we can break out of our narrow concern for ourselves and become genuinely concerned about others. The happiest people I know are those who really love others and are loved in return. Oh, love isn't always happiness. Often times it is anguish and suffering and being deeply hurt when others are hurt. But, in the long run it is an awareness that loving is what life is all about.

Is it any wonder then that the center of deep religious faith is to love God with all one's whole being and one's neighbor as oneself. When Jesus says to his disciples he wants to leave them a new commandment, in other words, a new way of dealing with life, he simply puts it, "that you love one another, even as I have loved you." That's what it's all about. #

Meditation 3

A lot of people are turned off by religion. It makes them uncomfortable, sometimes defensive, and sometimes apologetic. The very word "morning meditation" brings up for them an almost irresistible urge to turn off the radio or change the station.

I wonder why this is? I suppose there are many reasons. Some I have found are childhood experiences which were an overdose of piety, or the rantings and ravings of super salesmen for celestial fire insurance that played on childish insecurities and fears, or youthful awareness of the long distance between professed ideals and daily practices, or the narrow insistence that there was only one way, which by the way, always turned out to be the way of the person doing the insisting. A few are turned off because of bad experiences. Perhaps more are turned off from indifference; they just don't see why a person needs to get all worked up over it like some people do. Religion is seen by them as a full-time preoccupation in which the only value is becoming a pro much like becoming a pro in golf, football, basketball, or baseball. It is reserved for the superstars, not the regular players. It is so extraordinary that it has nothing to do with the ordinary affairs of everyday.

This approach bothered Jesus as indeed it bothers us. It was necessary to insist even to many pious and sincere people that "the Sabbath was made for man not man for the Sabbath." In other words, religion is for the sake of our humanity not our humanity for the sake of religion. It is easy to become so engrossed in religion that the world is divided into two parts with the religious one being the only one that matters.

All of life is God's gift and even the Christian faith is a way by which we realize and appreciate that gift. There has always been a problem when religion becomes more of a burden than life itself. A person's faith ought to open him or her to the divine resources for meeting life's conflicts, difficulties, sufferings, and tragedies without becoming bitter, disillusioned, or cynical. A sense of the presence of God doesn't insulate us from life's shocks, but it does keep us from being electrocuted by them.

A vital religious faith is also concerned with the brighter aspects of our existence. If our faith is adequate for our lives then it should open us to the goodness and beauty of creation – the natural world of delicacy and grandeur, the created world of design and fabrication, the human world of laughter and joy The divinely human experience of being co-creators with God reaches to the ordinary smiles and encouragements of everyday life which in their own unique way say to others, it really is a world worth living in after all. #

Meditation 4

Loneliness can kill you – at least that's the conclusion of a recently published book. Human beings have to have one another to be human. Broken relationships often result in broken lives. Broken homes are often like broken records, the music of life becomes an irritating repeat of the same old monotonous refrain. There is a lot we don't know about the effect of broken relationships on human lives, but this much we do know people can and do make one another sick. The phrase, "you make me sick," may not only be an angry blast, it may more accurately be a description of things to come. This is too large an area to give easy or simplistic answers but something needs to be said.

Along with the biological and chemical aspects of disease there is an elusive element which is hard to define and even harder to treat. We sometimes speak figuratively of a cancer of the spirit when a person's life becomes more destructive than constructive, more chaotic than creative, more pessimistic than affirmative. We also sometimes in a poetic way speak of a person having heart trouble when their only concern in life seems to be to look out for themselves and they become insensitive or oblivious to the needs, hurts, or desires of others.

Human beings are indeed strange creations. We are at once very fragile and very hearty. We can be withered by the angry heat of someone we respect and love. Yet, we can endure amazing punishment from someone on whose acceptance we don't depend. Every one of us needs a support system, even if it is only one other significant person whose very presence is an encouragement to us. Far too many lives are stunted by the drought of critical rejection.

Jesus had the remarkable ability to relate quickly, perceptively, accurately, and acceptingly to those he met. It was that way with the woman at the well whose several attempts at marriage had all ended in failure and left her almost hopeless of establishing any lasting and meaningful relationship.

Jesus was constantly moving about with people in such a way as to say, "life is for the living." God intends it to be full, rich, and free. Love – caring, sharing, involvement – is the way of life. Loneliness – isolation or detachment – is the way of death. Loneliness may not kill you but it is certain that it can make you sick, sometimes sick enough to wish you were dead.

May the divine reality be at work within us and among us today affirming the creative power of living with one another so as to heal the loneliness of at least someone else. #

Meditation 5

The 30s, 40s, and 50s were the decades of the great American musicals. There is a line from one of the most famous of these which goes, "If you don't have a dream, how you gonna have a dream come true?" We may not realize our dream, but no dream, no destiny.

One of the most poignant stories of the Old Testament is the story of Moses standing on Mount Nebo with the realization that after all the disappointment, agony, and failure the promised-land stretches out before him. The poignancy is in Moses' realization that he will never be able to take possession of his promised land.

That same theme was effectively portrayed in the movie _Midnight Cowboy_. After the desperate struggles of a chilling and impoverished life Reiso is on the bus headed for his promised land of Florida with the Cowboy. Here there would be sunshine and warmth, a new beginning free from embittering pain and cold. As the destiny awaits its realization, Reiso dies a rather inglorious death on the bus not even able to control his bodily functions. Was the dream of no avail? Hardly!

Alfred Lord Tennyson said the same thing when he wrote, "a

man's reach should exceed his grasp, else what's a heaven for." There is something pitiable in those lives that sacrifice their dreams for the dull reality of the easily attainable or for the cynical assessment of the popular song of a few years back, "is that all there is?"

Anticipation, another word for dreaming, is an important ingredient of enjoyment. If you don't expect much from life you probably will get what you expect. You may not be disappointed, but you probably won't be exhilarated either. On the other hand, if you expect a lot it may be like a promised land always on the distant horizon and somehow never fully in your grasp. Life's homely statements often turn out to be rather profound distillations of truth. "Expect great things from God, attempt great things for God" may be hard for the sophisticated and urbane to accept but it is still sound advice.

I may not be able to possess my promised land but its very glimpse may be enough to bring to life a radiance that somehow transforms it into something glorious. It may be that new heavens and a new earth is more than some far off future event. It may be that a change in ourselves gives us a vision of human life that makes morning break like the fresh dawning of the first day, new and vibrant with a destiny to be fashioned as co-creators with God. #

2. Second series of Meditations, March 10-14, 1986.

Meditation 1.

What do you remember of your childhood? The question is enough to send some of us into long flights of fantasy with sights and sounds and smells toppling over one another. But the memory I want to share with you this morning is of a camphorwood chest.

I was born during the Great Depression. My father, a plumber by trade, went to the Panama Canal Zone to work in construction there. Though it meant separation from his family, the prospects of a brighter future for them made the heartache bearable. When, in a couple of years he returned, he brought with him a few treasured objects – some silk kimonos with richly embroidered dragons on the back and a fabulously carved Chinese chest made of camphorwood. It fascinated me then; it still fascinates me.

Even when I had moved from childhood to youth, it was incredibly delightful to sit on the floor, run my hands over the ornately carved figures of strange people from a world unfamiliar to me and slowly lift the lid. Immediately the pungent odor of camphor would envelope me, delighting my sense of smell even more than running my fingers over those carved figures pleased my sense of touch, or their oriental features and costumes charmed my sense of sight. With the passing years that marvelous aroma never diminished.

When my mother died some years ago, I was stationed with the Destroyer Squadron at Yokosuka. I didn't go home for her funeral since I had been with her only a few months before as she slipped from the joy of life into the incapacitating control of her cancerous death. When I later returned to be with my father in route to my new duty station in the States he helped me put that camphorwood chest into my little hatchback car to take with me to California.

Mother had never forgotten how that chest had gladdened me as a child and youth and let it be known that it was to go with me as a happy memory of her.

From time to time now I open it to get something stored there – a piece of wrapping paper or a piece of linen. As the pleasant aroma floods my nostrils and bathes the room in its rare fragrance, I experience again the warmth and comfort of a loving home and the dreams of far off places not unlike those to which I have now been.

Strange isn't it that even as a child there was the preparation for experiences my parents could not have possibly known would happen and certainly not have deliberately planned for. That chest, like the *National Geographic* magazines they provided, was opening me to a world so much larger than Augusta, Georgia in the 1930s and 40s. At the same time, the church which was so much a part of their lives and of mine and my sister's was also opening vistas of God's incredibly diverse family. Missionaries came and painted word pictures of exotic lands of India and Africa, Latin America, China and Japan. We sang songs of "all the children of the world" who "red and yellow, black and white are precious in His sight." And the sounds and sights and smells were all preparing the

84

way for experiencing the amazing richness of God's one family I would in time experience to my surprise and delight. #

Meditation 2

"We become like what we love." That was the observation of St. Augustine, the renowned Bishop of Hippo in North Africa in the Fifth Century. Maybe we are not convinced that it is true. Perhaps we have to see for ourselves as Augustine had seen its truth over and over again in his own life.

How can it be? Let's take a clue from something around us in Japanese culture – the Sumo wrestler. The love of sumo causes him to gain the weight and the skill necessary to master himself and win out over his determined opponents. His love for it compels him to discipline himself to become what it demands.

A very long time ago someone in his wisdom said, "Train up a child in the way he should go and when he is older he will not depart from it." That's just another way of saying, "We become like what we love."

Perhaps you recall one or more of the many versions of a poem which affirms that loving, positive, supportively encouraging experiences and relationships for children are the foundations on which they become affirming, considerate, successful and loving adults. Abusive parents on the other hand produce abusive children who grow up to be abusive adults and so the cycle continues unless it is broken by becoming like what we love.

Not long ago after several frustrating minutes of trying to get a rather negative young man to see something good in life I asked him what he likes to do. He thought for a minute and replied, "I like to ski, yeah that's it, I like to ski." Hopeful for a breakthrough I continued by asking, "When was the last time you skied?" He mumbled that it had been about two years, at least not since he came to Japan. How preposterous. Here in a land where young people ski with almost fanatical zeal. What we do reveals what we love far more than what we say.

Have you ever heard someone say, "I don't see what he sees in her." They were right weren't they; for they don't love her as he does.

Love has a way of seeing which is all its own. When someone truly loves another person they see something which perhaps even that person has not yet seen or believed. That is as true of parents and children, teachers and students, doctors and patients as it is of a man and a woman.

When someone loves another person they encourage him or her to become their very best. While they accept them just as they are, they set free in them those special qualities which are uniquely theirs.

At the base of all this is a conviction that God is love seeking always the fullest development of our own individual characteristics which He created in us. We discover this primarily in our relationships with one another. As it is written, "How can a person love God whom he has not seen if he does not love his brother and sister whom he has seen?"

Indeed, we become like what we love. Loving God has a transforming power in us, not making us perfect in this life but at least opening us to hidden possibilities in ourselves and others which can only be seen through the eyes of love. #

Meditation 3

Where you stand determines what you see. Now that's simple enough isn't it. It's a plain matter of perspective and it's not always an easy matter to keep things in perspective.

Perspective in art adds depth, richness, and reality to a painting. Without it figures on a canvas appear flat and one dimensional. But, life is seldom flat and never one dimensional. There is always more going on than we can comprehend and assimilate unless we keep a sense of perspective.

One of the revolutions in modern art was the attempt of Pablo Picasso to look at things from several perspectives at once. The various dimensions of a table or a woman's face or body were put into strange juxtaposition causing some viewers to react with humor and others with dismay. But, Picasso was reflecting the age in which he worked as an artist, an age in which a single perspective or sense of values failed to dominate or give cohesion to onrushing events.

Indeed, we live in a world where events occur so rapidly that there is hardly time to absorb the impact of one terrorist act or one devastating coup d'etat before we are bombarded with happenings in another country which was probably not even in existence a decade ago.

Closer to home, few of us grow up as our grandparents did in the same hometown where we were born. It is a rare occurrence to talk with someone who has lived all his life in the same community much less the same house, attended a single school, or even lived with the same two parents to whom he was born. Is it any wonder that there is for so many a sense of homelessness, of being condemned to wander in search of some place or some person to which he belongs.

Ah, perspective that's it. Where we stand determines what we see. If I stand in front of an object I see only the features of the side facing me. As I move around it I get a sense of its wholeness, its immensity. That is what we experience when we visit the Daibutsu at Kamakura.

While an awareness of perspective is essential for understanding whatever I am engaged in knowing, I often have to engage it from different angles to see it whole.

An aircraft carrier is a very different thing to men who daily risk their lives on the flight deck launching and recovering planes and to men who deep below in an equally risky environment tend the boilers and engines which drive the shafts propelling it through the water. It is the same ship, to be sure, but experienced so differently.

Life is such a different experience to one who is happily married enjoying the comforts and pleasures of home, even the challenges and conflicts of aiding their children's growth, than it is for one whose marriage has fallen apart, or whose job has dead-ended or whose habits have taken control of him rather than he of them.

It makes a tremendous difference whether one's perspective affirms that she has come from God to whom she will ultimately return and who in all the journey in between birth and death is a co-creator with God of her destiny. She may not be able to say what will be around the next corner or what the next stop along life's way will be. However, it is enough to confidently believe that the journey is always with One who was and is and ever will be the Living God of here and now and there and then.   #

Meditation 4

There's a bit of folk wisdom which has helped me in many a situation. Perhaps you know it too. It goes, "you have to go from where you are." Every part of that is important. You are the one who has to make the move.

As the words of the Spiritual have it, "not my brother, not my sister, but it's me oh Lord, standing in the need of prayer." Or, as Frank Sinatra sang it with such feeling, "I did it my way." There are many things which happen to us over which we have little control, nevertheless we still have a responsibility.

I may fill in my dream sheet and get it to my detailer on time but he sends the orders for the new assignment. While I may have that choice made for me, I am still responsible for my attitude toward the opportunities and challenges it affords.

One of the marks of moral maturity is accepting as one's own the consequences of his decisions and acts. Sometimes it isn't easy to admit that, "I brought it on myself."

Bill Glasser, a psychiatrist in Los Angeles, has developed an approach called "Reality therapy". After the patient recounts the terrible things that happened to him as a child or even later in life Dr. Glasser leans across the desk, looks him in the eye and firmly asks, "And what are you doing about it?" The patient usually quickly wonders when they are going to deal with all his unhappy experiences. To this Dr. Glasser responds, "You are an adult now and the kind of life you live is your responsibility."

Take the second part of the saying after accepting it is you that has to go. Each one of us must not only be responsible for his life but he or she must also take the initiative or at least know what the decisions are and when they must be made. We have to go, move, decide, act. We are not pawns on some great chessboard moved against our will. Rather, we are players in the game of life, actors on its stage, and participants in its struggles. We are the movers and shapers of what we will yet become by God's grace.

We must remind ourselves from time to time that to refuse to make a choice is itself a choice. To be non-commital is a debilitating commitment to inaction and irresponsibility.

Life may not be a yellow brick road, nor a long and winding one for that matter, but it stretches out ahead of us. As Robert Frost reminded us, we are often standing where two roads diverge and we must travel one of them, whether it be a well-worn path or the road less taken. It makes all the difference how we choose which road we will take.

Always you are going on "from where you are". It is not from where you have been, though that has brought you to where you are now. Nor is it where we wish we were but in reality aren't. Try as we sometimes do, we cannot go back and live our life over again no matter how embarrassing or disastrous it might have been.

We have to go from where we are. That realization requires an ability to forgive ourselves and others and accept forgiveness from God and others. How beautiful is that biblical insight which affirms, "And God threw their sins over His shoulder and remembered them no more." With the hindsight, but without the burden of the past, we must keep pressing on. May God be with you as "you go from where you are." #
Meditation 5

What images do you use to think about life? One of my favorites is that of the aerial acrobat, the daring young man on the flying trapeze, if you will.

At times we stand poised secure and confident awaiting that moment when with adrenalin pumping we must take hold and launch out. Security must be left behind as we reach for the on-coming possibilities. Life then is a matter of holding on and letting go.

For the acrobat, timing is crucial. If he holds on too tightly and too long he will miss the bar he has swung out to catch which will take him to the next waiting platform. This daring to let go so as to hold on again isn't easy for anyone and appears almost impossible for some people.

Every one of us encounters disappointments in ourselves as well as in others. Some of us know first-hand the sorrow of crippling accidents or diseases. The tragedy of an untimely death may stalk us threatening to devour us. These and many other life experiences sometimes evoke in us anger, resentment, frustration or fear which we have a hard time letting go of.

I recently read a story of a young artist in New York City who was robbed and mugged in his own apartment. As his assailants were leaving they threw acid into his eyes permanently blinding him. Imagine the horror of the loss of sight for someone whose greatest joy has been painting what he sees. Yet, several years after that cruel blow he writes that his loss of sight has forced him to intensify the development of his other senses of sound and smell and touch. He maintains through all the terrible days that followed it was not the darkness that was his worst enemy. It was fear. It was fear he had to learn to let go of if he were to take hold of life again.

In the beginning days of World War II, President Franklin Delano Roosevelt movingly told the American people, "the only thing we have to fear is fear itself." Fear immobilizes us. If we cannot let go of it we are doomed to failure before we even start.

But fear is not alone. There is also anger, jealousy, envy, bitterness, frustration, and many other monsters of the spirit. They rush at us and for a moment threaten us. Who hasn't felt the hold of at least one of these? But, if we cannot let go of them we will never find the joy and satisfaction of a fully human life.

Anyone who experiences the loss of a person deeply loved whether through death or divorce must do her grief work so as to let go. Regular activities of life must be taken hold of or self-pity and the destruction of self-esteem will hold us to a fate worse than death, a fear greater than the darkness.

Anger too is a monster so powerful in its hold that it can make us physically, emotionally, and mentally ill. It is as life-threatening as a viral infection.

So Acrobats, we must let go of whatever keeps us from life so that in faith we can take hold of whatever is good, true, lovely, creative, constructive, and compassionate. We must let go of the negative images of ourselves and others expecting instead the best. We may not always get it but I would rather be disappointed at not getting the best than confirmed in receiving the worst. #

3. Third Series, Summer 1988 (exact dates unknown)

Meditation 1

Beautiful, incredibly beautiful! Whenever and from wherever we see Mount Fuji there is always a sense of its majestic grandeur. Whether we see it in the soft pastels of a winter's sunset or the sharp clarity of a crisp autumn morning, there is a special quality about it. It is easy to understand why Fuji San has been the inspiration for countless Japanese poets and painters. For centuries people have seen in it a remarkable mystique and fascinating religious aura.

A new dimension of the mountain opens when a person climbs it. The climb starts with great exhilaration from the fifth station. As climbers have their sticks branded at each successive station there is excitement about being there. The weather changes, the crowd dwindles, and the terrain alters as one goes higher. The smooth path gives way to irregular rocks which in turn are replaced by lava ash. Starting out in bright sunshine a person can go through rain, lightning, and thunder before being met with snow flurries at the top, even in August. One chooses the rock ahead carefully with an eye to the step beyond it. Beyond this the air gets thinner and the lava ash beneath one's feet demands repeated acts of determination not to give up and turn back. It may be seeing someone obviously older moving to pass him or the remembrance of how long he has intended to make the climb that keeps a person at it.

Fuji San becomes a parable of our lives. Beautiful, incredibly beautiful from a distance but hard going requiring sheer determination, physical stamina, and moral strength to reach the top.

How often we look at someone else's life – at their marriage, their children, their career, their friends – and say beautiful, incredibly beautiful. Yet, how little aware we are that they too must climb the challenging mountain putting one foot in front of the other, calling on resources deep within and a source of strength far greater than their own to reach their goal. We see the product, if you will, without knowing much, if anything about the process.

We can identify with the Hebrew poet who says, "I will lift up my eyes to the hill. From where does my help come? My help comes from the Lord, the maker of heaven and earth." The same God who created such incredible beauty and gave to us the capacity to appreciate and enjoy and be moved by it also is the source of the strength to handle life's obstacles as we keep on climbing. #

Meditation 2

A friend of mine retired recently after 36 years of naval service. Being an extremely creative, enthusiastic, and energetic person he never slowed down. There was certainly no short-termer's attitude about him. He was deeply involved in what he was doing right up to the time he left the Base to return to CONUS. Then, a week later he had begun work on his civilian job with the same exuberance. He could see opportunities ahead just waiting for his leadership.

What a contrast he is with another person with whom I worked. He also retired after many years of naval service. We hardly knew he was gone until we met his replacement. The kindest thing that could be said about him was that he retired on active duty several years ago. I didn't know him in his younger years but he must have been productive once because he had moved up the promotion ladder.

One of the major differences between these two men was their basic outlook on life. The first friend saw each new day as a chance to learn new things, explore new areas of life, and be involved with people in exciting tasks. The second acquaintance projected an attitude that anything any one asked him was an imposition. He didn't care to get directly involved and usually turned every request over to a subordinate. He basically let you know that for him life was a bummer. Nothing excited him, so far as I could tell, certainly not his job or the people around him.

One of these persons saw life as a gift and an opportunity to leave things a bit better than he had found them. The other saw life as an obligation and a chore to be done because you couldn't get out of it.

One of these was a co-creator with God of his destiny running into each new day with wide-eyed wonder. The other was serving a sentence with his head down and his eyes on the ground.

One of them retired <u>from</u> active duty to continue to pursue an active civilian human life. The other retired <u>on</u> active duty to withdraw from the demands of an active civilian human life.

These are two extremes. Maybe most of us are somewhere in between. As the poet John Oxenham observed:

To every man there opens
A way, and ways and a way,
And the high soul climbs the high way
And the low soul gropes the low,
And in between, on the misty flats,
The rest drift to and fro.

The choice is ours: time-servers sentenced to a dull death in life, drifters always being pushed along by someone else, or co-creators with God who makes all things new. #

Meditation 3

"But what have you done for me today?" That was the facetious question going around for a while. It implied that whatever good things you had done for me in the past didn't really count. What was really important was what favors you were doing for me right now. That's a pretty short sighted view, even if a popular one. If all we have is the present then we lose that vital sense of perspective as essential for life as it is for art. It is that lack of a realistic sense of past and future which makes the present so difficult.

Take the common problems of life most of us have to contend with such as not enough money to pay all the bills, or not enough time to get everything done we have to do. Or, disappointment when someone breaks a promise or disillusionment when someone we admired does something we find repulsive. Or, someone we love gets sick or dies and we feel so sad and lonely or grief-stricken and helpless. If all we have is what's happening to us now, is it any wonder that we sometimes get depressed and want to give up?

One of the great contributions of Judaism was a vivid sense of the past as the arena of God's activity. Over and over again, publically and privately, they recalled God's acts on their behalf: how He had called Abraham to become the father of a new people, how when the Jews had become slaves in Egypt God had freed them through the exodus, how He had brought them into the promised land and made with them a covenant that He would be their God and they would be his people.

One of the great contributions of Christianity was a vivid sense of the future to which God was calling all people; creating a kingdom beyond caste or color, race or nation. All the peoples of the earth would be one. They were called to serve one another in compassion seeking one another's welfare, contributing to meeting one another's deepest needs.

Vital religious faith always has dimensions of past and future enabling us to live in the present. Because God has been my strength and help in troubled times in my past – when one of my children was sick or my parents died or I failed at something in which I should have succeeded, I can say, "The Lord is my light and my salvation, a very present help in time of trouble." Because God wants the best for me and expects the best from me, I can face the unknown and uncertain future confident that "whether I live or whether I die, I am the Lord's."

As we continue our journey in faith, hope and love we gain a new sense of our own and other peoples worth. We discover what others before us have found: "surely the Lord is in this place and I wasn't even aware of it." We confidently affirm, "This is the day which the Lord has made, I will rejoice and be glad in it." #

Meditation 4

"Strangers in a strange land." Isn't that a great phrase! Someone ought to use it for a book title. Someone did. Robert Heinlein's *Strangers in a Strange Land* has become a science fiction classic. But we don't have to get into science fiction to appreciate what the title says. Some people go so far as to say that all human beings who ever lived, are living now, and who ever will live on this earth are strangers in a strange land.

Certainly you and I, living in Japan, know very well what it is to be strangers in a strange land. Whether we are newly arrived or old hands, we know we are and always will be gaijin, foreigners, strangers.

The author of the interesting book *Road to Sato* concludes with a conversation he had after walking from the northernmost tip of Hokkaido to the southernmost tip of Kyushu. He is an Englishman by birth who is married to a Japanese lady and has lived in Japan for the past seven years. He speaks Japanese fluently and is well read in the history and culture of his wife's native land. An old man asks him at the end of this walk why he had done it. The author replies that it was to understand the Japanese people. The old man replies that he could not understand the Japanese people by walking from one end of the country to the other, nor from talking with many different people, nor from reading many different books about them. The author still seeking understanding asks him, "then how can I understand them?" The old man replies simply, "You can't".

Now that's what we mean by being a stranger in a strange land.

Life is like that. We know even before we have gone very far that we will never get satisfactory answers to all our questions. We will never have all our hopes fulfilled. We will never have all our dreams come true. We know there is always a horizon which when we reach it gives way to a horizon farther on. Yet, that makes us more alert and vigilant. To become too comfortable is to become complacent and complacency leads to apathy and indifference – a sorry state of existence.

New worlds, whether geographic, intellectual or spiritual, are discovered and conquered by people who feel like strangers in a strange land. People who refuse to take everything for granted and seek new and better places to dwell. It isn't as the old saying has it that familiarity breeds contempt, so much as that taking the familiar for granted keeps us from seeing new and greater possibilities both in where we are and where we are to go.

Let us then, by God's grace, be strangers in a strange land who appreciate all the wonder, beauty, and difficulties of where we are now as we move on to where we must go. #

Meditation 5

Remember the last time you put out a candle? Remember how you did it? Did you blow out the flame? Did you moisten your fingers and pinch the wick? Did you use a candle snuffer to cover the flame until it stopped flickering and died. The result is the same – the flame deprived of oxygen can't burn, it loses its glow, its warmth, its light.

Candles need oxygen to burn just as people need air to breathe. That is so obvious. What isn't so obvious but is nevertheless just as true is that people need love to live. Deprived of love the light goes out of a person's eyes as surely as deprived of oxygen the flame of a candle flickers and dies.

Love then isn't a luxury, something nice to have after all the basic needs of life are met. How tragic when a person says, "I was too busy earning enough to put a roof over my family's heads, clothes on their backs, and food in their mouths to have time to give them a lot of love." Love isn't a commodity bought and sold like groceries or goodies. It is a positive expression of concern and care for another person in such a way that they know they are very special to you.

So many of the problems of adults, including the problems of alcoholism, obesity, sexual promiscuity, and violence relate to a deprivation of love in early life. A parent has no greater privilege and obligation than to nurture his or her children in love. It is such a sad experience to see an adult crying bitterly ready to destroy himself as he pleads with you, "not once did my old man say to me, 'I love you son'. He never said he was proud of me; I could never please him."

Nothing so threatens the light of life in us than the actual experience of not being loved or even the firm belief that someone special to us doesn't love us. Nothing, on the other hand sets us free to live creative, satisfying, and responsible lives more than the conviction that we are loved simply because we are who we are.

The heart of any genuine religious faith is the personal relationship of lovers, in which a man or woman is convinced that God loves them with a love that won't run out, or grow cold, or ever result in treating them with indifference. It is all so abstract, however, until it really

96

happens to us. Love poems are so embarrassing unless they are read by lovers, even when the lovers are God and human beings.

Like the candle, we need the love of God and one another if we are to glow with life.

St. Francis said it so eloquently a long time ago: "Lord make me an instrument of your peace... Where there is hatred let me sow love."#

4. Fourth Series, October 1989 – exact dates unknown.

Meditation 1

"Don't go into the lion's cage tonight, Mother. The lions are ferocious and they bite." That little song from America's Gilded Age brings all kinds of vivid images to mind.

Remember how you sat on the edge of your seat at the circus the first time you watched the lion tamer go into the cage with all those wild animals – lions, tigers, panthers, leopards, cheetahs. As each one was released from his or her cage into the big cage where the lion tamer stood with his chair and whip in hand, the big cats growled baring enormous teeth and you trembled for the tamer.

Life can be thought of as like a cage of wild animals – accidents, disease, natural disasters, unanticipated loss, and threat of nuclear annihilation – indeed a cage of ferocious beasts.

Each one of our lives also may be seen on the model of the wild animal cage. Inside each of us is the lion of anger, the tiger of fear, the panther of jealousy, the leopard of envy, the cheetah of greed.

Like the lion tamer we cannot tame them from the outside. We must confront them head on within the cage. It is a matter of courage and confidence, of deep conviction that they can be controlled, and the development of poise through persistence to find the means of taming them. Anger running riot is as destructive as the bounding lion mauling the tamer who has lost control. Under control it is as death-defying as when the tamer opens the lion's mouth and puts his head between the outstretched tooth-lined jaws.

Anger is part of the menagerie within a human being. But if it is simply the wild ranting of a person who has been inconvenienced or embarrassed, it is a rampaging lion. If, on the other hand, it is the impetus for change because we find the plight of the poor or the powerless, the victimized or the exploited, totally unacceptable, then its controlled use is as exciting as the paces the tamer puts the lion through as he leaps through the fiery hoop.

It took an act of faith, a conquering of fear, and dedication to mastering himself and the situation for the lion tamer to perfect his performance. That's life too isn't it? Faith, courage, commitment, reliance on God's creative gifts to tame the wild beasts within us lest they destroy us. #

Meditation 2

Normally everything goes along smoothly. We wake up on time, shower, get dressed, eat breakfast, go to work, have a few minutes to greet others and to collect ourselves before getting into the day's work. The work is pleasant, and we go home to enjoy dinner and have a relaxing evening before going to bed.

But, every now and then, one of those days leaps out of nowhere. We wake up late. The water in the shower is either too hot or too cold. We can't find what we had intended to wear. There isn't time for breakfast. When we rush in to work instead of the cheery good morning that usually greets us someone comes down on our case. There isn't time to get a sense of perspective. All day we run behind until we take the frustrations of work home with us ruining the evening meal and making ourselves unfit company for any one.

We have all had one of those days and it's a safe bet that we will have another. As simple as it sounds the most essential element of dealing with "just one of those days" is remembering that it is just one of those days. Even the smartest, best organized, or most capable people have them. They are not a judgment of God, or a punishment for our ignorance, or lack of discipline, or immature spirituality. They are simply a part of life. They are there like winds are part of storms or hot, humid days are part of summer.

If, however, they become frequent or get intense, it is time to take a hard look at not only ourselves but our situations.

If it is "just one of those days" we live through it with discomfort and frustration but wake-up the next day and find we are back to our normal experience of life. If however, the balance tips toward uneasiness, dissatisfaction, and depression then it is time to take spiritual inventory.

Maybe we've lost touch with the source and strength of life. Maybe the proper concern and care for others' welfare has been more and more eclipsed by a preoccupation with making sure I get what's mine. Maybe I've come to take the good days so much for granted that I've forgotten that each day is a gift from God to be accepted with gratitude and lived with joy. Maybe the situation in which I live or work has changed for the worse and I need to talk that over with someone who can do something about it?

"Just one of those days" is probably as important for us as rain for the growth of plants. When they come may we take the uneasiness and discomfort with the prayer, "Lord give me strength to just get through this one and make a new start tomorrow trusting in You the Lord and giver of life." #

Meditation 3

"Love means never having to say I'm sorry." That was a very popular line from a small but popular book (*Love Story* by Erich Segal)) which became an even more popular movie a few years back.

Unfortunately, it may make for good dramatic effect in a book or movie but it is a very misleading observation about the nature of love.

Built into the quality of life called love is the necessity of sorrow, regret, forgiveness, acceptance, renewal. It is precisely because I love that I have to say, "I'm sorry" when I realize I have made a mistake. It is an acceptance of the fact that I have, by my own action or words hurt someone else. Saying "I'm sorry" isn't so much an admission of guilt or an expression of weakness as a sign of acceptance of responsibility for my actions or words, thus a mark of strength or character.

How often conflict within families or between friends, at school or at work, is defused and reconciliation begins when one of the parties says and means it "I'm sorry". I stress that saying, "I'm sorry" has to be an element of love and thus of strength not the pathological weakness of

99

one who beaten by others has lost self-esteem and confidence and is afraid of becoming crushed further. He simply wants to avoid the pain of more conflict and thinks that quickly saying "I'm sorry" will help him to do just that.

It is important to keep in mind that somethings go wrong because of me. Others happen inspite of me. And some occur with no consideration of me whatsoever. In other words, sometimes I make a mistake. Other times I am the victim of someone else's mistake. Sometimes a bad situation develops in which I am involved but it wasn't directed toward me at all.

This all reminds me of Reinhold Niebuhr's famous prayer, "God grant me the courage to change those things which I can change, the serenity to accept those things I cannot, and the wisdom to know the difference."

Maybe our prayer in times of conflict or when mistakes have been made should be, "God help me to love enough to say 'I'm sorry' when I have made a mistake. Help me to deal with wrongs done to me without blaming myself. And grant me the peace of heart and life to solve problems more than the desire to place blame."

Saying "I'm sorry" shouldn't be the end of the matter. It is instead, the opening of opportunity for forgiveness, understanding, acceptance, reassessment, and better awareness of myself and others so that we can make new beginnings. #

Meditation 4

If you don't know where you're going how you gonna know when you get there? So often we are so busy doing the things that have to be done that we don't have much time for planning either what we would like to do or deciding what is really worth doing. It is hard to find fulfillment or satisfaction in such a life. We feel as if we are being lived rather than living our own lives, as if we are being used up rather than using ourselves for some purpose which means a lot to us.

When I was Chaplain on USS MIDWAY I conducted a course called self-awareness. It was a five hour course in three parts. Part one was a personal interview in which the other person shared with me his background, present situation, and future hopes so that we could establish trust and a helpful relationship. Part two was a group session in which we shared some of my own life's story, looked carefully at principles of successful living and ways of using our own unique resources in developing a purposeful life. Part three was again a one-on-one session in which the other person had the opportunity to discuss where he thought he was headed and how he intended to get there.

One of the road signs I used in part two for this travel map of life was a quotation from Joseph Fort Newton which I discovered as a college freshman forty years ago. It affirms, "Life is worth living when I have a self fit to live with, a work fit to live for, someone to love and be loved by." That simple summary has been for me such a permanent marker of the right course that I share it with confidence that it can help others.

The self-awareness course was open to anyone who wished to take it. In truth, most of those who were involved were there because they had been assigned either by the Executive Officer or the Commanding Officer as a result of their lives having gotten into dangerous waters.

One of the things that amazed me was that of the 400 or so men who took the course in a two year span, the vast majority had no idea either what they wanted from life or what they intended to use their lives for. In other words, they had no goal or plan which they could state clearly to themselves or to someone else. When asked what they wanted for themselves 20 years from now they laughed uneasily. When it was reduced to ten years it was still an impossible question for them to handle. Even five years or one year was baffling. It was little wonder that they were not able to recognize the dangers until they had been caught up in them. It was as if they were driving at high-speed down a highway where large signs kept saying, "Danger! Look Out!" but they couldn't read.

Planning ahead doesn't guarantee that a person is going to enjoy life or find it fulfilling, but it certainly increases the probability dramatically.

The wisdom of the ancient Hebrew prophet is still as accurate today as it ever has been: "Where there is no vision the people perish." That is to say, "When we have no goal, no dream, no hope, it is hard to get very far with a satisfying life." That is as true for each of us as individuals as for the nations of which we are citizens.

What is your vision, your dream? What do you hope for? #
Meditation 5

This is my third tour in Japan as a Navy Chaplain. I have served at sea and ashore. Several times I have deployed leaving my family behind and at other times I have been fortunate enough to be able to go home at the close of each work day. I have lived on the economy and on base. I have been deeply involved in the lives of single persons, young marrieds, and established families who are part of numerous commands. I tell you this hoping it will help you to take seriously, without defensiveness, what I'm going to say this morning.

One of the conclusions I have come to, based on these years of life as a Navy Chaplain stationed in Japan, is that involvement with others is essential for successfully completing a tour in Japan and leaving with pleasant memories to last a life-time.

I have worked with more families and individuals in these three tours than I prefer to remember who believed that early return to the United States was the only acceptable solution to their problems. I cannot recall working for early return of anyone who was personally involved in a religious community.

Listen carefully please. I did not say that people participating in religious communities over here don't have problems – their pay sometimes gets fouled up, they have to go on emergency leave, they have misunderstandings with their neighbors, they miscommunicate with their children or their children's teachers, they have the usual disappointments and failures which are the common lot of humanity. But, they also have two bed-rock foundations to see them through those hurts we are all subject to. First, they have a conviction that God is at work in the world and will sustain them in life no matter how rough it may get or where they are. Second, they believe that belief in God's presence translates into a community of people who care for one another. Sharing in experiences of worship gives them a sense of perspective. Participating in fellowship with others helps them to feel a part of an extended family. And using their abilities for the good of others brings with it a reciprocal concern expressed for them especially in time of need.

On the other hand, those who have felt there was no way out for them but to get out of here have been persons who imposed an exile on themselves. Not only were they foreigners in a foreign country, they became prisoners of their own problems. They had not established meaningful relationships with their neighbors and were either unable or unwilling to get involved in programs of family service or support centers or even, for that matter, into a hobby, craft, or special interest group.

Life alone is not even an option when we are far from home, family, and friends. If we are to make it we'll do so because we acknowledge that we need others and they need us. If you are active in a religious community I commend you and encourage you to invite others to share it with you. If you aren't, I invite you to give it a try – you don't have anything to lose but your isolation, self-pity, and that awful feeling of not being able to make it here. #

E Television broadcasts, KMID-TV, USS MIDWAY (CV41)

1. .February 23, 1991 (taped for broadcast later)

a. A familiar face has gone. Father Bill Dorwart, dearly beloved and respected by the whole crew, was identified with these TV moments for the past two years. Father Dorwart is a member of the Order of the Holy Cross and received orders from his Provincial to return to South Bend, Indiana for reassignment. The order wants to use him somewhere other than as a Navy Chaplain – that is our great loss. We were all blessed by his presence and spiritually enriched by his ministry among us. His earlier service as a Navy enlisted man, then later as a missionary in Bangladesh, prepared him to bring the unique gifts he so graciously gave to us on the MIDWAY. We are confident we shall always be in his prayers – and there is something comforting and reassuring in that.

b. Much of the material Father Dorwart used in these TV moments came from a series of resources titled PROV-Ns published by the Navy Chief of Chaplains Office. PROV-Ns stands for Positive Reinforcement of Values in the Naval Service. We will continue to use these resources because we are convinced every one of us can benefit from the positive reinforcement of sound cultural, moral, religious, and spiritual values in our everyday lives. Be a re-enforcer of the best, instead of a critic of the worst.

c. A Chinese proverb says, "Behind an able person there are always other able people." Have you ever noticed how generous really great people are in giving credit to other people for their success, while small minded people want all the credit for themselves? Very few good things can be done by one self. It takes a lot of able people to make good things happen.

d Henry Wadsworth Longfellow said: "We judge ourselves by what we feel capable of doing, while others judge us by what we have already done." The best predictor of future success is past success. Yet, some people still talk a better game than they actually play. In life, as in love, as the song from *My Fair Lady* has it, "don't talk of love, show me."

e. "Anger is momentary madness, so control your passion or it will control you," observed the ancient Roman Horace. Everybody has a temper. We just have different flash points and means of control. It would be a dull existence if we never got angry but it is a disastrous one if our anger controls our actions.

f. "He who waits to do a great deal of good at once, will never do anything." Samuel Johnson must have seen a lot of people waiting for the big chance which never came. Maybe life would have been better for them if they had really believed that doing little things well usually brings the opportunity for doing even bigger things. Maybe bigness is in how well any job is done.

g. I have a friend who jokes about something being against his religion. And when you ask what is his religion he replies, "Confirmed coward." He's only kidding, of course, because he learned the truth Shakespeare also noted, "Cowards die many times before their deaths; the valiant never taste death but once." Courage, confidence, and commitment are all defenses against the cowardice that threatens us all.

h. Abraham Lincoln once said, "I desire to conduct the affairs of this administration that if at the end, when I come to lay down the reins of power, I have lost every other friend on earth, I shall at least have one friend left, and that friend shall be down inside of me." A man who is friends with himself has a running start on making friends with others.

2. March 1991 (taped for broadcast later)

a. You don't have to be a philosopher to ask yourself the question, "What makes life worth the effort?" One of the best answers I've found jumped out at me almost forty years ago from a book by Joseph Fort Newton. He asked, "When is life worth living?" and replied: "Life is worth living when I have a self fit to live with, a work fit to live for, someone to love and be loved by." Not bad, eh?

b. As we get ready to return to the people we love, we become more reflective. Fathers, especially, think about what they can do to provide the very best for their children. I like this observation by the great former president of Notre Dame, Theodore Hesburgh: "the most important thing a father can do for his children is to love their mother."

c. You have heard it so often, "marriage is for adults." The more immature we are, the more we resent that statement. Being adult isn't the same as being 18 or 21. It is more a matter of willingness to be more concerned and involved in another person's happiness and well-being than my own. That's why Joseph Barth's comment that "marriage is our last, best chance to grow up," has a ring of truth to it.

d. Daydreaming is fun but skylarking is hazardous to your health on an aircraft carrier whether at sea or in port. Safety and productivity result from attention, persistence and an attitude that there is a direct correlation between my efforts and what happens after that. Ernest Newman observed, "The great composer does not set to work because he is inspired, but becomes inspired because he is working. Beethoven, Wagner, Bach, and Mozart settled down day after day to the job at hand with as much regularity as an accountant settles down each day to his figures. They didn't waste time waiting for an inspiration."

e. A famous Admiral always encouraged his officers to act on their own initiative. One day he received a message from one of the Captains in his fleet: "Am lost in fog, shall I proceed to destination or return to base?" The Admiral replied, "Yes". Soon another message arrived from the Captain, "Do you mean yes I should proceed to destination, or yes I should return to base?" This time the Admiral replied, "No". Now, there's a Zen approach if ever I saw one. Someone from Arkansas might have replied, "Every tub's got to sit on its own bottom."

f. I have always liked school and learning. When you like something it is easy to hear good things said about it. So, for as long as I can remember people have been saying, "get all the education you can because nobody can take that away from you." But it isn't only your education, it's also your character, your integrity, your honor which can't be taken away. William Lyon Phelps once pointed out, "You can be deprived of your money, your job, and your home by someone else, but remember that no one can ever take away your honor."

g. Ralph Waldo Emerson stated: "There is no limit to what can be accomplished if it doesn't matter who gets the credit." We recently were awarded the Battle "E". We would have never gotten it if everybody had been out for himself or was asking all the time, "What's in it for me?" One of the best things about MIDWAY's "E" is that it is a visible reminder of that willingness to say, "Let's give it all we've got because that's the right way to do things."

h. "If you have something to do that is worthwhile doing, don't talk about it – do it. After you have done it, your friends and your enemies alike will talk about it," said George Blunt. There are talkers and there are doers. Which one are you?

II. Writing

A. Writing isn't easy

Writing isn't easy, at least for me. It is a discipline one imposes upon oneself and requires tenacity. I suppose it is somewhat like the requirement for getting a Ph.D. a colleague once described to me: "all it takes is a leather bottom." In other words you just have to sit there until you get it right, or at least as close to right as you are willing to expose to public readership. Many well-known writers have expressed a similar sentiment and say such things as "I find it necessary to make myself write for a designated time each and every day without fail," or "I must sit there with pen and paper, (now computer keyboard) for at least an hour each day whether anything productive comes or not."

There are things written, just as there as things spoken which seem to be gifts. To the religiously oriented speaker or writer those are considered gifts of the Holy Spirit. To others they are nevertheless considered inspired or intuitive and come unsought and almost fully developed.

On the other hand much writing requires developing some specific objective or purpose, an outline of whatever form for getting there, and a conclusion which follows necessarily from the development of one's thoughts. Good writing still reflects Aristotle's observation that what is written must have a beginning, a middle, and an end. There is so much more, of course, but those are the basic building blocks.

It is important to have a specific audience in mind when one writes just as it is crucial to be aware of the make-up of the audience to whom one is going to speak. Random shots, either written or spoken, may hit indiscriminate targets but the chances of what is being written or spoken having an impact are greater if the writer or speaker has not only something to say, that is something worthwhile, but knows to some degree to whom he wishes to speak or write.

There are any number of helps for good writing, particularly writing fiction, which one may find simply by "googling" tips to good writing. I will not attempt in this volume to provide even a rudimentary

107

approach to good writing. It is a skill I am still trying to improve on. I will, however, express by views on what one must consider to write to fulfill the purpose for which the piece is being written. Having done that I will present some of my own efforts at writing including books, articles, papers, and book reviews.

B. The discipline of Writing

As we noted in the section on public speaking, there are many helpful guides to the process which are readily available online so that I do no need to repeat them here. Maybe, however I should point out a model or too that affect both speaking and writing. The most common and least effective is the bow and arrow approach in which the speaker or writer sends his or her message out into the air aiming at a specific target and feels it has been successful when someone says, in effect, "I get it."

A second model is the loop model when the speaker or writer is sending out important points and completing them as far as possible so as to pull the hearer or reader into the loop. In effect, the response is "I'm with you."

A third model is dialogue in which the speaker or writer expects some response, even if it is tacit. The speech or article is basically linear but it may wander off into by-paths if both parties find that fruitful. The response to this is "Let's see where we are going with this."

In these and as many more as you care to enumerate there is what experts in the field call "noise". That is such a broad term but it basically means anything that interferes with clear reception whether that be previous life experiences, mind wandering otherwise known as wool gathering, distractions from within or without, or even the physical setting of the place and means of presentation.

Like so much else that I have referred to in previous volumes of this series writing is both an art and a craft. As a writer one should think of himself or herself as an artist, not with marble, canvas, musical score, architectural form or any other medium but with words. I have often been deeply gratified when someone has said they found what I had written beautifully expressed. That is certainly not always the case. But when it happens the writer knows the joy of creative artistry. Then there is the craft of writing. A great compliment to a serious writer is that he or she is a consummate Wordsmith. That conjures up images of blacksmith and that is a good thing. It is sometimes hot, sweaty, grueling grappling with the task at hand until the words are shaped into the intended form or object. One who is a good wordsmith of prose is not necessarily a great poet. Nor, for that matter is an accomplished writer of non-fiction, say document writing, concomitantly good at fiction. A writer may be gifted and quite accomplished in certain forms or genres of writing but be unable to reach the desired level of competency in other areas. His short stories may intrigue the reader and leave him or her yearning for more when all is said and done. On the other hand, her ventures into humor or satire may require a mind-set like the writer's to appreciate what is written.

I have never tried my hand at fiction except in a few flights of fancy here and there. I marvel at how good fiction writers are able to keep so many balls in the air as they juggle the story with its plots and subplots, place, people, events, things are blending harmoniously into a satisfying whole. Many writers, both historical and contemporary, have distinguished themselves and made their protagonists almost "household names" through the long series of their exploits. While reading and appreciating a certain author's works is idiosyncratic it is good that the author is able to find so many eager readers waiting for their next publication.

One of the many things I enjoy about living at Country Meadows is our monthly book club which I have facilitated for the past four years or so. We are supplied with books by the Kitsap Regional Library and plan out the year in advance so as to present ourselves with a wide array of books to consider. Some of them are thrilling, some we wish we had not wasted our time reading. But all of them provide occasion for us to stretch our minds as we enter into the world of the writer. Indeed, learning is life-long and this is another expression of it. Like any discriminating reader we have our favorite authors, some well-known and many others new to us. One of the members of the club told me recently that he liked the work of an author we recently discussed so much that he resourced his additional works and is working his way through them. The one we shared together is still his favorite but he is finding his own reading venture personally satisfying. Good readers do not necessarily make good writers, but it is like a tool-kit in any field of endeavor. The more there is in the tool kit the more sophisticated and refined the work that can be done with it. Children should begin reading early and never stop. What great rewards it brings.

A personal aside here if I may. I was so engrossed in my professional reading all through college and graduate school and then even into college teaching that I considered reading fiction a luxury I could not afford. It was not until I took a course, Literature for Adults, for my master's degree in library science that I discovered the joy, and great value fiction reading holds. I have since then included it in my reading diet and am so happy that I have.

I have loved to read since a very early age and before that being read to. I have written in an earlier volume of the premium my wife and I placed on reading to our children from their earliest years and the rich rewards that has brought. However, lots of reading doesn't guarantee that one will be a good writer.

I vividly remember my painful progression in writing from elementary school through graduate school.

In elementary school I won a county-wide contest sponsored by the Women's Christian Temperance Union on the evils of alcohol. That was ironic since one of my grandfathers was a saloon keeper and several of my dad's brothers were alcoholics. It is also notable in that the writing was probably not all that good. I do not have a copy of that essay but wonder from this vantage point about the quality of the other entries.

A second remarkable good fortune in writing was in my senior year of high school when the Navy League of Augusta and the daily morning newspaper, *The Augusta Chronicle,* sponsored a contest for thirty-three surrounding counties (Georgia still has a lot of small counties) on the topic "Why Naval Aviation must be strong." I was fortunate to have a good friend, Charles Hoover, who was a student at Augusta Junior College who was a mentor for me. I researched the topic and I wrote the essay with a lot of helpful guidance from my patient and knowledgeable friend. I won for Richmond County and along with the other 32 recipients had a three day trip to Pensacola Naval Air Station which made a profound impression on me. Again I regret not being able to locate a copy of that essay. That was, of course, in the days before computers when the original is on the computer and may be retrieved at will. I expect I made a carbon copy of the essay which disappeared over the years.

I do not remember writing many papers for high school classes. I was on the staff of the high school newspaper and was the Public Affairs Officer for the ROTC program which was made up of the entire student body of the Academy of Richmond County. There were press releases which were printable. There were no signs of an embryonic Pulitzer here.

In college I wrote many papers as did my fellow students. What I remember most about those was the almost, and I emphasize almost, irresistible urge to tear the finished paper up and throw it in the waste basket. I never felt any of them were as good as I wanted them to be though I cannot remember getting a grade lower than a B and most were A or A-. Though, for some reason, I still have a few of these I do not consider any of them worthy of inclusion in this volume. These all display a very florid writing style. The sentences were long and convoluted. Wordy in the extreme.

The papers in seminary and graduate school were more complex and I was rescued from mediocrity by Dr. Roger Lincoln Shinn, one of my theology professors, painstakingly steering me in the right direction with Rudolph Flesch's *The Art of Clear Speaking* and *The Art of Clear Writing* and E.B. White's *The Elements of Style,* this latter title is absolutely essential for any writer. In the process of writing the Ph.D. dissertation I had to rely on the *Chicago Manual of Style* which established the parameters of acceptable doctoral writing. Though I mentioned Dr. Shinn's invaluable help in the previous volume it was appropriate to mention it here also.

Writing is usually for some definite purpose. We write assignments in school all the way from the earliest grades on through post-graduate courses. The number of essays in any person's life is immense. In mine it is colossal since I went on to get a BA (Bachelor of

Arts), M.Div (Master of Divinity), MSLS (Master of Science in Library Science), MBA (Master of Business Administration) and Ph..D (Doctor of Philosophy). I think many of those papers particularly for the MSLS and MBA would have been worthy of publication with a little bit of polishing. I shall include a few papers as representative and list many, though not all, of them in the Bibliography.

C. A look at some of what I have written

1. Books

The writer of Ecclesiastes was right: "of the making of books there is no end."

I have read several compilations of writers on writing and find their approaches, especially to writing books, are as varied as the writers themselves. Some write with a determined sense of purpose in a strictly linear fashion moving from start to finish as rapidly as possible. Others amass great piles of material which they sort into manageable categories before even developing an outline. Others have a clear notion of where they are going but are not sure how they are going to get there thus rely heavily upon an outline which they revise often. Still others see writing a book as a mystical, almost magical, experience in which the whole notion of the work appears to them as in a dream or a vision and once they have begun the writing process it is as if an unseen hand is guiding them throughout.

Thomas Alva Edison was famous for many things besides the light bulb. One of his most famous sayings is, "Genius is 1% inspiration and 99% perspiration." Maybe the numbers are off a bit but we get the point. For most of us, including those of us who happen not to be a genius, know that writing, like most other things we do depends on our setting our sights on a goal and working persistently and consistently in accomplishing it.

I am not a great writer of books, probably not a great writer at all, but I have tried my hand at it.

A list of the books I have written appears in the Bibliography in Appendix II. There would be no benefit to you, the reader, for me to excerpt from the books I have written. If you are interested in perusing them you can find them with a little searching. They like, most of the material in the bibliography have been given to the Disciples of Christ Historical Society where they may be located by the Archivist, presently Shelley Jacobs to whom I am deeply grateful for providing copies of some of the papers which are included in a section further on. Before her Sara Harwell was the Archivist and assisted me when I needed help in locating something I thought I had kept a copy of but had in fact already sent to the DCHS.

The first book I wrote and had published was *Decide – Act*. This was curricular material for senior high youth and was written according to well-defined guidelines and with the remarkable assistance of one of the best editors I could have had, Neil Topliffe. There was a student's book and another book for teachers. Some of the articles which follow in the next section were attempts to provide support resources for teachers using that material.

I had ambitions for writing and publishing other full length books but my reach exceeded my grasp and nothing came of it. I even had a commitment from a publisher to publish a book on Christian Ethics but never got around to completing the project. I had a workable manuscript for another book on death and dying but was unable to find a publisher. That project would stay with me and result in two books I published after retirement: *Living Life – Facing Death*, Lucas Park Books, 2011 and *Death and Dying: Bibliographic Resources*, Create Space, 2013. I tried all the major religious presses for *Living Life – Facing Death* but received kind words of encouragement but no offers to publish. After the experience with Lucas Park Books I discovered Create Space, a subsidiary of Amazon and have found it the best way for me to go. As far as I am concerned it has the most genuinely personal and professional help anytime you need it, there is no minimum number of books to be published, the author has complete editorial control, the service is fast and efficient.

I ambitiously undertook to publish a series of books on my experiences as a Navy Chaplain focusing on prayers, especially evening prayers at sea and prayers for ceremonial occasions like change of command. An index is a help to persons searching for someone who might be included in a book. I did not compile one when writing the three volumes of *Sacred Moments: Prayers of a Navy Chaplain at Sea and Ashore*. I decided it would be worthwhile to compile one as volume IV and it worked out well. It was a pleasure to write that series of books since I already had most of the material readily available. Though the books are available through the usual outlets there has been no rush to make them come anywhere near a best seller list.

A few years ago I decided while I still had good health and satisfying mental ability I would write a series of books for my progeny. That, of course, is this series of *Thoughts along the Way*. Initially I wrote the basic outline and tried to find appropriate material for each volume. I was amazed at how much was still available to me even with all the geographic moves I had made. However, I was just as appalled at the absence of some material I would especially have liked to include. Oh well, as they say, "You have to go from where you are." As with the previous series there has been no rush to acquire these books any more than their predecessors. I sell a few from time to time mainly to fellow residents here at Country Meadows and to Summit Avenue Presbyterian Church members. The greatest joy is that I may publish them and purchase copies at a reasonable cost which then may be shared with family and as gifts from time to time. I shall never grow rich from the royalties. Total royalties run less than $10.00 a month in case you are interested. In other words, the books I have written have not been written either for scholarly acclaim or for financial gain. They have rather been an opportunity for sharing with others some of the thoughts, ideas, and experiences which have made up my life and helped mold me into the person I have become.

2. Articles

Most of my writing was occasional – not meaning once in a while, or not very often, instead meaning intended for a specific occasion. As I see it most of the writings of Augustine, Luther, Wesley and many other theologians were occasional in this sense. Of course, there are more systematic approaches as in the development of systematic theologies by such luminaries as Paul Tillich and Karl Barth, but even then their eye was on the contemporary context in which the words would be read and received. The references to great theologians focus primarily on their books or extended treatments. However they all wrote voluminous articles. I think it is in their articles that we find them grappling earnestly with issues or concerns of their readers. Most articles are written with a specific readership in mind and use language and illustrations which will resonate with those readers. I hope these articles I am including convey some of what I mean by articles being primarily a focused expression of the author's thought so as to respond to even if not answer his or her readers' questions or needs.

a. Articles on teaching and learning

This section could just as well have appeared in the previous volume, *To teach is to learn* but I have chosen to include it in this volume. It was only natural that some of my writing would be about teaching and learning. After all, my vocational commitment was to the ministry of teaching and I had been Minister of Education at Woodmont Christian Church prior to beginning college teaching. It was appropriate that some of my time and energies should be devoted to helping others to teach and to learn in the educational ministry of the church.

As I noted above I was asked by the Christian Board of Publication to write a textbook on Christian ethics for high school students. Along with the students book I also wrote a textbook for teachers. Once these were available I was asked to write three related articles for t*he Bethany Guide*, my denomination's magazine edited by Sherman R. Hanson supporting the curriculum of church education.

The process of writing the textbooks was a long and detailed one. There was a conference for writers of curricula material held in Philadelphia in which we were given explicit guidelines as to the parameters of the works on which we were working. Each of us was assigned an editor to work with us throughout the process. I was fortunate in getting Neil Topliffe as my editor who patiently worked with me and polished my submissions until they were ready for publication. The books served their purpose and were I think no better nor worse than the rest of the curricular material for that cycle. They are now, of course, out of print, having served their purpose and been superseded by more appropriate subsequent offerings. There is no need to include any of that material here. What follows are edited versions of the three articles.

Let me observe that the use of the masculine was not a deliberate attempt to exclude women teachers. It was rather the standard practice at the time to use the masculine to include members of both genders.

The first of the three articles. "Technods and Methiques for Teachers of Youth," appeared in *the Bethany Guide*, April 1971, pages 32-35. It was an article on approaches to teaching, in other words, techniques and methods for effective teaching. The editor gave the article the funky title "Technods and Methiques for Teachers of Youth." I shall present here an edited, in other words shortened, version of that article.

Sherman Hanson's question to me was "Where are the *handles?*" "We've got to do more in showing teachers *how* to use this course!" "Paul, in your revision, please reduce the pages on content and increase those devoted to process." Over the years, writers like myself have become used to getting communications like the above from our editors. We have all been working together at the task of creating the resources for our church's new Christian Life Curriculum, and the leaders of our editorial teams have constantly stressed the importance of putting usable processes into our images of teaching steps. Words like "techniques" and "methods" have become our daily companions.

The point, of course, is that in Christian education we must always be marrying two things: something to be learned has to be wedded to a means by which it can be learned. The means involves techniques and methods, or, just to help us be sure we are looking at the whole matter creatively, technods and methiques. Here is the article which I wrote in response.

Techniques and methods are the ways and means of teaching, not the ends with which one deals. Mastery of techniques will not assure a person becoming an excellent teacher. However, an understanding of the uses and limits of "handles" contributes directly to the efficiency and power of one's teaching. No single method is adequate for the learning experience of any group. A variety of techniques should be mastered so any one of them will be available for use at the appropriate time. Once a teacher has mastered a number of technods and methiques, they become a part of the resources he regularly utilizes in his teaching. He does not then self-consciously have to call to mind ways available in presenting, developing, or dealing with a given topic. He does this naturally and automatically.

In Moliere's play, *The Would-be Gentleman,* Monsieur Jourdain seeks to become an aristocratic gentleman. He believes the mastery of certain techniques of music, fencing, dancing and philosophy will contribute to his being received in a higher social class. One of the most pathetically comical scenes is that in which the philosopher instructs Mr. Jourdain in rhetoric, or the correct ways of speaking. He indicates that one may speak either in poetry or in prose. Mr. Jourdain inquires whether these are the only two available forms of speech. The philosopher, somewhat meticulously, explains the difference between the two. With utter amazement Mr. Jourdain exclaims that he has always spoken prose. 'What a marvelous accomplishment,' he declares.

Well, lest we appear equally foolish, let all of us who write, edit, and teach CLC courses for young people call to mind that we have participated in experiences of learning in which all or at least most of the techniques appearing below have been utilized. They are so familiar to us that it comes almost with amazement that we have actually been using them. For the sake of convenience we will list them without giving any particular preference to the order: [In the article each item has a descriptive paragraph. I omit those descriptions and simply list the items by number.]

1. Lecture, 2. Guest speaker, 3. Questions and answers, 4. Discussion, 5. Dialogue, 6. Panel, 7. Symposium, 8. Debate, 9, Buzz groups, 10. Task groups, 11. Assignments, 12. Research, 13. Interviews, 14. Quizzes, 15. Tests, 16. Creative activities, 17. Storytelling, 18. Music, 19. Drama or play, 20. Role plays, 21. Pantomime or charades, 22. Demonstrations, 23. Exhibits, 24. Book reviews, 25. Tapes, 26. Phonograph records, 27. Projected visual-aids, 28. Flat visual aids, 29. Field trips, 30. Personal example or witness.

Teachers of church school CLC youth-level courses, and leaders of Christian Living Encounters, Chi Rho Fellowship, and CYF study-action courses have discovered that these material do try to marry given chunks of content with appropriate technods and methiques. The teachers, however, due to the special and unique natures of the groups with which they work, must always double-check any suggested marriage. They must decide, in light of the situations in their classrooms and the capacities and bents of their young people, what technod or methique to use in any part of a lesson or session. It is advisable, therefore, for teachers to keep some kind of real or mental inventory of processes with which they feel comfortable always at hand. For, just as the editors have helped me see, so I'd now like to help teachers see: 'It isn't enough to see *what* you want to teach; you have to see just as clearly *how* it can best be taught.' You have to know your Bible; you have to know your church history; you have to know doctrine. But, teaching youth, you also have to know your technods and methiques. #

The second of the three related articles on teaching and learning using the book *Decide – Act* deliberately addressed the relationship of these two emphases 1) deciding or thinking, and 2) acting. The article, "Think and Act; Act and Think," appeared in *the Bethany Guide*, May 1971. Pages 21-23.

The lead-in supplied by the editor follows: "*Like horse and carriage, bacon and eggs, gift and giver, studying a matter and doing something about it go together. In all teaching and learning, therefore, elements of 'analysis' and 'engagement' must complement one another.*

Education today is in a state of ferment. Colleges and universities seek increasingly better ways to assist in educating students. Businesses and corporations try new techniques of teaching their personnel how better to succeed in today's world. Workshops, seminars, and discussion groups have become a part of the way of life of an increasing number of persons. The church, too, finds itself in a time of transition and change. It is difficult for us to remain satisfied with our old and conventional ways of teaching. This is not to say that they have not had value, or that they may not even in the present have great value for us. It is rather to say that we must find the best ways of teaching and learning and make changes when these assist in this aim. How one goes about teaching in a given situation is determined by a large number of factors.

One of the factors to be considered is the context itself, the fact that a given class is a part of a school whether that be a public school or the church school.

Another factor is the nature of the students who make up the class.....

Another factor is the interests of teacher and students....

Another factor is the abilities of those engaged in learning....

Time is a factor in 'learning through involvement.'....

There are two basic emphases in teaching the Christian 'Way'. One may put the emphasis on thinking. Or the emphasis may fall on acting. This is not to say that thinking is done without acting, or that acting does not involve us in thinking. It is rather to say that the matter of priority or emphasis needs to be clear to the teacher and the learners. All need to be aware too, that the emphasis may change from time to time, back and forth, as the class moves along. In each of these areas there are two further approaches that may be noted.

I. Emphasis on thinking:

This approach will be preferred by those who feel their time, abilities, and interests will be served if most of their study of a given theme is done in the classroom situation. ...

II. Emphasis on acting:

This is a less conventional approach and assumes some variation in the time and place of meetings as well as a difference in the objectives.....

Using either of these two basic emphases without the other leads to sterility, of course. Acting without thinking often leads us to lose sight of what it means to be a person or to be a Christian in the world. Thinking without a concern for acting is a deception which sometimes leaves us with the illusion that as long as we are able to understand a problem we have already begun to solve it. What we must search for is an appropriate interrelationship of these emphases at a time when youth are eagerly excited and enthusiastic about a given theme, problem, issue, or crisis….. #

The third and final article in the series appeared in *the Bethany Guide*, April 1972, Pages 29-33. My apologies for the unintentional sexist language. I should have known better since I had had many dedicated women teachers throughout my church or Sunday School involvement.

The qualities of the good teacher, as they are applicable to Christian education, may be summarily stated:

1. He believes in the importance of Christian education in the church.
2. He measures up well as a person.
3. He has convictions and reasons for teaching Christian ethics.
4. He understands the nature of teaching.
5. He has sufficient knowledge to teach others.
6. He invites others to share in learning with him.
7. He develops good human relationships with his students.
8. He understands and appreciates how people learn, and is able to deal with their individual differences in learning.
9. He seeks to deepen his own faith as he explores its meaning with others.
10. He has an appreciation for learning as a process in which God's love becomes ever more meaningful. (Adapted from *If Teaching is Your Job*, by J.L. Lobingier. Pilgrim Press, 1956. Pages 28-41.)

Sometimes it is helpful to ask very specific questions about oneself as a teacher. Here is a checklist of such pertinent questions.

I. The teacher is also a learner:

1. Do I regularly read books or articles on Christian education and on Christian ethics?
2. Do I occasionally read Christian education magazines or journals dealing with Christian ethics?
3. Do I participate in various kinds of leadership education activities regularly?
4. Do I participate in faculty meetings in my church?

II. The good teacher makes adequate preparation:

5. Do I make general preparation for teaching by studying the course as a whole in advance and by finding supplementary material?

6. Do I study the teacher's material and also become acquainted with the student's material?

7. Do I look ahead in planning so as to be able to take advantage of audio-visual resources and utilize a variety of methods of teaching?

III. As a part of advance preparation the good teacher makes a lesson plan:

8. Do I write out a plan for each session?

9. Do I try to make the plan fit the class rather than the class the plan?

10. Do I make the plan far enough ahead of time to add material to enrich it?

IV. The teacher approaches each session with confidence:

11. Do I pray God to help me recognize opportunities for learning, to be patient and to keep me from being defensive about the material?

12. Do I arrive early – either before the students or at least fifteen minutes before class is scheduled to begin?

13. Do I arrange the room for good learning, taking care of proper ventilation, light, heat or cooling, chairs and table, pictures, and chalkboards?

14. Do I keep sufficient supplies such as pencils and paper on hand for effective use?

V. The growing teacher is always trying to improve:

15. Do I become familiar enough with material that I do not have to read out of the book all the time?

16. Do I try to practice the art of listening as well as talking so that conversation and discussion contribute to learning and better understanding?

17. Do I try to find out from others who teach senior high youth what approaches or methods they have used effectively?

VI. The effective teacher realizes that the student must be an active participant, not a passive spectator:

18. Do I encourage my students to be at the least active listeners and even better, active contributors to the session?

19. Do I occasionally discuss class plans and goals with the class?

20. Do I work at drawing out the reticent student and seek to find other ways he may contribute if he does not wish to engage in discussion?

VII. The good teacher brings variety into the procedure and thus introduces the element of surprise:

21. Do I vary the approach so as not to follow the same pattern every session?

22. Do I make good use of enthusiasm and interest of the class, occasionally devoting the session to some form of creative activity?

23. Do I once in a while rearrange the room to keep it from being monotonous?

VIII. The effective teacher gives more thought to the students than to materials, curriculum, or any other matter:

24. Do I know my students – their names, families, schools, work, and interests?

25. Do I express genuine interest in them as persons, letting them know they are missed when they are absent and recognizing both their accomplishments and problems?

26. Do I seek to gain the respect and confidence of my students and work with them rather than treating them with indifference?

IX. The successful teacher recognizes the importance of his own personality and personal living:

27. Do I have genuine convictions about the importance of Christian education and Christian ethics and the particular kind of learning we are engaged in?

28. Do I see my teaching as strengthened by the total life of the congregation and my own participation in it, especially in worship and investment of time, energy, and money?

29. Do I keep before myself as well as my students ever more inspiring ideals of Christian living?

30. Do I have an appropriate appreciation of my appearance and teaching?

X. The teacher is a member of a team:

31. Do I work with other faculty members and the staff, encouraging others in our ministry of Christian education?

32. Do I teach so as to invite others to consider the joys and values of teaching?

33. Do I try to learn from others while I am teaching them?

XI. The wise teacher recognizes the importance of the home:

34. Do I know my students well enough to make the session relevant to their daily lives?

35. Do I invite parents or others members of the student's family to occasionally visit the class or assist in the learning process?

36. Do I encourage my students to realize the class is but a part of the Christian life and needs their wider involvement?

37. Do I talk over problems with the parents of my students?

XII. The thoughtful teacher is critical of self even more than of the students when faced with noncooperation and disciplinary problems:

38. Do I try to find the cause of a discipline problem and remedy it?

39. Do I take the problem student as a challenge and seek to find what he has to contribute to the class?

40. Do I occasionally review and evaluate my teaching to see how it can become more interesting to all my students?

XIII. The good teacher always looks for positive results:

41. Do I measure success in part by my students' growing knowledge and understanding of the content of the course?

42. Do I measure success in part by the developing attitudes of my students – their appreciation of others, including persons of different ideas, races, cultures, religions than their own and by their understanding of the problems involved in ethical issues?

43. Do I measure success in part by the quality of my students' everyday lives and their leadership in church, community, and school?

44. Do I measure success in part by the willingness of my students to discuss controversial subjects without anger or dissension?

45. Do I measure success by the eagerness of my students to learn and their willingness to take some personal responsibility for the quality of the class?

(Basic structure and idea adapted from *If Teaching is Your Job*, Pages 145-150)

Now let's look specifically at four areas of concern: the physical setting, preparation, sessions, and evaluation. [I am shortening each of these]

The physical setting

It is so easy to make too much, or too little, of the physical setting for teaching. People have learned in situations which the educational experts would have written off as hopeless. Just having an excellent facility for teaching will not guarantee good teaching and learning any more than using good material will assure adequate learning. But, both good materials and a good physical context are aids to better learning....

Preparation

Preparation for teaching is cumulative. All the experiences you have had and the things you yourself have learned up to this point in your life are part of your preparation for teaching this course. The books you have read and the persons you have talked with have played their part. ...

It is necessary, however, if one is going to teach a specific course, to be concerned to know what the course is about. Consequently, you will want to try to assess your own knowledge and experience, strengthen the weak points, enrich the others so as to engage with your class in a meaningful dialogue regarding Christian ethics.... [A few specific books were suggested for getting a better grasp of Christian ethics]

Do not be afraid to admit that there are many things that you do not know. Be able to express with the students a willingness to search out ways by which pertinent knowledge may be acquired....

Sessions

You note in the outline of sample sessions that a lesson plan is recommended for the sessions. Beginning teachers will find it well worth the time spent to develop rather full or elaborate written lesson plans. More experienced teachers will find their own way of shortening the process and perhaps only outlining their plan. More advanced teachers will have learned the art of planning much of this mentally, using only a minimum of written material as they go into class sessions. The need for making lesson plans cannot be emphasized too much….. [Specific elements to be included in a good lesson plan were then set forth]

Evaluation

Teaching is both an art and a science. As a science one learns explicit methods by which he proceeds. He learns to use terms clearly and precisely. He learns through repeated practice what results he may expect from certain practices or acts. He learns how to move from the simple to the complex. He learns how to check himself as he moves along to provide correctives for wrong, inappropriate, or inadequate procedures so as to make these more effective.

As an art he learns a love or an appreciation for that which he seeks to perfect. He is willing to invest the necessary energies for acquiring greater proficiency in his art. He learns how to perform his art with grace and beauty. The practice and performance are heightened or improved as he develops a reservoir from which he draws.

Part of the teacher's evaluation is an evaluation of specific techniques, methods, or procedures. Part of it is assessment of whether or not the aims are being fulfilled and whether the consistency of the performance measures up to his desired aim….

….Evaluation is for the purpose of better teaching in the future and for a sense of satisfaction as one reflects on the teaching and learning of the past. Perspective or distance is needed for accurate evaluation…. By all means evaluate, but let evaluation be for the sake of learning and teaching. #

b. Articles for a college newspaper

Here are two articles I wrote for the Transylvania newspaper, *The Rambler.*

i. "Few Surprised to learn that 'God is Dead'", February 18, 1966, page 3. (Ed. Note: This is the first of a two-part essay written for *The Rambler* by Dr. Paul Murphey. The second part will appear February 25).

The announcement that God is dead came as no surprise to a number of persons waiting quietly for confirmation of what they had assumed all along. Indeed, as Dave Meade, writing in the *Chicago Daily News* said, "If 1965 was the year God died most people didn't know it. They kept right on living as if nothing had happened." Why, Orson Welles had caused more panic in the antiquated days of radio with his dramatic and unexpected declaration of an invasion, then taking place, of strange creatures from another planet.

But there were some for whom it was big news. When *The New York Times, Time, Newsweek,* and *the New Yorker* began to fan it, it was no longer a theological intra-fraternity fight. The widely circulated *Christian Century* brought out issue after issue in the style of a neighborhood hassle over "my old man can lick your old man" in the taunting refrain, God is dead, no he isn't, yes he is, etc., etc. By then the Avant-garde of many a college campus saw a new rallying cry and gleefully met with religious fervor to discuss what to them was the irreligious question. They were sometimes gathered reverently round three bright young professors whose boldness was applauded in the collegiate courts of the gentiles and ruefully discussed in the holy of holies of the theological elite.

The reaction hasn't been like solid stone rolled out of place, rather more like rocks in the cement mixer of the campus whirl:

So, God is dead? Yes, well, what else is new?

I didn't even know that he was sick.

When's the funeral?

How can you tell?

Who told you? —The theologians, man, you're out of your mind.

How ridiculous! Why that's nothing but blasphemy. Go gargle with Listerine.

Don't tell my mother, it'd be the death of her.

Alright, what do we do now?

I can't believe it. What do you mean anyway?

What **do** you, or they, or whoever is saying mean? We mean for one thing that it is not **new** news.

Even austere John (Calvin, that is) in the 16th century could tell the citizens of Geneva that their godlessness was indicative of a practical atheism. Since they lived as if there were no God why didn't they go on and say God is dead. Or take a look at loquacious Martin (Luther, naturally) whose wife Katherine responded to one of his black mooded silences with the observation that God must be dead for Martin to be so sullen. Johannes Rist in a 17th century hymn blurted it out – "O grosse not! Gott selbst ist tot." And Hegel, that systematizer par excellence, kept things turning til Nietzsche, with journalistic flair, popped out his madman in the Gay Science (*Frohliche Wissenschaft*):

Have you not heard of the madman who lit a lantern at noonday, ran to the market-place, and cried unceasingly? "I am looking for God! I am looking for God!" Since it happened that there were many standing there who did not believe in God, he roused great laughter. Is he lost? Said one. Or gone astray like a child? Said another. Or has he hidden himself? Is he afraid of us? Has he gone on a voyage? Or emigrated? So they shouted and laughed. The madman leaped into their midst and pierced them with his glance. "Where has God gone?" he cried. "I will tell you. **We have slain him –** you and I. We are all his murderers. But how did we do it? How could we drink up the sea? Who gave us the sponge to wipe out the whole horizon? What did we do, when we unchained this earth from its sun? Where is it moving to now? And where are we moving to now? Away from all suns? Do we not stumble all the time? Backwards, sideways, forwards, in every direction? Is there an above and a below anymore? Are we not wandering as through infinite nothingness? Does empty space not breathe upon us? Is it not colder now? Is not night coming, and ever more night? Must we not light lanterns at noon? Do we not hear the noise of the gravediggers, as they bury God? Do we not smell God decaying? – Gods too decay! God is dead. God stays dead. And we have slain him. How shall we console ourselves, chief of all murderers? The holiest and most powerful that the world has ever possessed ebbed its blood away beneath our knives – who will wipe this blood from our fingers? What water can make us clean? What propitiations and sacred rites will we have to invent? Is not the greatness of this deed too great for us? Must we not ourselves become gods in order to seem worthy of them? There was never a greater deed, and, because of it, all who are born after us are part of a higher history than ever was before!

The madman fell silent, and looked at his hearers again. They too were silent, and looked at him with shocked eyes. At last he threw his lantern on the ground, so that it broke in pieces, and went out. "I came too early he said, "it is not yet my time. This monstrous event is still on the way – it has not yet penetrated men's years. Lightning and thunder need time, even after they have been done, in order to be seen and heard. This deed is still further from men than the remotest stars – and yet they have done it! The story goes that the madman went into several churches on the same day, and sang his **requiem aeternam Deo.** Led out and questioned he replied just the one thing: "What are the churches, if not the tombs and sepulchers of God? (*Frohliche Wissenschft,* tr. Ronald Gregor Smith and quoted in *The Nature of Faith* by Gerhard Ebeling.)

We have quoted this extensive passage from Nietzsche because it is the Shema of the present movement, the Gospel of the "God is dead boys". It is this from which they preach and to which they turn for their basic emphasis. The madman has at last come into his own. His time has come and the world listens attentively.

A more somber and pathetic note than Nietzsche's was struck by the novelist Jean Paul when he wrote of the impact of the death of God on man the believer:

The scene is that of a cemetery surrounding a church, through the open door of which is seen a corpse on a flat bier. The corpse raises its hands and folds them in prayer, but the arms stretch longer till they drop off, the hands still clasped in prayer. In the church's steeple is a clock, symbolic of eternity. On its face are no numbers, nor are there hands to indicate the time for which the dead await.

A noble figure emerges above the altar within the church and the dead cry out to him, "Christ, is there no God?"

He answers, "There is none. I have been through the worlds, ascended to the suns and flown along the milky ways through the wastes of heaven but there is no God. I have descended as far as existence casts its shadow and looked into the abyss and cried: "Father where art Thou?" But I have heard only the eternal tempest which none controls, and with no sun to fashion it the glistening rainbow from the west stood over the abyss and dripped down. And when I searched the immeasurable world for the divine eye it fixed me with an empty and unfathomable socket, and eternity lay on chaos and gnawed it away and repeated itself. Lament and cry through the shadows for He is not."

The vision continues as the dead infants crawl to Christ and utter, "Jesus, have we no Father?" With tears he haltingly bemoans. "We are all orphans, I and you, we have no Father .... Do you know this? When will you destroy the building and me? ... Oh, if each I is his own father and creator, why not his own destroying angel?" (quoted in *The Silence of God* by Helmut Thielicke, tr. By G.W. Bromiley)

The pathos has not yet overtaken the young "Christian Radicals", as Langdon Gilkey of the University of Chicago calls them. They still ride the full swell of ecstasy in the impact of what is received as new. They have come into their own and are not at all averse to the public eye. For three or four years they had been writing in the secluded pages of theological journals and even in the much respected interdisciplinary periodical, *The Christian Scholar*. But it was not until *Time*, et al set them on a larger stage that they began to be taken seriously. Who are they?

ii. "In absence of God, Jesus seen as Father Image," *The Rambler*, February 25, 1966. Pages 3-4.

Professor Gabriel Vahanian treats the death of God as a cultural phenomenon descriptive of our culture. The others will readily admit this but wish to go further. Vahanian re-declares what Nietzsche's madman had come too early to proclaim: contemporary culture as scientifically and technologically oriented finds God an extraneous factor in axiomatic and empirical explanation. Since most of present day man's questions are raised and answered in the framework of the physical and quantitative, God is an embarrassing intrusion. Consequently, if God is not taken seriously as a reason or a source or even a means of meaning it is legitimate to see him as non-existent, or more graphically put, dead. This is clear enough but what about the message of the real vanguard?

Professor William Hamilton quickly admits he is in the most vulnerable position since he feeds himself on the salary of a seminary professor charged with preparing men for the Christian ministry. He is reported to have commented that if things get too hard to bear he can always become an undergraduate religion professor since many of them don't believe in God anyway. Hamilton is the easiest to read of the three – there is a touch of humor and an apparent tongue-in-cheek approach here and there. However, he is ambiguous, though not nearly so much as Thomas Altizer whom some theological colleagues call "a madman obviously in need of a psychiatrist." Hamilton seems not to wish to say God is dead in the usual sense of the word of death as finality. He insists he is saying more than that God is absent, separated, away, but this is what comes through nevertheless. Here we have an old refrain, only it was from the other team in I Kings 18. Hamilton, it appears, is really saying God is on vacation and we'll just have to get along without him while he's gone. While waiting for a return unknown and unscheduled, we should make the most of it and prove ourselves to be men. Hamilton says he is using the phrase God is dead metaphorically and its meaning is apparently separation. Since God is dead, that is, separated from us, we can have no recourse to him. We must honestly admit that **for us** God is dead. However, we don't have to go it alone as orphans in this dark world. Jesus is emphatically the man for us. (I can't help but think at this point of a plethora of "gospel songs" that must be ruminating in Hamilton's church heritage, e.g. "he keeps me singing as I go," "he walks with me and talks with me and tells me I am his own," "by looking to Jesus, like him thou shalt be, thy friends in thy conduct his likeness shall see": and on and on).

You might put it this way: Poppa is away on vacation so Sonny is running the store but since Sonny is a man himself he doesn't need to call Poppa for every transaction. He can keep things moving as long as he needs to so that they'll be in order when and if Poppa gets back.

God is dead but Jesus takes over the responsibilities and functions of God avoiding any supernatural connotation. He is indeed the man-for-others whom men should follow into the city streets or wherever men in this world need a champion. Theology now gets identified with ethics tested by involvement in the revolutionary struggles of contemporary human existence.

130

Professor Paul Van Buren would have no mistake about the fact that the phrase God is dead is not a metaphor. The very heart of the problem lies just there – it is linguistic and semantic. The three letters g-o-d in that order with appropriate closeness to one another and with the first one capitalized (thus God) have become as a word, so hopelessly confused and individualized by a multiplicity of meanings that human communication utilizing this word is an absolute impossibility without precise definition each time it is used. The problem goes further than communication, however, for the term God has no verifiable referent and consequently cannot be used intelligibly. The objectifiability of an existent reality to which the symbol God refers and corresponds is unseen and unknown empirically. Since there is no definite coincidence of reality and word, or referent and symbol, then it is nonsense or meaningless to use it in human discourse.

Van Buren, no more than Hamilton, wishes to leave man in a hopeless void. Man's attention must be turned from the impossible to the possible, from the unknown and for that matter unknowable to the known. In other words from God to Jesus.

For Van Buren, then, God is dead linguistically. This raises more problems than we care to deal with, not the least of which is that it leaves quite a lot of frustrated novelists, dramatist, poets, construction workers, college students, and such to find some more legitimate oath

The query whether God **is** or **is not** is actually rather extraneous since there is no correspondence of reality and word which may be confirmed and thus employed. Therefore, the usual supernatural trappings of traditional religion, such as prayer, worship, doctrine, etc. have to be secularized, that is, turned to exclusive reference in "this world." Categories associated with traditional religion, as for instance, supernatural and theistic must be abandoned. But, once again, the news isn't new. There has been reaction for a long time to man's tendency to make God into an old man with flowing beard, or a celestial book-keeper, or a cosmic cop. Transylvania has been among those colleges which have presented the necessity of such realism in religion in facing this need.

Whenever God is so **super** that there is no correspondence between the term and the reality, false motives and relationships have to be countered. It is legitimate to say that God is dead if one is saying that old ideas of God hiding under every bed or behind every closet door, or hurling thunderbolts at grown-up naughty children, or giving high post-mortem interest for low present investment are meaningless. Van Buren is saying more than this, however, in that since no attainable referent presents itself to verify the word it must be assumed that there is no such reality, or once again God is dead.

Professor Altizer contends what he is saying is not that God is dead (metaphorically) or God is dead (linguistically). For him God is dead is an historic event. Altizer seems to have little regard for precision in language and one is not quite sure what is really intended by such an assertion. He goes on to amplify this by insisting either we become the murderers of God or we have no right to call ourselves men in a world come-of-age (blatant shades of Nietzsche!) Either the present must be grasped as fully in the hands of man or lost in terms of any creative possibilities. For him, God is associated with the past, with need, with deficiency and even with evasive irresponsibility.

Surely part of Altizer's dramatic and flamboyant style is a gathering rejection of the neo-orthodoxy which reigned supreme in the immediate past with its stress on the supremacy of God, the sinfulness of man, and the continual and culminating judgment of God over human history. Altizer is saying, at least in part, "I'm a grown man now and I don't need you telling me what to do" It has all the rings of the boy who is becoming a man and must stand over against his father – except he goes a bit further and insists that I'll always be a lad as long as there's a dad. I can't really live till he's dead, so if I'm going to become head of this territory I'll have to bury him.

Man come-of-age must stop cringing before a God who has the powers of life and death, of grace and wrath, of forgiveness and judgment for there is no such God since man has murdered him.

There can be no solace from the silence, nothing but languishing in the loneliness. There isn't even a guilt-feeling to fill the emptiness. We

had to kill God, it was a necessary part of the rite of maturation, the rite necessary to become ourselves in a world of our own making for the fulfillment of our own purposes. But, surprise! Though we have killed God we still have Jesus! All the fervor devoted to the Father now goes to the Son, whatever that word means, because he's been around and he knows what it's all about. He was really the man-for-his-time as we must be men for ours. Just as he seized the situation to make it meaningful for himself and others so must contemporary man.

So, what of all of this? Even if the God-is-dead movement is a theological fad or if these bright young theologians are religion's counterpart to drama's angry young men, what is to become of it? Is it as Harvey Cox says, "the maudlin celebration of the demise of deity," or the sychophantic "He's dead, he isn't stalemate?" Is Cox, who teaches at Harvard, right in saying, "it is theology not You Know Who that is dead?"

I think the very clamor of the cry is a possibility of a new acceptance of theology as really concerned with the world. Surely at the base of the God-is-dead movement there lies a gnawing problem for twentieth century man. There are at least three facets which are being opened by the present debate: 1. The absence of God as a meaningful aspect of contemporary man's way of looking at things, 2. The mass confusion and wholesale misunderstanding resulting from hazy language about God, and 3. The necessity of seeing religion in terms of man's maturity in his world.

One does not, obviously, have to accept the conclusions of the "Christian radicals" to recognize the legitimacy of the problem with which religious, and for that matter, irreligious men will have to deal for an indefinite future. The raucous voice of the belligerent blurters should be heard, but with the insistence that they make clearer what they are shouting about and write so an intelligent man can make some coherent sense of what they are saying.

It may be that from the death-of-God furor there will come a more genuine religious faith, a more urgent commitment with integrity to the divine reality of the present cognizant of the meaningfulness of the past and the awareness of the future, and a reappraisal of the prospects and limitations of a sometimes myopic scientific-technological orientation or preoccupation of contemporary man.

I feel responsible for saying one thing further before concluding this article since it was probably a reaction to the following which prompted the invitation to write the article in the first place.

A recent convocation speaker sweepingly laid all the ills of the present state of misaffairs in America at the feet of Darwin, Freud, and Marx whom he held as the culprits in the God-is-dead fracas. We have tried to take note of the theological dimensions of this battle consequently have not referred to the illustrious three. They have their rightful place in the cultural malaise so well described by Vahanian. Whether one deplores some of the consequences of their genius he would hardly wish to live in a world without them where there was instant creation (just add water) or actions were only what they seemed, or exploitation of the masses was fair game for those who had a running head start because of family wealth. They were but three modern men, though a highly significant three, who must be continually revised and reinterpreted. Little is to be gained by railing against them as wholly responsible for unleashing upon us uncontrollable forces of destruction. Their appearance, as is well known, did stir up angry diatribes between "religious" and "scientific" men and even worse harangues between "pseudo-religious and pseudo-scientific" men. It may be that they, like "the Christian radicals" raised issues which had been too long ignored, or found approaches which were put to both fruitful and perverted use. It may be also that one runs the risk in admitting that they might be saying something worth hearing that he is then forced into accepting their conclusions. But this is part of the risk that makes life, especially in an academic community, an open-ended experience of excitement and joy.#

c. An unpublished journal article:

In the Fall of 1981 I was invited to submit an article to *Military Chaplains' Review* for its Spring 1982 issue on Ethics. I was then on assignment as Chaplain on USS PELELIU (LHA5) and did not finish the article before we left on extended deployment to the western Pacific. Computers were not yet readily available so I was restricted to regular mail for submission rather than email.. By the time I finished writing and typing the article and mailed it the issue had already gone to press. I am including it because of its subject matter or content. The article was written in traditional format with footnotes. As included here the "footnotes" appear in parenthesis after the section that was footnoted in the original.

"The Military Chaplain as Ethicist"
The context of military chaplaincy.

Extensive literature is available on the military chaplain's role expectations in preaching, counseling, teaching, and administration. However, little has been written on the military chaplain as ethicist. Yet, one's influence and effectiveness, as well as his or her vocational involvement make this a vital aspect of the profession. The exercise of this function varies in degree, though not in kind, with the type and level of assignment. The role of ethicist, one who consciously and deliberately seeks clearer understanding of the ethical implications of human actions, is inherent in the task. It is not a question of whether or not the chaplain will function as an ethicist but only a matter of the quality, thoroughness, and adequacy of that functioning.

The military chaplain lives and works as servant of the church while at the same time as servant of the state. This duality sets a condition peculiar to this form of ministry. In the military he or she is involved directly in the structure of existence which is intimately, inescapably, and daily shared with other participants in the system. In the civilian pastorate he or she consciously ministers within the context of a religious organization whose members share a common heritage and hope. Whether that ministry is within an authoritarian and hierarchical religious organization or a voluntaristic and egalitarian community of believers, ministry is defined by service to God's people in the church in the world. Beyond the realm of the political structure of the church in which he or she ministers involvement is in the structures or orders of existence of those to and with whom he ministers primarily as observer, spectator, or critic.

In preaching he or she may or may not probe aspects of societal existence detrimental to fuller realization of a more just and humanely productive realm. When he or she does so it is primarily by the avowed, even if reluctant, assumption of the role of prophet steeped in the biblical heritage. Professional responsibilities do not, however, put him or her at a point at which involvement as ethicist makes him or her an integral mover in the system which is critiqued.

In counseling the dynamics of unethical situations impacting negatively upon the wholeness of human life may be explored but the counselor's orientation is towards openness to the person affected by such conditions rather than to the conditions themselves. The purpose is to assist the counselee to become open to and avail himself or herself of the spiritual and psychological resources for dealing realistically with actions imperiling or impeding his or her life as a mature person. The desired change is in the person who in turn may then conclude that a healthily stable existence requires some change in context. Such change may come about by the counselee acting as an agent for such change, or if necessary, withdrawing from a perceived debilitating situation. It is the counselee and not the counselor who exists within a given context to which he or she either adjusts, seeks alteration of, or withdraws from.

As an ethicist the military chaplain has identified with a particular institution or system in which he or she is involved as participant rather than observer. This kenotic character of the chaplain's role (see Philippians 2:7) is vital to functioning effectively within it. The chaplain wears the uniform, lives under the orders and regulations and is subject to the traditions, customs and obligations of the specific branch of military service to which he or she belongs. The chaplain is morally responsible for supporting the prosecution of the mission and objectives of the unit in which he or she ministers. As an officer, the chaplain is bound by the same requirements for loyalty and adherence to regulations which control the destiny of other officers and enlisted men and women. The fact that the chaplain wears the uniform and insignia, receives the same pay and benefits of others in his or her pay-grade, and lives under the same regimen as those with whom he or she lives and works involves him or her in that institution in a way without parallel in a civilian pastorate. As a chaplain he or she is aware that such participation is one of tension and ambiguity. It raises the necessity of serious reflection on whether or not a person can serve two masters when the demands and obligations of the two are not coincident. This question is not unique to the chaplain but is one which men and women of deep faith who have chosen the profession of arms also ponder. It is a point at which the role of chaplain as ethicist may be explored. (A professional resource summarizing approaches and issues of military ethics is a research paper, "Military Professionalism and Ethics," by Francis B. Galligan. Reproduced by the Center for Advanced Research, Naval War College, 1979)

The military chaplain may preach to few hearers by comparison with the congregations in which he or she preached in a civilian pastorate. He or she may even cease preaching regularly with advancement in rank and supervisory responsibility. A similar diminution occurs in pastoral involvement with advancement in rank. Nevertheless, the spiritual and moral welfare of the men and women for whom the chaplain bears an assigned responsibility does not diminish.

The chaplain's role as ethicist is a constant whether serving a field unit or ministering to an entire branch of military service. The chaplain may not be asked specifically to function as an ethicist and at times may be challenged for doing so. However, it is incumbent upon him or her to seek clarity and understanding of the moral ends and purposes of procedures, programs, and policies. The forms such consideration take involve the obvious issues of abuse (alcohol, drug, personal), perversity (sexual, managerial, conditional), and conflict (racial, obedience to orders, personal desires, and institutional demands). They also cluster around less immediate issues of the uses, purposes, and limits of war, the extent, proliferation or limitation of nuclear arms, the rights and obligations of military persons in a free society, and the responsibilities for humaneness in the structures of control and the exercise of power.

The chaplain's professional responsibility as ethicist

If the chaplain has a responsibility to perform as a professional ethicist it is important to have some grasp of what that entails. Among the marks of a profession is that one does it for some goal beyond immediate gratification. Members of a profession perform a service for the benefit of those with whom, on whom, or for whom they practice their skill or art. In doing so it is recognized that a specialized body of knowledge contributes to that practice. (Adam Yarmolinsky, "The Professional in American Society," *Daedelus*, 107, no. 1, Winter, 1978. Quoted in Richard Hutcheson, Jr. *Wheel within the Wheel.* John Knox Press, 1979. Page 39. In addition to "special knowledge" Yarmolinsky also cites "special skills, special resources, and special responsibility' as marks of a profession. Page 159) While there are many ways to approach such knowledge, for instance, from a historical perspective, there are certain primary categories or concepts which are recurrent and explicatory. Three of these which appear in various forms are concepts of the good, the right, and the appropriate.

The good may be variously defined dependent upon the theological or philosophical orientation of the ethicist. The good may be defined as "doing the will of God," "avoiding pain and gaining pleasure," "achieving ends which are creative rather than destructive," "contributing to conditions which maximize justice," and so forth. The good may be as abstract as a Platonic ideal discovered in time because it exists in eternity, or an Aristotelian actualization of reality which moves from particularity to universality. The good may likewise be as concrete as the acceptance of the legitimate necessity of providing assistance for accomplishing a task which could not be completed without such assistance. Whatever the content of the concept, the good denotes a given-ness or end toward which actions move. Whether one approximates, realizes, discovers, actualizes, or creates it the good is the object of ethical involvement.

The concept of the right denotes obligation. Rightness is a category of the imperative. The right is what one ought to do to achieve the good. To do something because "it is the right thing to do" is to commit oneself to a course of action with the expectation that whatever the consequences the good will be obtained. It implies an acknowledgment,, if not a consensus, by persons acting in good faith that it is a proper course to pursue to reach the desired good. Ancient struggles over the nature of the good whether in Plato or Paul and the difficulties of attaining it invariably imply a course of right action. To reach the good one must do the right thing whether this is a wise exercise of virtue or a mystical identification with one whose life is seen as the embodiment of what is right about human existence.

While the good is the category of ethical ends and the right is the category of ethical means, a third category is also essential. Appropriateness is acknowledgment of the contextual dimensions and the interplay of actions in the three dimensions of time and the reality of given space.

Human actions are never in the abstract. They occur in specific contexts where consistency and coherence are primary considerations. Appropriateness as an ethical category safeguards the rightness to pursue different courses of action toward realization of the good under different circumstances. While it is right to speak the truth about a person's past, it may not be right to do so in a given context when one's knowledge is limited to hearsay and the probability of the disclosure contributing to any future good for him or her, or for others, is minimal.

Ethical discussions in given situations are always "under the circumstances" in much the same way that theologically one speaks of human existence always being *coram Deo*. Such circumstances or contexts define the parameters of ethical discourse and decision dependent upon both the primary and derivative human values to which actors adhere either explicitly or implicitly.

The actual process is not so neatly systematized as this would have it appear. However, the three dimensions of ethical discourse and decision all contribute to clearer understanding. The good is the end, often an ideal value, toward which ethical actions intentionally move. The right is the obligatory means chosen for progress toward such a goal. The appropriate is the contextual instrumentality of the exercise of the chosen right in pursuit of the desired good. Rarely are ethical decisions so simple as to preclude the possibility of other viable options. Other ethicists may, indeed often will, discern alternative rights and other appropriate courses of action. This is the also the case with goods held *prima facie* which may also conflict. (Treatment of *prima facie* obligations with wide ethical implications but focused on the "just war" argument is found in "Just War Criteria," by James F. Childress in *War or Peace?* Edited by T.A. Shannon. Orbis Books, 1980. Pages 40-58.)

Illustrations of this may be found in any chaplain's experience. One has only to reflect upon the case of the newly reporting serviceman or woman who believes he or she has made a serious mistake in enlisting for military service but who has no legitimate means of reversing that decision until the contractual obligation has been fulfilled. Is the good always adherence to the contract as a *prima facie* obligation? Is it right for him or her to seek legitimate means such as psychiatric evaluation with the hope of being diagnosed as immature personality disorder to be absolved of that obligation? Is it right, in every case, for the Command because it has the power to do so to insist that there always be adherence to the contractual demand? What are the relevant ethical factors which would significantly affect the situation to make legitimate means of discharge possible? If no legitimate means are available does the service member have a moral option of pursuing illegitimate means? If he perceives the good for him to be release from military service does he have the right to seek that good in a manner which will result in discharge under less than honorable conditions? Is it appropriate to consider such factors as immaturity of the individual, non-productive burden on the Command, family background and circumstances including the lack of stability and support, failure to successfully complete any obligation to himself or others in school or work over a significant period of time?

Let us in too brief, but hopefully not too simplistically a fashion see at least one ethically defensible approach. The good of the person is moral maturity. The right would be the honoring of his or her voluntary commitment. It is then appropriate that he or she accept responsibility for such an obligation even at the cost of discomfort or displeasure to himself. However, even that good, while ethically desirable, may not be possible if he or she will not assume responsibility for himself and through deviant behavior becomes a detriment to himself and the Command. While the good and the right remain the same, if clarity of understanding of his or her present situation and the options within that context, the availability of resources for coping and the actualized support of the chain of command in pursuit of the right and the good have not elicited personal responsibility on his part, it may become appropriate to acknowledge a conflict of institutional and personal goals and seek a mutually beneficial resolution..

This case introduces an element which often inheres in ethical decisions, the element of regret, if not moral guilt. A discernible good may not be persistently sought by oneself or by others. Such a choice may entail regret at the inability or unwillingness to exercise sufficient rights to appropriate action.

The chaplain as ethicist functions in the military system as a staff officer, an adviser to the line. His or her responsibility is to provide as much clarity, consistency, and coherence of ethical analysis as he or she is capable. The utilization of such information is a Command prerogative. Effectiveness of that role is dependent upon a number of variables such as the chaplain's expertize and the Command's receptivity to acceptance and utilization of that expertize. Willingness to accept the limitations and legitimatization of his or her ethical analyses are prerequisites to recurrent acceptance of that counsel. A relationship of mutual respect leaves both chaplain and Command free for the exercise of their areas of responsibility and accountability. Without that mutual respect the chaplain has little chance of functioning effectively as ethicist in that Command at least at that wider level.

Morals, ethics, and meta-ethics

The terms morals, ethics, and meta-ethics bear exploration in the quest for clarity and understanding in ethical analysis.

Morals are the actions of human beings relative to the good through the pursuit of the right within the context of the appropriate. Morals are universal in that they belong to human beings because of their humanness. Their universality is in their "that-ness", that is, in action itself, rather than in their "what-ness", that is, in the content of that action. Even if one's actions are adjudged to be immoral or amoral it is against the universality of human moral accountability that such an

141

assessment is made. The choice of one action vis-à-vis another in terms of its effect on human life is a moral act. Morals are the given with which ethics must contend for clarity, understanding and expansion.

Ethics treats these moral actions in a reflective and disciplined manner. That reflection need not be subsequent to the actions brought into focus. In fact, the reflective character of ethics involves the three dimensions of time: reflection upon (past), reflection toward (future), and reflection in (present) moral activity. One of the legitimate responsibilities of an ethicist is to anticipate areas of probable conflict and possible resolution.

Ethics are particularistic in contrast to the universality of morals. While it is correct to speak of human morality it is too inclusive to refer to a human ethic. Ethics derive from historical, cultural, religious, and philosophical traditions. One properly acknowledges a Christian ethic, a Jewish ethic, a Muslim ethic, an Aristotelian ethic, a Utilitarian ethic, a Hedonistic ethic, a Pragmatic ethic, and so on. (For a review of various ethical orientations see *Approaches to Ethics,* 2nd edition by W.T. Jones, F. Sontag, M.O. Beckner, and R.J. Fogelin. McGraw-Hill, 1969) Ethics is always performed in terms of one or more intellectual and particularistic understandings of the meaningfulness and relatedness of moral action.

Though morality is an apt category for all human beings, not all human beings engage deliberately in ethical reflection, at least not to the degree of maturity that seeks comprehension of the impact of isolated or sustained actions on the past, present, and future of either an individual or of corporate entities. Ethical reflection may lack the depth and breadth to warrant its consideration as systematic but by its nature it necessitates disciplined examination of such matters as consistency, coherence, adequacy, and appropriateness.

The chaplain is an ethicist rather than a moralist. In spite of his or her penchant for assuming the role of arbiter of morals or the pressures of others upon him to exercise that role, the chaplain is an ethicist not a moralist. While it is tempting to either sanction or condemn actions as moral or immoral the sphere of influence is so drastically reduced in doing so that the applicability of his or her professional resources is severely

142

limited thereby. It is one thing for the chaplain to hold to a personal morality regarding alcohol consumption, for instance, but it is quite another for him as an ethicist to explore with or for the Command the impact of alcohol abuse upon the individual, the family, the Command, the military itself and society. The same would be true in any area where as a human being he or she must make choices as to what he or she considers the good, the right, and the appropriate. As a professional ethicist he or she bears a responsibility to scrutinize even that morality in terms of the ethical implications for himself and others in a pluralistic context.

There may be times, when the chaplain like Martin Luther must say, "Here I stand, God help me I can do no other." But when he does, he does so as a responsible person rather than as an ethicist. He or she may reach the conclusion that he has no other legitimate choice if he is to preserve his integrity than to say with Sir Thomas More, "I die the king's good servant, but God's first." But, as an ethicist his or her responsibility is to make as clear as possible the ramifications of a specific policy, program, or procedure on both the persons who pursue it and those on whom it is to be utilized.

It is at this point that the third category, that of meta-ethics should be introduced. Ethics presupposes values which are so fundamental or basic that they are **prima facie**; they cannot be violated without destroying the ethical validity of the whole enterprise. This derives from a commitment to human values which while necessitating rational reflection transcends the limitations of that reflection. There is a point at which one realizes all rational arguments must be concluded and a commitment to a particular course taken up. This is what is meant by meta-ethics. It has the same necessity in regards to moral reality which metaphysics has for physical reality. The multi-dimensional unity of human experience necessitates a transcendent or meta-ethical dimension which the complexity of physical phenomena poses in seeking relational connections beyond the immediately observable data.

Ethics is more akin to a science dependent upon observation of phenomena while meta-ethics is more akin to a religious explication which posits on faith a reality to which one gives himself or herself fully in commitment. Meta-ethics may be either theological or philosophical. Every person comes at some time or times to a place where he or she says, "this far and no further". Such a stand may be for the simple reason that to do so would crush his sense of respectability just as he may take such a position because he believes God's actions in the world demand a commensurate reaction from him.

It is obvious that in meta-ethics as in ethics there is no single exclusive position. Indeed just as John recognized, "The crowd standing by heard it and said that it had thundered. Others said, 'an angel has spoken to him'" (John 12:19 RSV). For those who heard the angel there could be no argument sufficient to convince them otherwise. It is this metaphysical "hearing an angel speak," this commitment to the good as one perceives it with a sense of ultimacy that underlies any ethical system. Men give their lives literally or symbolically to those values which underlie their ethic, whether for God or country or some other cause they are willing to live or die for.

Context of ethical behavior.

Ethics is a contextual discipline. The context for military chaplaincy is the military system or institution. This expansive system moves the chaplain from the smallest unit to which he or she is assigned up through the chain of command to the branch of service, the Department of Defense and the Nation itself. Familiarization with that system is requisite to functioning effectively as an ethicist within it.

The authoritarian nature of the institution establishes the parameters of operation. For instance, the chaplain serving a field unit of Marines will have little occasion to pursue, in other than an academic sense, such issues as troop rotation, family separation, accompanied or unaccompanied tours, and the like. The Chaplain to the Marine Corps, on the other hand, would find such issues a dimension of his or her professional opportunity and responsibility. A ship's chaplain will likewise have little occasion to pursue such issues as nuclear arms, selective conscientious objection, deployment schedules and inspection requirements relative to operational commitments. The Chief of

Chaplains, on the other hand, has at least the possibility of performing the role of ethicist relative to such issues.

At whatever level of professional operation the military chaplain functions there are appropriate ethical issues regarding the moral climate of the Command, the processes of due recourse, tensions between the individual and the institution, the methods or procedures employed in exercising policy objectives, legitimately humanizing leadership in contrast with dehumanizing management technology.

Operating principles for the chaplain as ethicist

Though it is improbable that a list of ethical operating principles could be drawn up to which all chaplains would assent, the following is offered for consideration.

1. Command accountability and chaplain responsibility. The chaplain as ethicist is a staff officer with responsibility to the Command which bears the burden of accountability for actions affecting human lives. Such a position does not guarantee an interdependent relationship in ethical matters but it does at least offer the possibility of such a relationship. The Command may or may not accept as legitimate the role of the chaplain as ethicist. It may also be that the chaplain fails to effectively fulfill such a role even if the opportunity is afforded him or her.

While the chaplain's meta-ethics may predispose him or her to a position of championing the powerless in an institution where power is prominent, his role as ethicist can hardly be effective if such a predisposition predetermines that in any given situation the chaplain will see the underdog as always ethically in the right. On the other hand, he or she loses credibility as an ethicist if his analysis is always but a rationale for issues, programs, or policies already determined with the weight of Command authority. The right lies neither with the powerless nor with the powerful simply because of their position. As ethicist the chaplain is seeking understanding of ways by which objectives of the good may be achieved by those who have the responsibility of Command which require neither submission to power without reason nor the exercise of power without clarity of appropriate ethical dimensions.

2. Explications of implications. Any ethical process discloses not only the obvious and apparent right but often expresses more compelling though less apparent implications. It is of the nature of the ethical experience to inquire "if this, then what?" It may be that an immediate punitive action as a result of racial conflict will act as a deterrent to further outbreaks of such intolerable violence. It may also be that such action may exacerbate resentment and reaction if grievances are not promptly and effectively addressed and redressed.

The ethicist's concern with implications is in part a concern for the integrity of his or her discipline for it is the implications even more than the consequences which give some clue to coherence, consistency, and adequacy. If a certain course is decided upon what factors would be sufficient to cause a reconsideration of that course?

It is sometimes a tragic flaw of persons in positions of authority to exercise that authority disproportionately to the offense. A case in point is the widely used reduction in rate in non-judicial punishment. Such a far ranging punishment often has punitive rather than restorative implications. It is ethically defensible in a situation where the circumstance, the effect on the man or woman and his or her family, the impact on others in the Command are such that other lesser means have proven ineffective, or would appear to do so. It is not ethically defensible in an initial reactionary move.

3. Consistency and coherence. The maintenance and continuation of any institution demands consistent and coherent programs and policies. Disintegration results from isolated and insulated actions. Change is essential for growth. However, too radical, ill-timed, or inappropriate change may produce not growth but death. Change incorporates interrelated continuity and discontinuity. What **is** is derivative from what **was** even as it is proleptic of what will yet be.

Confidence in any exercise of command control can only be weakened by inattention to consistency and coherence. All offenses do not have to receive the same consequences for a system to be ethically viable. However, the factions affecting the differences in results have to be reasonable or at least acceptable, understandable, and proportionate.

146

While "good guys" may get more breaks it must be apparent to all what constitutes or is accepted as goodness and this must be more than the mood or feeling of the person making the decision.

Coherence encourages maturity and responsibility in that it establishes the limits of freedom. Without recognition of such limits freedom degenerates into moral anarchy. At least two very different interpretations of the statement, "and each did what was right in his own eyes" derive from the role of coherence. On the one hand each does right in his own eyes because a sense of rightness within the community has broken down and each person is dependent upon his or her own resources. Each has become disenchanted with the ability of the community's values to satisfy his or her needs. On the other hand, each may do what is right in his or her own eyes because there has developed within him or her a sense of consistency and coherence of past, present, and future so that external control or coercion is not at that point required for acceptance of the rightness of a given action. As Kant would have it, it comes from "the moral law within."

4. Expediency and expeditiousness. Expediency, the selection of one course of action as most probable under the circumstances, is an important ethical principle. Expediency may simply become an acceptance of the path of least resistance. However, it is not necessarily so. The expedient may be the acceptance of what is possible under the circumstances though one is aware of the limitations of such a choice or the distance remaining between fuller realization of a desired or intended good. Expediency should not connote, as it sometimes does in common speech, doing whatever one can get by with or acting from no higher motive than intent to see that what one desires is achieved at any cost.

Expeditiousness may be a less freighted term which acknowledges that rarely is it possible to fully actualize the ideal in any given situation. Expeditiousness recognizes that in a given situation something will be done, indeed **must** be done. There are times when the action taken may be taken with regret: "regret may be appropriate but not remorse." (Childress, Page 44) Ethics accepts the rarity of moral purity even while

147

incurring regrets signifies that a more adequate moral course may not be available in the situation or under the circumstances.

Expediency and expeditiousness occur in an ethical arena where norms are operative giving a referent to rightness and goodness in the course pursued. To avow that one must do the right thing because it is right implies an acceptance of the meaningfulness of the good to which the right points. It is right within the context of the goal sought by the one who acts as well as those for or to whom such action is done.

5. Critique and insight. One of the ethical functions on which wise decisions may be based is that of insightful critique. Critique and criticism are two very distinct categories. Criticism usually is an action tearing down or dismantling something. A critique is an analysis of a given issue, proposition, proposal, or policy pointing out both strengths and weaknesses. A critique cannot take place in an atmosphere where personal or professional insecurity precludes the possibility of acknowledging inadequacies, deficiencies, or weaknesses as well as strengths. A critique is not an exercise in moral judgment in which one slips from the ethical to the prophetic role declaring the wrongness of a course of action. The chaplain as ethicist has no more advantageous position than any other person to issue universal dicta. Indeed, in his or her personal morality he or she may adhere to a Kantian categorical imperative to act so that the maxim of his or her action could become universal law. Or he or she may be operating from some other fundamental ethical foundation. As an ethicist he or she accepts both the staff advisory or supportive posture allowing the legitimacy of ethical critique and the reality of the locus of ethical decision making.

I saw the difference between critique and criticism in serving in the same Command under two different Commanding Officers. The first approached each "hot wash-up" as an opportunity for genuine critique of the exercise for the purpose of improving. All participants were encouraged to be open and honest about both what went right and what could have been improved. That Commanding Officer was followed by one who in the first "hot wash-up" made it abundantly clear that he would entertain no criticism and was not interested in a critique. When the first participant pointed out an area for improvement the Commanding Officer's response was "I didn't hear that; now let's move on to the next person." Since they were quick learners they knew the days of critique were over and what was being demanded of them was telling the Commanding Officer only what he wanted to hear. Needless-to-say such leadership styles reverberated profoundly throughout the Command.

    6. Lowest level of resolution. One further operating principle, that of "lowest level of resolution", is suggested as important for the chaplain as ethicist.

    Institutions inevitability involve tensions between the rights of individuals or subunits within the whole. Resolution of such conflicts, so far as possible, is essential for the growth and health of the institution. Often conflicts can be resolved quickly by the interposition of maximum authority from the highest level of command. However, while this may be an occasional necessity it has a deleterious effect as a normative mode of conflict resolution. Systems operate effectively and efficiently when there is clear understanding of the limits of power at each given level within the system. The effective functioning of a chain of command is not just a matter of managerial process; it is also one expression of the ethical dynamic whereby persons are called upon to exercise mature leadership within the given sphere of their responsibility. By its operation a sense of trust and loyalty is built up which contributes to fuller realization of stipulated goals or the successful accomplishment of the assigned mission.

    Contributing to the effective operation of the principle of lowest level of resolution will be a clear distinction between leadership and management (Abraham Zaleznik, "Managers and Leaders: are they different?" *Harvard Business Review,* 55, no. 3, May-June, 1977. An articulate advocate for military leadership has been Vice Admiral James B. Stockdale whose "Taking Stock" introductions to issues of the *Naval War College Review* during his tenure as President of the Naval War College were exemplarily concise applications of ethical insight.)

    Persons are led; resources are managed. There is a derivative of proportionality to consider vis-à-vis leadership. A biblical principle is apropos: "to whom much is given from him much is required." The ethical requisites of consistency, coherence, and adequacy are expected at any level of operation. The opportunity for the exercise of such concerns is a matter of differences in degree rather than in kind.

The ethical responsibility of leadership is as obligatory for the work-center supervisor as for the unit commander except that as the hierarchy of leadership ascends, the deliberative functions play an ever increasing role in that the decisions become more open to wider surveillance while at the same time they impact more lives. To risk the life of one other person is an ethically serious matter; to risk the lives of millions is almost imponderable. The ethical burden is serious whether for the Marine sergeant sending one of his men on reconnaissance against inestimable odds of his safe return or President Harry S. Truman having to make the final decision for the dropping of nuclear bombs on Hiroshima and Nagasaki. Again, a difference in ethical degree but not of kind.

Lowest level of resolution is a highly respected operating principle in the military. However, if the issue cannot be resolved at the lowest level and it is of ethical significance it may be necessary to move up the chain of command even though the risk to one personally increases with each advance. Not every issue needs to be brought to the Senior Enlisted Member in the chain of command any more than it should be taken directly to the Executive Officer or the Commanding Officer. However, if the ethical stakes are high enough and the chaplain as ethicist has the will and character to do it then advancing the cause may become a matter of personal integrity.

I remember well the advice I received from a line Admiral when I first went on active duty at the age of 44. "Remember Chaplain, anything that Congress mandates you cannot do anything about. But in all other cases, if you consider it urgent enough, it may be necessary to keep moving up until you find the right person. Someone has the power to listen and to make changes. You just have to find the right person."

Conclusion

In conclusion, let me summarize. We began with a contention that the military chaplain's role as ethicist is one which needs to be acknowledged and taken as seriously as his or her role as preacher, counselor, or administrator. That role is one which he or she did not and could not exercise in the civilian parish in that he or she was not identified with the system at the point at which ethical decisions affecting an institution were made. The focus and purview of that ethical responsibility is dependent upon his or her assignment within the military institution.

The professional responsibility of the chaplain as ethicist was then examined in terms of specific categories: the good, the right, and the appropriate. It was recognized that such ethical reflection is a disciplined if not a systematic task. In order to further clarify the resources for ethical analysis the terms morals, ethics, and meta-ethics were examined.

It was then emphasized that ethics is a contextual discipline occurring for the chaplain within the bounds of the military institution of which he or she is a part. Several operating principles were given: 1. Command accountability and chaplain responsibility, 2. Explications of implications, 3. Consistency and coherence, 4. Expediency and expeditiousness, 5. Critique and insight, and 5. Lowest level of resolution.

While several issues were alluded to none was explored in depth. Many others of equal or greater consequence have been left untouched. The purpose of the article will have been fulfilled if it has stimulated thinking about the chaplain's vocation as ethicist encouraging even wider exploration and practice.

Bibliography

Childress, James F., "Just War Criteria," in Shannon, T.A., *War or Peace?* Orbis Books, 1980. Pages 40-58.

Galligan, Francis B., *Military Professionalism and Ethics.* Center for Advanced Research, Naval War College, 1979.

Hutcherson, Richard G., Jr. *Wheel within the Wheel.* John Knox Press, 1979.

Jones, W.T., F. Sontag, M. O. Beckner, and R.J. Fogelin. *Approaches to Ethics.* 2nd ed. McGraw Hill, 1969

Shannon, Thomas A., ed. *War or Peace?* Orbis Books, 1980.

Yarmolinsky, Adam, "The Professional in American Society," *Daedalus*, 107, no. 1, Winter, 1978.

Zaleznik, Abraham, "Managers and Leaders: are they different?" *Harvard Business Review*, 55, no. 3, May-June, 1977. Pages 70-75.

d. A series of articles on Business Ethics:

If writing is not easy, then writing collaboratively, or with someone else, is especially difficult. Even when the two writers know one another well there is still much room for misunderstanding and a great deal of time has to be devoted to making sure they have the same goal in mind and are working toward its achievement in a compatible way. I found this to be true in the series of articles which follow. The first article was no problem but as we progressed we found it necessary to spend more time either face to face or on the phone clarifying where we were coming from and where we wanted to go.

I suppose that there are natural pairings which bring great satisfaction as the two or more writers work together. It is another matter when someone works with a writer to produce something in his name, in other words as a "ghost writer." Some of those are quite successful and some are shamefully misleading. These are different types of collaborative writing and I will not pursue them here.

What follows here are those collaborative articles which I wrote with Jim Kendall beginning with the first one.

But first a description of the authors as it appeared in the *Kitsap Business Journal* following the first article:

Jim Kendall is President of Telebyte Northwest Internet Services, headquartered in Silverdale, Washington. He has been in business since retiring from the U.S. Navy in 1986 and is President of the Washington Association of Internet Service Providers, a state-wide trade association. He earned a Bachelor of Science degree in Electrical Engineering and has completed post-graduate courses in Systems Management.

Paul Murphey earned a Ph.D. degree from Vanderbilt University and holds Masters Degrees in Business Administration, Library Science, and Divinity as well as a Bachelor of Arts degree. He is a member of the Society for Business Ethics, the Association for Practical and Professional Ethics, the American Philosophical Association, and the Society of Christian Ethics. He regularly teaches for Chapman University and

Olympic College and has taught both undergraduate and graduate courses for City University of Seattle.

1. "Yes, but is it right", July 2003, pages 42-43.

JIM: A few months ago I was invited by a college professor to address his class. The class was "Leadership and Professional Ethics," – it is now titled "Business and Professional Ethics," – and was taught by Paul Murphey. He has been teaching that course at Chapman for the past five years.

To enrich the course local business and professional leaders are invited to share their experiences about ethics with the students. It was a very interesting and challenging experience for me. In fact, it was so interesting that I invited Dr. Murphey to address my Rotary Club. His presentation was one of the best, if not the best, presentations I have ever experienced.

One thing he said early in his talk nearly struck me dumb (and that is a real accomplishment!). In the course of teaching his class, Paul very early on surveys his students. One of his most remarkable findings is that consistently about 80 percent of his students, whose average age, by the way, would be in the early thirties, state their opinion that in order to be successful in business, you cannot be ethical. I was stunned when he made that statement.

When challenged, he reaffirmed his findings. That one single observation speaks volumes about why businesses and business men and women experience such hostility with some of their customers.

Out of that presentation, and subsequent conversations, we decided to write a series of articles on the subject. We will relate examples and present different tools and philosophies on the nuts and bolts of how businesses and business people deal with each other and with their customers, and the ethical decisions and processes they use.

One of the issues that seems to recur is that while something may be legal, it very certainly can be viewed as not right. That is to say, it is not ethical. There are any number of viewpoints on what is or is not ethical, but the measuring stick I found most frequently useful is to ask, "If the roles were reversed, how would I like this problem resolved? Would that resolution be fair to me?" Very often I don't like the answer I get, and modify my response to a given situation. That is one measure of "ethics" and there are many more. We hope to explore ethical tools and relate some real world situations that arise and suggest tools for dealing with them.

Paul: Jim, let me interrupt you here to clarify the issue which startled you. At the beginning of the course students complete both a Personal Ethical Audit and an Internal Ethical Audit from Robert C. Solomon's fine book, *Its Good Business*. Dr. Solomon has strong convictions about the crucial role of ethics in business. In fact he says that most business failures are not due to managerial or technical incompetence but to moral ignorance.

Most people, including my students, have strong opinions about the word ethics but many of them have very little understanding of what ethics is all about. Our views on ethics affect all of us because they undergird the way we live our lives, including the way we conduct our businesses or carry on our professions. As you suggested earlier, you can think of ethics like a tool kit. You can do a lot of jobs with just a hammer, a pair of pliers, and a screwdriver, but the more complicated the task, the more sophisticated the tools required to accomplish it.

So, as I see it, these conversations you and I will have will be focused on the jobs to be done, in other words, the ethical situations, problems, or dilemmas and the tools we might use to do them right. A whole lot of writers in business ethics agree with Peter Drucker that management is about doing things right and leadership is about doing the right thing.

Ethics is about doing the right thing and doing it the right way. Context is awfully important and that takes into account laws, regulations, current practices, persons involved and affected, as well as various philosophical approaches. What we do is largely dependent on what we think or believe so we need to get as clear a picture of ethical thinking as we can if we are going to be able to turn the question, "Yes, but is it right?" into the affirmation, "Yes, it is right and that is what I will do."

One of my recent students, David Herr, a business man himself, said it well, "At the end of the day all you have is your reputation which is based on your work ethic and the values and principles you display and hold to." That to me, is what you and I are concerned to discuss with one another and hope others will find as exciting and helpful for them as it is for us.

2. "Part 1: Contract? What's a Contract," August 2003, page 11. (Editor's Note: This is part of an ongoing discussion series on the subject of business ethics)

JIM: Paul, we had a discussion a while ago about the foundations of business ethics. You made the statement that two foundations of (presumably good) business practices in our modern society are laws and contracts. You certainly touched a nerve with me, especially in regards to contracts.

Business contracts form the basis of a business agreement between parties. A contract should be fairly specific about what each party is expected to provide, and what each party will receive. Put very simply, it usually is an agreement of a client to pay a specified amount of money over a set period of time, in return for which the vendor agrees to provide goods and/or services.

The incentive to enter into contract will vary somewhat, but the benefits to a business are that a "guaranteed" revenue stream will exist for a known period of time. This allows the business to amortize any upfront expenses, calculate ongoing expenses, and from that, determine a reasonable profit.

The benefit to a customer frequently is a reduction in the prices of a good or service, which is offered because they promise to provide a revenue stream for a set period of time. The customer benefits and the business benefits. Is that about right?

Paul: Jim, as you noted contracts are essential to successful business operations. But contracts, like laws, may be advantageous, disadvantageous, or neutral from a moral or ethical perspective for one or both parties.

Contracts, as legal documents, are designed to assure that the terms agreed upon by both parties are appropriately carried out. They are necessary for the type society in which we live – we move a lot, do not quickly form or identify with communities, are concerned with more immediate matters than with long-term relationships, often have a hard time even making contact with a real live person to discuss matters of dispute.

You know the familiar picture all too well. It is not nostalgia nor pining for the good old days, which sees the moral context for our business and personal lives today differently than a generation or so ago.

Jim: Yeah, the "Good Old Day's" when a man's word was his bond." We don't see much of that any more.

Paul: When your father or mother, or certainly your grandfather or grandmother were doing business in their day, in most cases they were doing so in a culture which was "up close and personal." There are still some pockets of that, as a student reminded me recently. He related how when he was growing up in a small mid-western community, he and his younger sister crossed a busy four lane highway to get to the little Mom and Pop Grocery to get some candy. No sooner had they gotten safely across than the store owner called their parents who immediately came and got them.

Those people knew one another and their moral code demanded their doing all they could to protect one another and advance one another's welfare. If they went back on their word, or cheated in what had been promised, or misrepresented not just the facts but even the expectation, or lied about what they could or would do, or took unfair advantage of someone, whether willfully or not, word would spread like wildfire throughout their close-knit community.

They would have to deal then, with not only loss of business but even more with the loss of their good name, acceptance in the community, and reputation.

Written contracts were not the basis of those business relationships. Integrity, honor, and trust were even more fundamental. Scrupulous business persons and equally scrupulous customers often transacted costly deals with nothing more than one another's word. The scurrilous ones were quickly found out and dealt with accordingly.

Jim: "I don't think we are in Kansas anymore, Toto!" Contracts now are almost essential for doing any sort of complex business in today's fast-paced world. Failing to honor a contract is every bit as bad as "breaking your word" was in the "good old days." Yet we see more and more that some individuals and businesses just don't want to treat a contract as much more than a suggestion. When that happens, any hope for a future business relationship is gone, probably forever. And that sure is "no way to run a railroad!"

3. "Part 2: Contract? What's a Contract?" September 2003, page 5.

JIM: When one thinks "contract" one tends to remember the admonition to "read the fine print." Page after page of legalese stacked together for the simplest project. It is almost as if they are designed to trap the unwary. "What's a contract?" The average person probably unconsciously thinks of a sales contract at the car dealership, or if lucky enough to buy a home, the real estate contract. But really, contracts come in all shapes, sizes, and formats and we deal with them every day of our lives, don't we?

Paul: Actually yes, there is a progression of contracts.

Here is a simple outline: At ground level it is simply two people making eye contact and saying and meaning "I agree." Sort of like a covenant – "I don't know for sure what lies ahead, but whatever it is we are in this together." Emphasis is perhaps given by an emphatic nod of the head. A firm handshake follows and acts as a confirmation of their intent, desires, and expectations. Then a piece of paper with a few simple facts such as cost and time are exchanged.

As distance between the parties becomes greater and they begin to represent companies, it becomes necessary for mutual protection to spell out in ever-greater detail the terms of the agreement. Then we can reach the stage where government contracts, for instance, fill multiple volumes and require experts to write and interpret. It all becomes pretty complicated. It's time to wrap this up with a few points to consider:

First, contracts are basically morally neutral, though they can be written with unethical elements in them. Notice, I said unethical rather than illegal. Morality and legality are not always the same. Legality is the floor beneath which you cannot go; morality is the way you operate or move things around on that floor or above it.

Second, contracts are essential from a strategic business perspective to anticipate revenue, project products and services, and assure a minimum level of acceptable relationships. Keeping them, by both parties, is a moral obligation.

JIM: Paul, I would contend that keeping or meeting contractual obligations is not only a moral (and legal!) obligation, but a very real tool for long-term success. I agree that there is a real moral obligation to meet the letter of the contract (unless circumstances arise making it impossible to do so, but more on that later), but I contend that failure to do your absolute best to live up to your obligations to vendor as well as customer, in spirit as well as by specific "letter of the law" detail, harms your company every bit as much as it harms your customers and vendors.

Paul: Indeed. My third point would be that contracts are indispensable in the highly mobile (or transient), often impersonal, litigious, and automated context of contemporary business. A single business matter may take us several phone conversations to locales around the country or abroad where we rarely speak with the same person a second time. Add to this the frequently ineffective influence of a community including its basic institutions such as family, school, and religious bodies, in establishing or concurring on, much less forming and maintaining high personal and social moral values.

Fourth, contracts allow us to "get what we pay for" and "deliver what we promise" to the benefit of both consumers and companies and that is a moral matter of justice and fairness.

Finally, contracts encourage a high level of moral responsibility such as keeping one's promises and accepting responsibility for one's actions so that when these moral elements break down there is recourse for either party to take legitimate steps to rectify the situation. There is so much more to be said on the moral elements of contracts, but at least this provides something to consider when it comes to morality and contracts.

Jim: I would say that what it all seems to boil down to is that "it is a jungle out there" and personal integrity still has a role to play in day to day business. Everything from software licensing to observing a copyright (a form of contract), to mandatory labeling on a variety of products to simple handshake agreements; we deal with contracts every day of our lives. How well we do that has a very real impact on health and happiness. Which brings us to our next part of this discussion: some examples of the type of "contractual disconnects" that happen, and a discussion of how to deal with them. Call it "defining the business ethics toolbox".

4. "I'm not getting sentimental over you... I'm in business," October 2003, page 11.

Jim: When you get down to it, a "hard-headed" business person can't be sentimental. There has to be a bottom-line reason for doing anything and everything related to the business. That is at least the image that many people, even many business people, have of the "successful business person". Hiring, firing, advertising, charity, purchasing, selling, product or service selection, personnel decisions are all grist for the mill. They think that morality and ethics need not enter into the decision process. That really is not the case. But sentimentality is a luxury.

Paul: Jim, before tackling that head-on, let's figuratively "take a walk down Business Street." The first thing we notice is that the buildings are not like the song of a half-century ago "all made of ticky-tacky" and they do not all "look just the same." There are incredible arrays of styles and materials, sizes and colors. The people coming in and out of those building are just as varied.

Look at this impressive building. It has a sign identifying it as the Business Hall of Fame. Once inside we find a pantheon of business leaders. Some of them had business dealings that were questionable. Some of them such as Andrew Carnegie apparently tried to assuage guilty moral sensitivities by incredible philanthropic contributions and endowments. Others, like James Cash Penney don't carry that kind of baggage. Here was a man who was legendary in his frugality. One story is about him stopping to instruct a clerk in exactly how to wrap a package so as to not waste a centimeter of wrapping. He had an eye on the bottom line and the bottom line was for him the Golden Rule.

Here is a picture that is unusual because the subject is still alive. It is Aaron Feuerstein, CEO of Malden Mills. When New England mill owners were heading out of town faster than yuppies on Labor Day weekend, Malden Mills said "we're staying put" and made its Polartec fabric ever more profitable even with higher production costs. Then disaster struck in December 1995 when a fire destroyed the mill. Feuerstein didn't hesitate. At great personal sacrifice and because he had deep spiritual resources for his ethics he kept his employees on the payroll and set about rebuilding.

In late November 2001 Malden Mills filed for bankruptcy. When I get to this point in my classroom some of the more outspoken students agree with what you stated at the beginning, "See you can't be sentimental and successful at the same time. It's people or profits; you can't have both."

That's wrong for a number of reasons. Those students especially don't have the foggiest notion of business strategy. Bankruptcy, at least corporate bankruptcy, is not necessarily an indication of fiscal, managerial, or moral failure. In many cases it is a deliberately calculated approach to reposition the firm more advantageously and allow it to pursue its mission. Whether that mission reflects noble ethical values or not is not built into it. It is interesting to me that the major creditors for Malden Mill are also, for the most part, the same corporations who are lending the venture capital to help this phoenix rise from the ashes. Today they are back in business and on the road to success.

Now let's cross the street and take a quick look at the "Business Hall of Shame." We only have time to ponder one portrait. It's "Chainsaw" Al Dunlap, the man *Business Week* in 1996 called "A Corporate Tough Guy." Boy, there was a guy no one would accuse of being sentimental. I have to admit he was successful – ruthlessly so, but successful. That was the story of his life. Then the Board of Sunbeam said in effect, "that's enough". Either we lose you or we lose our integrity, which is another way of saying we lose our corporate soul and they said "Sayonara" to Al.

JIM: To restate the question, "do business and ethics go together?" I can see that is going to be a recurring theme. Hopefully, in the meantime, we got rid of a stereotype or two. It is clear from your examples that ethical conduct or lack thereof in the market place is not a sure indicator of success or failure. What I hope to demonstrate in our future conversations is that, while the evidence is not yet all in, there is enough to suggest that an ethically guided company has a much better chance of success than one that is not, all else being equal.

5. "Business + Ethics: Not an option," November 2003, page 11.

JIM: Paul, in my view every organization has "ethical standards," whether or not they are stated. They come from the owners and managers, from law, custom, and the "company culture." What most companies, especially small companies, do not have is a formal statement of ethical standards, or philosophy of doing business, or whatever we care to call it. More often than not, it is because the business management doesn't know where to start. Or more to the point have not made it a matter of priority in the battle to survive.

We said that we would get to resources, but there are a ton of resources. Perhaps if we go through the steps of drafting a "business ethics" program, we can narrow the list. So, where do we start? Or for that matter, how do we start?

Paul: Jim, you can't reduce business ethics to simple and simplistic data, which can be fed into a handy-dandy, pocket ethical calculator which will then immediately display the ethical answer. "Ethics" is hard, painstaking, difficult often complicated, and sometimes risky. It requires willingness to face facts, probe issues, challenge popular beliefs, critically examine options, and courage to act on the best available alternative within the context.

You are right that we must have tools if we are to do a good job. It is no different than woodworking, computer repairing, gardening, or any other task. Having the right tools, and knowing how to use them

161

properly is essential for doing a proper job. The more complete the tool kit the easier and better the performance. The tools we use not only affect the product we come up with, but the kind of worker we are.

Jim: I'm with you there, Paul. If anyone thought this would be easy, they weren't paying attention. Which is all the more reason that a business owner or manager needs to approach the task with as many tools as possible, and hopefully the tool-bag will be full of high quality tools.

Paul: Let me give you a couple of good resources as we start assembling our tool kit. Anthony Weston has a book titled, *A 21st Century Ethical Toolbox* (Oxford University Press, 2001) in which he examines ethics as a learning experience, ethics and religion, paying attention to values, families of moral values, some traditional ethical theories, theoretical and integrative approaches when values clash before pointing out specific tools for critical thinking (finding the facts, watching words, and judging like cases alike), creativity (multiplying options, and problem-shifting), and ethical action (knowing your goals, matching tools to goals, learning by dialogue, and learning by service.). He also has a chapter devoted to Business and Professional Ethics.

Jim, If I could persuade you and our readers to read one book on business ethics it would be Robert C. Solomon's, *Its Good Business: Ethics and Free Enterprise for the New Millennium* (Rowman & Littlefield, 1997). See what you think of these few gems: "Business is an ethical activity. That is the premise of this book." (Page xiii) "Ethical errors end more careers more quickly and more definitively than any other mistake in judgment or accounting…. What makes such career calamities so pathetic is that they are not the product of greed or immorality or wickedness. They are the result of ethical naiveté." (Pages 16-17)

I think Solomon has overstated his case here. What I think Solomon is referring to however, is the ordinary activity of most of the business persons you and I know and deal with. They are not out to do us in by unethical manipulation. They are, for the most part, wanting to do the right thing and doing it to the best of their ability most of the time, but even good intentions need good tools to get the job done.

Jim: All of which supports my contention that adopting a formal statement of business ethical standards or practices is important to the success of the business. In other word, it isn't an option; it is a requirement.

Paul: Here are a few more of Solomon's thoughts: "Unethical thinking isn't just "bad business" it is an invitation to disaster in business.... Ethics provides the broader framework within which business life must be understood." (Page 17) . "Nothing is more dangerous to a business -- or to business in general – than a tarnished public image.... The fact is that a tarnished image has direct consequences for sales, for profits, for morale, for the day-to-day running of the business." (Page 19)

More resources to check into: Center for Business Ethics, Bentley College, Waltham, MA http://ecampus.bentley.edu/dept/cbe/, Ethics on the WWW: ttp://commfaculty.fullerton.edu/lester/ethics/ethic_list.html. and Ethics resources at *Questia – Online Library of Books and Journals:* www.questia.com.

6. "The Business-Ethics Plan: Where to start", February 2004, page 6.

JIM: Paul, we have covered a lot of territory, mostly philosophic in nature. I still want to get to the nuts and bolts. When I first took over as OIC of a small shore facility, I created a "Common Philosophy" document, using example "CO Statements" I received at ComSubPac Submarine PCO School (Prospective Commanding Officer) to use as the outline. There is no way I could have written such a document from scratch, yet I was able to personalize it for myself and for the facility. A document that was designed to be applied to Submarines and Submarine crews was adapted (quite successfully, I might add) to a Navy Laboratory shore facility. I would contend that we could find or concoct such a template for a small business to use that is adaptable to most businesses.

For example, such a document would state how that business's employees are expected to treat their customers. It would include guidelines on how employees will treat each other, And yes, you might expect such statements as "employees are to treat each other with respect" would be a "given" and yet I contend those statements need to be in writing and every employee acknowledge that that is one of the standards of conduct.

With that as a premise, what elements should all business "ethical standards statements" include? That is, what elements would you say are universal, recognizing that each will need to be tailored to the specific business and industry? For example I might start with "This business will deal in strict honesty with our customers, our vendors and our employees."

Paul: Jim, it seems to me you have not only stated your expectations but have answered your own questions as well. So, instead of my responding directly, let me suggest a few more things to consider.

1) Any existing business already has a culture, which expresses its values. It is seen every time a transaction takes place whether within the firm among employees or as the firm interacts with customers and other stakeholders.

2) Any business which wants to take ethics seriously and articulate its values will need to make a commitment to this and dedicate time and other resources to making it happen just as it does with any other aspect of the firm's operations.

3) There is plenty of help available for those who really want it.

4) In addition to the great number of books and articles on business ethics there are business ethics courses available from local and area colleges and universities as well as online at both the undergraduate and graduate level.

5) Engaging a consultant to do an ethics audit in much the same way a firm hires an accounting firm to do a fiscal audit may someday be considered a justified business expense, not a frill.

6) Contact firms who have made ethics a priority in both personnel and programs to learn what is involved. I am impressed with the work Weyerhaeuser has done. Nancy Thomas-Moore, a Central Kitsap High School graduate by the way before going on to college and graduate school, is in charge of their program. If you would like a copy of their 6th edition code of ethics, contact Jeff Conner at jconner@precisiondirect.com Upon request, you will receive a beautiful

and useful brochure titled: "Our Reputation: a Shared Responsibility. Code of Ethics, 6th edition"

7) Get all the members of the business together in a retreat devoted exclusively to exploring the firm's ethical climate and formulating basic ethical statements including a code of ethics and policy and procedure guidelines.

8) Select the most astute and dedicated workers from all levels and form a task group to tackle this task on company time and with the resources to make it worthwhile.

9) Appoint an ethics officer – several large firms now have vice presidential level officers in charge of their ethics programs – to develop, give direction to, and maintain the ethical focus of the firm. Even a small business can profit from empowering one of its members as its ethics officer.

Jim, **we** have run out of room and will have to postpone the checklist of "universals". In the meantime you may want to check out the Josephson Institute's website at www.josephsoninstitute.org for "Six pillars of Character," and "Ten Core Values."

Jim: What a great resource list! I must admit that I am remiss in requesting the booklet you suggest, but I am going to do so right now. I am also going to begin the process of formalizing an ethics, or standard of conduct program in my own small business. While we certainly have set ethical standards and have even put some of them in writing, it is not on the level you recommend. Yet! I'll let you know how it goes!

7. "The Business-Ethics Plan: Taking Your Business Ethics Temperature," March 2004.

JIM: Paul, we left off last time talking about a sort of "check list" as a starting place for evaluating our approach to conducting business ethically. While I am sure that it sounds a bit simplistic, a periodic review or "self-evaluation" certainly is not harmful, and may do some real good. And when we get into those gray situations where it really is not all that clear what the "right" thing is to do (and no honest businessman can deny that those situations occur) it would be helpful to have a sort of measuring stick to use other than a simple wish or intent to "do what's right".

PAUL: Jim, first let me respond directly to your request for a checklist of sorts. Whatever else it may have, I think the following are the "universals" you are looking for:

1 Will this action strengthen the positive image of our business in the community and beyond?

2 Will this action enhance the business' reputation for providing exceptional quality goods and/or services?

3 Does this action reflect our desire to treat all persons with whom we do business, including our employees and customers, as well as other stakeholders in the way we want to be treated?

4 Would we be proud to have this action written up in the local Newspaper or appear on the evening television news?

5 Does this action make us feel good about what we have done?

6 Is this action legal and in compliance with pertinent regulations?

7 Is this action morally defensible?

8 Will this action make a positive difference in the long-run in both the profitability of the business and the betterment of the community?

What words go with these questions? Words like integrity, honesty, consideration, concern, awareness, commitment, compliance, contribution, fairness, equity, justice.

JIM: That is a pretty comprehensive list of questions to ask of oneself when facing tough business decisions. I suppose one could say that it is a more complex way of stating the Golden Rule, and that is not a bad thing. The Rotary four-way test is another approach to take as well, and perhaps warrants some elaboration.

1. Is it the truth? Well I would say that is a very solid starting point, and not as simplistic as it appears. My personal experience is that it is all too easy to lie to yourself in a number of ways, from acting from incorrect information, wrong assumptions, to plain old bullheaded unwillingness to admit you are wrong. I have been guilty of all of that at

one time or another, and I suspect we all have episodes in our history that we don't look back upon with any pride.

2. Is it fair to all concerned? Whoops! There's that fairness thing again. Now we are getting into that pesky subjective territory in a golden ruleish sort of way. What may be fair to me is not fair to you, and vice-versa. An ethical approach to business will provide a guideline on how to conduct yourself when a dispute arises over what your idea of fair is if it does not agree with mine? Which view will prevail? Will we compromise? Will I automatically defer to your view every time?

3. Will it build good will and better friendships? . More of that golden rule type stuff. That is, "do unto others as you would have them do unto you." Generally speaking, an ethical approach takes into consideration building long-term business and personal relationships over short term gain. Maybe the situation is not fair to you, in your view, but maintaining a good relationship or friendship dictates deferring to the other party. (Hey, nobody said this was going to be easy or fun!)

4. Is it beneficial to all concerned? The fundamental concept of a business transaction is that of exchanging value for value. Currency, money, cash, gelt: whatever form of value exchange one party offers in an amount that is acceptable to the other party, is exchanged for an agreed upon good or service. Simply agreeing on what and how much is to be exchanged is not a guarantee that the transaction is beneficial to all concerned, however. We can easily think of situations where an "agreed upon transaction" is not beneficial to all concerned.

Whew! Well. That is a lot of food for thought, Paul, and without building a generic one-size-fits-all ethics program (impossible), I think this is a pretty cracking good set of beginning guidelines!

3. Papers:

During my long involvement in attaining academic degrees I wrote a lot of papers. No papers from my undergraduate days at Texas Christian University are included here. They were important to me then but would add little if anything to the way my writing exemplifies my thought progression or beliefs. I also am not including papers from seminary and graduate school in pursuit of the Ph.D. I took a hard look at several of them and decided the length of this volume would not make it possible to include them. A fuller list of papers appears in Appendix II: Bibliography. I especially wish there had been room to include the following: *The Holy Spirit in the theology of Nels F.S. Ferre, Calvin's concept of the Holy Spirit, Revelational and Philosophical Formulations of the Self*, *The Evangelical Alliance in the Nineteenth Century, American Democratic Culture and Locally Autonomous Church Polity.*

I restricted papers from the MSLS degree program. One paper I would have liked to share was *Academic Libraries in the South, 1850-1900* . I chose instead to include *Death is not dead yet: a bibliographic essay.*

I have included several papers written for courses in the MBA Program.. They convey my thoughts and are examples of my writing on a wider range of subjects than my previous volumes which are more deliberately theologically oriented. I actually enjoyed writing these papers. By the time they were written I had been teaching and learning for quite some time. I had gained confidence in my writing and the ability to convey my thoughts clearly and accurately, at least that was my assessment. I will make a brief comment on each of the articles to put them in context. The articles appear in chronological order.

a. *Death is not dead yet: a bibliographic essay.* LS 602 University of Kentucky. 1975.

The following bibliographic essay or annotated bibliography was done as part of the requirements for a graduate course in bibliography. .It enabled me to bring together a number of resources I was familiar with and had used over the years. Even more it enabled me to bring my resources up to date and expand my treatment of a subject that had been with me since my graduate years in the doctoral program. It was especially helpful when I prepared the manuscript for *Death and Dying: Bibliographic Resources* (Create Space, 2013)

I enjoyed compiling bibliographies and did many of them for courses I taught. I taught a course on Bibliography in the Humanities for the School of Library Science after I completed my MSLS degree.

Among the many bibliographies over the years was a lengthy one on Bibliography of Business and Professional Ethics which I revised from time to time for a course I taught in that area at Chapman University. It is too long to include here.

I am including this particular bibliography because I have found it useful in other work. Soon after I completed it I was able to use portions of it in a presentation to Medical and Chaplaincy staff at the Naval Hospital. United States Marine Corps Base, Camp Lejeune, North Carolina in August 1975. Obviously it is dated and would need considerable work to bring it up-to-date.

The literature on death and dying has reached phenomenal proportions in the past twenty-five years. To include all references currently available would result in a sizable book rather than an essay, especially if works in the humanities were included. Consequently, we have concentrated on those works which may be considered as basically of a social scientific, medical, and ministerial orientation. Even then we are aware of an extensive array of materials not included. The focus is primarily on books, with some notable articles, but no attempt has been made to cite the individual essays found in the collected works referred to.

The essay is divided into the following sections: bibliographical, reference works, pioneers and popularizers, works by a single author on several aspects, defining death, denial of death, attitudes toward death, education for death, psychology of death and dying, sociology of death, ethical and moral issues, euthanasia, suicide, ministering to the dying, patient care, grief and bereavement, funerals, death of the aging, death of children and youth, personal reflections, comparative religions, history and mythology, films, and conclusion.

Bibliographical: Two journals are now appearing devoted exclusively to the study of death: *Archives of the Foundation of Thanatology* which began with volume 1 in 1969 and *Omega* volume 1, *1970*. Both are devoted to "the study of dying, death, bereavement, suicide and other lethal behaviors." *Archives,* published by the Foundation of Thanatology of the Columbia College of Physicians and Surgeons contains more medically oriented articles. *Omega* has more of a psychological, sociological, and anthropological intent. Many journals, including several

169

popular magazines, have either published an entire issue on death or have included substantial and frequent articles on death and dying.

The general bibliographical tools have increasingly provided material for heightened awareness of the literature both descriptively and evaluatively. Invaluable in a search of the literature are the standard works: *Book Review Digest, Humanities Index, New York Times Book Review, Readers Guide to Periodical Literature, Social Science Index, Subject Guide to Books in Print*, and the *Times Literary Supplement*. Essential for a search of medical literature is *Index Medicus* and for ministerial literature the *Catholic Periodical Index*, the *Index to Religious Periodical Literature, Religious and Theological Abstracts*, and *Religious Periodical Index*.

The most thorough basic bibliography of death and related topics is edited by A.H. Kutscher, Jr. and A. H. Kutscher, *A Bibliography of Books on Death, Bereavement, Loss and Grief, 1935-1968* (Health Science, 1969) and *Supplement I, 1968-1972* edited by A. H. Kutscher, Jr. and Martin Kutscher (Health Science, 1974). As the title indicates, the references are to books rather than articles, essays, or non-print material. A similar valuable bibliography was compiled by J. Vernick, *Selected Bibliography on Death and Dying* (U.S. Department of Health Education and Welfare, 1971). Among the basic bibliographical resources, especially of a psychological and sociological nature is Richard A. Kalish's, "Death and Bereavement," which appeared in the *Journal of Human Relations* (1965), pp. 118-141 (370 citations).

Several review essays have appeared: G. Nettler wrote a "Review Essay: On Death and Dying," *Social Casework* (Winter, 1967) pp. 335-344 from a sociological perspective. Among the review articles for the medical profession is L.R. Shusterman's, "Death and Dying: a Critical Review of the Literature," *Nursing Outlook* (July 1973) pp. 467-471. The literature searches of the National Library of Medicine – "Attitudes toward Death, (pp, 71-74, 295 citations) and "Reactions to Infant Death by Family and Social and Legal Institutions," (pp74-75, 92 citations) are essential.

Many of the books on death and dying have extensive bibliographies. Especially notable are the works by Feifel, Fulton, Hendin, Kubler-Ross, Weisman, and Williams which appear later in this essay.

Three brief, but helpful, evaluative annotated bibliographies for ministerial personnel are those of Perry Lefevre, "Recent Books on Death and Dying," *Chicago Theological Seminary Register* (December 1966, pp. 26-27), Randolph C. Miller, *Live Until You Die* (United Church Press, 1973. pp. 149-152) and Robert E. Neale's *The Art of Dying* (Harper & Row, 1973., pp. 151-158). Most of the articles in the following reference section also contain brief selected bibliographies.

Reference works: The standard English language encyclopedias have been revised in the past few years. These revisions evidence the changed emphasis on the treatment of death. This is especially obvious in the *International Encyclopedia of the Social Sciences* which was published in 1968. Two major articles appear in volume 4: "Death and Bereavement," pp. 19-26 by John W. Riley, Jr. and "Social Organization of Death," pp. 26-28 by Robert Habenstein. This is in marked contrast to the emphasis on death rites and customs which was the content of the article in the older *Encyclopedia of the Social Sciences.*

Encyclopedia Americana (volume 8) in its 1973 edition has three short articles: "Death," p. 564 by Milton Helpern, "Legal Aspects of Death," pp. 565-566 by Oliver Schroeder, Jr. and "Death Customs and Rites," pp. 567-568 by John Middleton. *Encyclopedia Britannica* (volume 15) was able to secure three leading authorities for its 15th edition (1974): "Death", pp. 526-529 by Elisabeth Kubler-Ross, "Death and Gift Taxes," pp. 530-533 by Harold M. Somers, and "Death Rites and Customs," pp. 533-539 by S.G.F. Brandon. The Micropedia of the *Encyclopedia Britannica* (volume 3, p. 415) has an extensive outline in addition to these articles.

Encyclopedia of Mental Health secured Herman Feifel to wirte a lengthy popular article, without bibliography, in question and answer format (pp. 427-450). *The Encyclopedia of Philosophy,* published in 1967, has a historical and topical article by Robert G. Olson (volume 2, pp. 307-309). Similar but with an even more deliberate historical intent is the article, "Death and Immortality," by Jacques Choron in the *Dictionary of the History of Ideas* (1973, volume 1, pp. 634-646). A French work, not yet translated into English, which adds to the reference resources is Robert Sabatier's *Dictionnaire de la Mort* (A. Michel, 1967).

The reference works in religion reflect the same more psychologically and sociologically oriented revisions. *Encyclopedia Judaica* (1971, volume 5), the *Interpreter's Dictionary of the Bible* (1962, volume 1), the *New Catholic Encyclopedia* (1967, volume 4) and Karl Rahner's (ed.) *Encyclopedia of Theology* (Seabury, 1975) all have newly written material. Still basic for religious anthropology is the extensive treatment of "Death and Disposal of the Dead," (volume 4, pp. 411-511) in the *Encyclopedia of Religion and Ethics* (1908-1927) which treats several religious or geographical areas by specialists in these fields.

Encyclopedia articles provide an excellent introduction to or summary of current thought on death and dying.

Pioneers and popularizers: In 1959 Herman Feifel edited *The Meaning of Death* (McGraw Hill), a collection of philosophical, theological, psychological, sociological, anthropological and humanities essays, some original but most previously appeared in journals. This marked the beginning of a new era in the literature of death and dying. It has been reissued in paperback (1965) and is widely used in college courses. Its closest parallel is *Death and Identity*, edited by Robert L. Fulton (Wiley, 1965) containing some of the same articles in Feifel but many additional ones appearing for the first time in book form. Along with Feifel and Fulton credit for opening up the new concern for death goes to Jessica Mitford, whose *The American Way of Death* (Simon and Schuster, 1963) was resistently received as iconoclastic. However, the challenge she posed for American culture in its denial, by excessive expenditures and practices, of the reality of death could not be ignored.

No one has risen to the fore as rapidly and with such generally acclaimed success as Elisabeth Kubler-Ross. Her *On Death and Dying* (Macmillan, 1969) has become the standard text. It has been followed by *Questions and Answers on Death and Dying* (Macmillan, 1974) and a collection of essays reflecting her stance, *Death – the Final Stage of Growth* (Prentice-Hall, 1975). She has become known as "the death lady" and is in constant demand as a consultant for seminars, conferences, films, cassettes, and filmstrips. She is in great demand as a speaker for symposia and conventions and is a prolific writer with almost a hundred articles drawn from her pioneering efforts to her credit. Robert Kavanaugh has gained fame in applying Kubler-Ross' approach to college courses and integrating his personal experiences with her's in his *Facing Death* (Penguin, 1967)

David Hendin has used his journalistic expertize in presenting a summarization of current developments in his *Death as a Fact of Life* (Norton, 1973; Warner, 1974). An appeal to personal responsibility for preparation for dying is Stanley Keleman's, *Living Your Dying* (Random House, 1974). John Langone has contributed two books to the current exploration of death in America: *Death is a Noun: a view of the end of Life* (Little, Brown, 1972) and *Vital Signs: the way we die in America* (Little, Brown, 1974). Parallel to Langone's second work is that edited by Arien Mack, *Death in American Experience* (Schocken, 1973). These are primarily popularizations, though with substance, of the major developments in the literature of death.

<u>Works by a single author on several aspects of death and dying</u>
In 1951 Jean Charlot published a collection of satiric cartoons called *The Dance of Death* (Sheed & Ward). These raised questions, not about the Medieval World, but about twentieth century America's handling of the final experience. Several articles, or series of articles, have appeared in the popular press calling attention to death. Among these are Victor Cohn's, "Our Old Concepts of Death seen changing," *Washington Post* (May 29, 1972), Melvin Maddock's, "Death's a Finale, so make it good," *National Observer* (February 15, 1975), Connie Rosenbaum's four part series in the *St. Louis Post-Dispatch* (September 13-16, 1971), and James L. Adam's, "Facing Death," a six part series in the *Cincinnati Post* (January 11, 13-17, 1975).

Among the recent works of a single author covering a broad expanse of related topics are Ray Arvio's, *The Facts of Death* (Harper & Row, 1974), Fred Curren's, *Coming to Terms with Death* (Nelson-Hall, 1974), Robert Jay Lifton and Eric Olson's, *Living and Dying* (Praeger, 1974), and Warren Shibles', *Death: an interdisciplinary analysis* (Language Printer 1973.

A few voices express a mood of tiring of so much attention to death: Nathan Schnaper, "Death and dying: has the topic been beaten to death," *Journal of Nervous and Mental Disease* (March 1975), pp. 157-158, and

Samuel Vaisrub, "Dying is worked to death," *Journal of the American Medical Association* (September 30, 1974), pp. 1909-1910.

Edited works on several aspects. In addition to works already cited, several significant collected works have appeared. Foremost among these is Arnold Toynbee, et al's, *Man's Concern with Death* (McGraw-Hill, 1969) which concentrates on religious, medical, and anthropological aspects. A more ethically probing collection is *Facing Death* which appeared as volume 2, number 2 of the *Hastings Center Studies* in May 1974. This is one of the published works of the Institute of Society, Ethics, and the Life Sciences, one research section of which is devoted to death and dying. David Bender edited *Problems of Death* (Greenhaven, 1974) as a dialogue of the pros and cons of current treatment. Henrik Ruitenbeck's *Death: interpretations* (Delta, 1969) brings together diverse viewpoints. Robert H. Williams is editor for several scholarly and provocative essays with the title, *To Live or to Die? When, how, and why?* (Springer, 1973). The ethical issues treated in this work are not limited to death and dying. Edith Wyschogrod performed a similar task to Ruitenbeck in her *The Phenomenon of Death* (Harper & Row, 1973).

While it falls more appropriately in the humanities bibliography Nathan A. Scott, Jr's *The Modern Vision of Death* (Knox, 1967) has among its noteworthy essays what has already become a classic: "The Time My Father Died," by Joseph Mathews. This memorable essay first appeared in *Motive* magazine in its January/February 1964 issue which was devoted to death. Papers from a seminar at Vanderbilt were edited by Liston O. Mills in *Perspectives on Death* (Abingdon, 1969) with biblical, theological, and religious-historical dimensions. The December 1966 issue of *Zygon* brought together several exceptional essays in the continuing dialogue of religion and science.

Defining death One of the most insistent and elusive areas for exploration today is an acceptable definition of death. It must meet the demands of both law and medicine in a scientific-technologically advanced culture. Many works are available grappling with this facet of death. Significant among them are Dallas M. High's, "Death: its conceptual illusiveness," *Soundings* (Winter, 1972), pp. 438-458, Gunnar

174

Biorck's, "On the definition of death," *World Medical Journal* (November 1967), M. Martin Hailey and William F. Harvey's, "Medical vs. Legal Definitions of Death?", *Journal of the American Medical Association* (May 6, 1968), pp. 423-425, and "Refinements on Criteria for the Determination of Death: an appraisal," *Journal of the American Medical Association* (July 3, 1972), pp. 48-53. The symposium, *The Moment of Death* (C.C. Thomas, 1969) edited by Arthur Winter is a basic reference work with a diversity of viewpoints ably presented.

Denial of death An insistent claim for the past twenty-five years has been that modern man, particularly in American culture, is bent on denying the reality of death. Ernest Becker's *The Denial of Death* (Free Press, 1973) probes the great depth of the psychological roots of such ingrained denial. Similar to Becker, but with a more medical orientation is Avery Weisman's, *On Dying and Denying: a psychiatric study of terminality* (Behavioral Publications, 1972). R. Levin expresses a parallel concern in "Truth versus illusion in relation to death," *Psychiatric Review* (1964), pp. 22-32. Richard G. Dumont looks at *The American View of Death* (Schocken, 1972) and asks whether it is one of acceptance or denial. Jacques Choron approaches the same issue in his widely read *Death and Modern Man* (Macmillan, 1972)

Attitudes toward death Recent years have seen a stress on the interrelation of the attitude of dying persons with those of physicians, nurses, ministers, families and others involved with the terminally ill. This is a primary concern of Kubler-Ross repeated in all her work. It has been approached from a variety of perspectives as may be seen in Stacey B. Day's, *Death and Attitudes toward Death* (Bell Museum of Pathology, University of Minnesota, 1972). Specifically directed to the physician are a number of works including Louis Lasagna's, *Life, Death and the Doctor* (Knopf, 1962) and his "The Doctor and the Dying Patient," *Journal of Chronic Diseases* (1969), pp. 65-68, R.J. Bugler's, "Doctors and Dying," *Archives of Internal Medicine* (1963), pp. 327-332. *Advances in Psychiatry* (1965) dealt with "Death and Dying: attitudes of patient and doctor". Still another of the many articles is Bryant M. Wedge and Robert H. Dovenmuchle's, "Death and Dying: attitudes of patients and doctors,

(*Mental Health Center*, 1965). The results of an extensive study of attitudes of nurses appeared in the August and September issues of *Nursing 75* and was edited by David Popoff. More sociologically oriented is B. Chasin's, "Neglected variables in study of death attitudes," *Sociology*, Winter, 1971), pp. 107-113, and D. Martin, et al, "The relationship between religious behavior and concern about death," *Journal of Social Psychology* (April, 1965), pp. 317-323.

Education for death   Until very recently anyone seriously advocating education for death would have been suspected of morbid obsessions or dire psychic disorders. However, the climate has changed dramatically so that not only in hospitals, medical schools, and seminaries but in undergraduate colleges and high schools, as well, death education now rivals courses in sex education for popularity and enrollment. The most substantial work yet to appear is Betty R. Green and Donald P. Irish's, *Death Education preparation for living* (Schenkman, 1971), the sub-title of which expresses the generally accepted conviction that death education is for the sake of more adequate human life. Again Kubler-Ross has been in the vanguard with her "Facing up to death," *Today's Education* (January 1972), pp. 30-32 the journal of the National Education Association, and "A Teaching Approach to the issue of death and dying,", *Archives of the Foundation of Thanatology* (Fall 1970), pp. 125-127. J.A. Sadwith shows how "An Interdisciplinary approach to death education," might be taken in the *Journal of School Health* (October 1974), pp. 455-458. Phillip W. Seman surveys the more than 600 college courses which were taught in 1973-74 in his article in *The Chronicle of Higher Education* (March 11, 1974), p. 8 titled, "Death, once a taboo topic is the subject of a growing number of college courses." D. Barton pleads for more death education in medical schools in his "The need for including instruction in death and dying in the medical curriculum," *Journal of Medical Education* (March 1972), pp. 169-175, as does E.H. Easton in "Education of death and dying: a survey of American medical schools," pp. 577-578 in the June 1973 issue of the same journal. An example of a positive approach to death education with appropriate exercises used in a seminary class is Robert E. Neale's *The Art of Dying* (Harper & Row, 1973).

176

<u>Psychology of Death and Dying</u> Attitudes are but one aspect of psychology of death and dying which is a far more complete phenomenon. The most thorough treatment is the *Psychology of Death* (Springer, 1972) by Robert Kastenbaum and Ruth Aisenberg. Ignace Lepp's, *Death and its Mysteries* is a beautifully illuminating approach to the fears and feelings of death's effect on life. The pervasiveness of death for life, so persistent a theme for existentialism is made the center of essays by Peter Koestenbaum in his *Vitality of Death: essays in existential psychology and philosophy* (Greenwood, 1971). A notable work with a Freudian base is Joseph C. Rheingold's, *The Mother, Anxiety and Death: the catastrophic death complex* (Little, Brown, 1967). Concern with the fear of death appears in many works including David C. Gordon's *Overcoming the Fear of Death* (Macmillan, 1970). The separate essays, articles, and chapters in the collected works mentioned above dealing with psychological aspects of death and dying are abundant.

<u>Sociology of death</u>   Even more abundant are the resources which are directly sociological. A less than original, but still extensive approach is that of Glenn Vernon's, *Sociology of Death: an analysis of death-related behavior* (Ronald, 1971). A more adequate and perceptive study is D. Sudnow's *Passing On: the social organization of dying* (Prentice-Hall, 1967). *Social Research* (August 1972) devoted the entire lengthy issue (200 pages) to "Death in American Experience". Talcott Parsons, William F. May, Roy Eckart and several others wrote articles which cover a wide variety of sociological aspects of death and dying which are not only functionally descriptive but insightful speculative, symbolic, and metaphysical as well. "Death in American Experience," *Sociological Review* (August 1972) pp. 367-567. W. Lloyd Warner, renowned American sociologist, also looks beyond the acts and events to the meanings symbolized and values expressed in his *The Living and the Dead: a study of the symbolic life of Americans* (Yale, 1959). Perhaps no single work, particularly one so short, has had the widespread acclaim of Oscar Lewis' *A Death in the Sanchez Family* (Random House, 1967) its shear magnitude is astounding.

<u>Ethical and moral issues</u>   Descriptive studies often shade into normative ones as the values expressed by the events described are

177

critically examined. There is a plethora of ethical issues surrounding death, two of which are euthanasia and suicide. These will be given separate treatment below.

An early exploration of a number of death-related moral issues was Joseph Fletcher's *Morals and Medicine* (Beacon, 1960). Donald R. Cutler edited a work on several issues in his *Updating Life and Death* (Beacon, 1969). Similar to Cutler's book, but receiving even greater use by medical personnel is Edward Shil, et al, *Life or Death: ethics and options* (University of Washington, 1968). The question of "who shall live?" has been dealt with repeatedly, especially in reference to abortion, organ transplants, and indefinite prolongation of life technologically. Among the more provocative of the works are: *Who Shall Live? Man's Control over Birth and Death* (Hill & Wang, 1970) produced by the American Friends Service Committee. Kenneth Vaux's edited work by the same title – *Who Shall Live?* (Fortress, 1970), and Renee Fox's *Experiment Perilous* (Free Press, 1959).

One of the most penetrating, scholarly treatments is Paul Ramsey's *The Patient as Person: explorations in medical ethics* (Yale, 1970). Ramsey is a prolific writer conversant not only with philosophy and theology but with medicine and law as well.

While articles are too plentiful to catalog, at least a few should be mentioned: Richard A. McCormick, "To Save or Let Die: the dilemma of modern medicine," *Journal of the American Medical Association* (July 1974) pp. 172-176, anonymous articles, "The Right to live and the right to die," *Medical Times* (November 1967) pp. 1171-1196, and "When do we let the patient die?" *Annals of Internal Medicine* (March 1968) pp. 695-700, and F. William Williamson, "Life or death – whose decision?" *Journal of the American Medical Association* (September, 1966) pp. 793-795.

A somewhat oblique issue but one which has attracted much attention is that of cryogenics, the freezing of bodies immediately at death anticipating their resuscitation at some future date. The basic work in this area is M. McClintock's *Cryogenics* (Reinhold, 1964). Robert C.W. Ettinger raises relevant questions about the meaning of this in his article,

"Cryogenics and the purpose of life," *Christian Century* (October 4, 1967) pp. 1250-1253.

Euthanasia "A good death," "the right to die," "death with dignity" these have become the slogans of a new and vitalized consideration of euthanasia. The Euthanasia Educational Council, 250 West 57th Street, New York 10019 carries on a vigorous campaign of information, exploration, and dissemination providing resources for individuals and classes, holding conferences, and publishing advocacy materials such as "the living will", Proceedings of their annual conferences, the first of which was held in 1968 around the theme "The Right to die with dignity". They also publish a selective annotated bibliography

This area has contributed some of the most constructive thought in the literature on death and dying. An extraordinary treatment is Daniel C. Maguire's, *Death by Choice* (Schocken, 1975). A.B. Downing edited *Euthanasia and the Right to Die: the case for voluntary euthanasia* (Humanities, 1970), a splendid collection of provocative essays. Marvin Kohl, whose perceptive reviews of much of the death literature has made him knowledgeable of the material, has contributed a thoughtful work, *The Morality of Killing: sanctity of life, abortion, and euthanasia* (Peter Owen, 1974). Marya Mannes', *Last Rights* (W. Morrow, 1974) has had wide popular appeal and is emotionally penetrating. Popular magazines have found this area one of great reader interest. Among Joseph Fletcher's numerous writings is his article, "The Patient's right to die," *Harper's* magazine (October 1960). Focusing on religious and legal interaction is C.F. Preston and J. Horton's, "Attitudes among clergy and lawyers toward euthanasia", *Journal of Pastoral Care* (June 1972) pp. 108-115.

Suicide Related to euthanasia but constituting another area of intense concern is the treatment of suicide. The leading authority in this field is Edwin S. Shneidman. His *Psychology of Suicide* (Science House, 1970) is a landmark. He edited an extensive study, *Essays in Self-Destruction* (Science House, 1967) and collaborated with Norman L. Farberow in *Clues to Suicide* (McGraw-Hill, 1957) utilizing clinical material from the Los Angeles Crisis Intervention Center.

An early sociological study still beneficial is Andrew F. Henry and James F. Short's, *Suicide and Homicide: some economic, sociological, and psychological aspects of aggression* (Free Press, 1954). A more recent updating of relevant material is David Lester's, *Why People Kill themselves: a summary of research findings on suicidal behavior* (C.C. Thomas, 1972). From a deliberate religious perspective two works stand out: James Hillman's *Suicide and the Soul* (Harper & Row, 1964) and E.V. Stern's, "Faith, hope, and suicide", *Journal of Religion and Health* (July 1971) pp. 214-225.

A couple of popular articles on adolescent suicides give important summaries: J. Marie Hoag's, "When the cry for help comes," *Seventeen* magazine (March 1973) pp. 118-119, 154-155, and Pamela Cantor's, "Adolescent suicide: results of a study," *Time* magazine (June 3, 1974) page 24.

<u>Ministering to the dying</u> Russell L. Dicks and Thomas S. Kepler wrote an early work, *And Peace at the Last* (Westminster, 1953) which made an impact on this important dimension of ministry. Carl J. Scherzer's, *Ministering to the Dying* (Prentice Hall, 1963) continued this concern. More recently R.B. Reeves, Jr., et al, edited, *Pastoral Care of the Dying and Bereaved: selected readings* (Health Science, 1974) a book which will find enormous use. Two articles which emphasize the contextual or interdependent family involvement in ministering to the dying are: S.B. Goldberg's, "Family tasks and reactions in the crisis of death," *Social Casework* (July 1974) pp. 398-405, and G.W. Krieger and L.O. Bascue's, "Terminal Illness: counseling with a family Perspective," *The Family Coordinator* (July 1975) pp. 351-355.

Geoffrey Gorer did an extensive study of grief manifestations in England: *Death, Grief, and Mourning* (Doubleday, 1965). His compatriot C. Murray Parkes has also done influential work: "Effects of Bereavement on physical and in-patient care_ The literature of patient care in the face of death is growing at an incredible rate. Leonard Pearson's, *Death and Dying: current issues in the treatment of the dying person* (Case Western Reserve, 1969) is an erudite study for professionals. Barney G. Glaser's, *Time for Dying* (Aldine, 1969) and with Anselm Straus, *Awareness of Dying* (Aldine, 1965) are two remarkable books. A companion to the latter which is already a classic for nurses is Jeanne C. Quint's, *The Nurse and the Dying Patient* (Macmillan, 1969). These works derived from detailed clinical practice in San Francisco. An abbreviated presentation of the basic contention of Quint's book appears in her article, "The Threat of Death: some consequences for patients and nurses", *Nursing Forum* (1969) pp. 286-300.

Orville Brim, Jr., et al, brought forth an exceptional work, *The Dying Patient* (Russell Sage Foundation, 1970) which is cited often by others in the field. In the May 31, 1970 issue of *Patient Care* magazine many facets of this concern are explored. Melvin Krant's, "The Organized care of the dying patient", *Hospital Practice* (January 1972) and Russell Noyes, Jr's, "The Care and management of the dying," *Archives of Internal Medicine* (August 1971) pp. 299-303 are but two of many fine articles calling attention to the need for a fresh examination of patient care.

The leading authority in this area is Ciceley Saunders, Director of St. Christopher's Hospice, London. In addition to numerous articles, two of her books explain the viable alternative which she has used instead of the depersonalized practices still too prevalent: *Care of the Dying* (Macmillan, 1959) and *The Management of Terminal Illness* (Hospital Medicine, 1967).

Of particular concern in medical literature is the treatment of cardiac and cancer patients. Many references to this area may be found in *Index Medicus*, including E. G. Litin, et al "Symposium: what shall we tell the cancer patient?" *Proceedings of the Staff Meetings of the Mayo Clinic* (a960) and Borys Surawicz and E. Pelligrino's edited work, *Sudden Cardiac Death* (Crone and Stratton, 1964). Clarence McConkey, out of his personal experiences has written a helpful book directed not to the physician or nurse, so much as to the patient and his family: *When Cancer Comes* (Westminster, 1974).

Psychiatry more properly belongs here than with psychology and the classic in the field is Kurt Eissler's, *The Psychiatrist and the Dying Patient* (International Universities Press, 1955). In addition, among the many available resources are Magretta K. Bowers, et al, *Counseling the Dying* (Nelson, 1964. A.D. Weisman's, "Misgivings and misconceptions in the psychiatric care of terminal patients," *Psychiatry* (1970) pp. 670-681, and J. Zinker and S. Fink's, "The possibility of psychological growth in a dying person," *Journal of General Psychology* (1966) pp. 185-199.

Grief and bereavement The classic study on grief appeared six years before the time span covered by this essay, but it has exerted such profound influence that it should be noted. Erich Lindemann's, "Symptomatology and management of acute grief," *American Journal of Psychiatry* (1944) pp. 141-148 has often been reprinted and is included in Fulton's *Death and Identity* referred to earlier. "Mental health a study of the medical records of widows," *British Medical Journal* (1964), and "The First Year of bereavement: a longitudinal study of the reactions of London widows to the death of their husbands," *Psychiatry* (November 1970) pp. 444-467. B. Schoenberg, et al, edited a significant work for medical personnel: *Loss and Grief: psychological management in medical practice* (Columbia, 1970). Similar in depth and coverage is Austin H. Kutscher's, *Death and Bereavement* (C.C. Thomas, 1969).

Edgar N. Jackson has written many works on grief, the most influential of which is his *Understanding Grief: its roots, dynamics, and treatment* (Abingdon, 1957). Written primarily for self-awareness and help to the bereaved is Bernadine Kreis and Alice Pattie's, *Up from Grief: patterns of recovery* (Seabury, 1969) and Granger Westberg's marvelous, little book, *Good Grief* (Augustana, 1962).

Lynn Caine, using her own experiences and personal knowledge of others in grief, has contributed *Widows* (W. Morrow, 1974). A concentrated study is S. Roxanne Hiltz's, "Helping widows: group discussion as a therapeutic technique," *The Family Coordinator* (July 1975) pp. 331-336. A companion piece is P.R. Silverman's, "The widow as a caregiver in a program of preventive intervention with other widows," *Mental Hygiene* (October 1970) pp. 540-547.

Austin H. Kutscher collaborated with others in his recent *Acute Grief and the Funeral* (Health Science, 1974).

Funerals: Kutscher's book examines the positive role of the funeral in grief management. Paul Irion pursues this goal in his *The Funeral – Vestige or Value?* (Abingdon, 1957). Jessica Mitford's, *The American Way of Death* (Simon and Schuster, 1963) already referred to, was a major breakthrough in reappraisal of funerals. Leroy E. Bowman wrote, *The American Funeral* in 1959 and it was reissued by Greenwood in 1973.

A historical/sociological study was done by Robert Habenstein and William Lamers, *The History of American Funeral Directing* (Bulfin, 1959). C.J. Polson, et al, examined with thoroughness, *The Disposal of the Dead* (C.C. Thomas, 1962) with concentration on contemporary American practices. Maurice R. Davies has brought together a handbook on *Laws of Burial, Cremation, and Exhumation* (Finch, 1956). Paul Irion focuses on *Cremation* (Fortress, 1968) a practice which has had reticent acceptance in American culture. The varied religious functions funerals perform are set out in J.D. Forest's, "The Major Emphasis of the Funeral," *Pastoral Psychology* (1963) pp. 19-24.

<u>Death of the aging</u>   The basic work in this area is a challenge to the ill-conceived and widespread contention that people die of old age: *Nobody Ever Died of Old Age* (Little, Brown, 1973 by Sharon R. Curtin. *Geriatrics* devoted its August 1972 issue to a symposium on death and attitudes toward death. Joseph Paton deals with, "The Art of Aging and Dying," in *Gerontologist* (1964) pp. 94-100. Richard A. Kalish comes at this from a sociological perspective in, "The Aged and the Dying Process," *Social Issues* (October 1956) pp. 87-96.

Personal responsibility and the process of death among the aging is explored by M.B. Miller in, "Decision-making in the death process of the ill aged," *Geriatrics* (May 1971) pp. 105-116. C.E. Preston, et al, continues this theme in, "Views of the aged on the timing of death," *Gerontologist* (Winter 1971) pp. 300-304. Striking correspondences to time of death and personal objectives is maintained by H.K. Fischer, et al in "Man's determination of his time of illness or death: anniversary reactions and emotional deadlines," *Geriatrics* (July 1971) pp. 89-94. The plight of the aging, particularly in nursing homes, as they move toward death was examined in hearings before the special Committee of the 92nd Congress in August 1972 on the topic, "Death with Dignity: an inquiry into related public issues." The committee was chaired by Senator Frank Church.

Death of children and youth   At the other end of the life continuum is the death of children and youth. Again, there is abundant literature with diverse considerations. In the medical field alone the literature is staggering. One of the most scholarly studies for professionals is Erna Furman's, *A Child's Parent Dies: studies in childhood bereavement* (Yale, 1974). William M. Easson has contributed a significant work focusing not on bereavement but on the child' death: *The Dying Child: the management of the child or adolescent who is dying* (C.C. Thomas, 1970). Easson earlier explored this area in his article, "Care of the Young Patient who is dying," *Journal of the American Medical Association* (July 22, 1968) pp. 63-67. The ways children conceptualize their death is the focus of W. Gartley and M. Bernasconi in their article, "The concept of death in children," *Journal of Genetic Psychology* (March 1967) pp. 71-85. Maria Nagy was a pioneer in studies of children's conceptualization of death and her work has often been reprinted, e.g. in both Feifel's, *The Meaning of Death* and Fulton's, *Death and Identity.*

As is true of many of the other aspects of death treated in this bibliographic essay, so with the death of children and youth articles, essays, and chapters may be found in the collected works mentioned earlier; see especially the works by Kavanaugh, Miller, and Toynbee.

A Maurer concentrates on youth in, "Adolescent attitudes toward death," *Journal of Genetic Psychology* (September 1964) pp. 75-9-. Edwin S. Shneidman has edited papers written by Harvard University students in his seminar on a variety of topics in the book, *Death and the College Student* (Behavioral Publications, 1972).

Marjorie F. Mitchell, from her observations in clinical practice with children, has written, *The Child's Attitude to Death* (Schocken, 1967). Herbert S. Zim and Soma Bleeker have contributed a brief but instructive work for parents and others involved with children who raise questions about the meaning of death: *Life and Death* (W. Morrow, 1969). Also of brief compass but with a more specific religious perspective are Edgar N. Jackson's, *Telling a Child about Death* (Channel, 1966), Earl A. Grollman's (editor) *Explaining death to children* (Beacon, 1967), Linda J. Vogel's, *Helping a Child to Understand Death* (Fortress, 1975), and Marie Fargue's, *The Child and the Mystery of Death* (Newman, 1966).

Two pertinent books written intentionally for children are John B. Coburn's, *Anne and the Sand Dobbies* (Seabury, 1964) and Joan Fassler's, *My Grandpa died today* (Behavioral Publications, 1971), both of which have proven extremely beneficial. #

b. *"The College Connection."* MB545, City University of Seattle, 1995.

Here is an interesting and innovative approach to assisting adults find their way into college either for the first time or in continuation of a program already begun but abandoned due to circumstances. The full title of the paper was Marketing Plan for an Educational Broker for Adult Learners to operate as The College Connection. It was a plan or proposal never brought to fruition. Most of the supporting data in the appendices has been omitted due to length. It should be noted that the paper does not explore the extent of student involvement in online courses through programs such as those offered by University of Phoenix and similar institutions.

Marketing Plan for an Education Broker for Adult Learners
to operate as The College Connection
Overview of The College Connection

The College Connection would be an educational brokerage firm for assisting adults in assessing their educational backgrounds, experiences, and resources providing them with comparative information on higher education opportunities available in Kitsap County, and assisting them in making application to their chosen institution and applying for financial aid as desired.

Kitsap County is a semi-rural area of approximately 360 square miles west of Puget Sound in the Seattle-Tacoma metropolitan area. Its population of 189,731 is expected to double within the next 20 years. Of that number 117,021 persons are 25 years of age or older. Only 6% of them have graduate or professional degrees, 13.9% have bachelor's degrees, 8.2% have associate degrees and another 29.0% have some college courses completed but no degree. In 1993 9,599 persons were enrolled in college. 7,923 were in publicly supported institutions and 1,676 were in private academic institutions. (Appendix A)

Olympic College, the only state-supported institution, is a Community College which enrolled 6, 635 students for the Fall Term 1993. (Appendix B) The remaining 1,288 students enrolled in public institutions were either engaged in external degree programs or enrolled in academic institutions in other counties, most likely King and Pierce.

The private institutions in Kitsap County are Chapman University Bangor Academic Center, City University of Seattle Kitsap Site, Southern Illinois University Bangor and Northwest College of Art. Comparable enrollments for the Fall Term 1993 were respectively 170, 65, 66, and 85 for a total of 386 leaving 1290 either enrolled in external degree programs or taking courses in other counties.

A number of academic institutions in neighboring counties, particularly King and Pierce, offer a wide array of evening and week-end programs for adult learners seeking vocational or academic experiences either for non-credit or for credit leading toward an associate, baccalaureate, or graduate degree. ("A Guide to Evening and Weekend Degree Options for Residents of Kitsap County" 1995)

The potential for increased enrollment of adults in higher education, the nature of available programs, the cooperation of academic institutions in Kitsap County, and specific aspects of the proposed educational brokerage service will be dealt with in the following sections.

Evaluation of Market and Company

The College Connection would provide an opportunity for an adult learner to get full-service higher educational brokerage services in close proximity to his or her home with a minimal expenditure of time and for a reasonable fee. Familiarity with resources for adult learning such as those indicated in the Reference section of this Plan (e.g. Bear 1988, Macmillan 1993, Sullivan 1993, Thorson 1992) and first-hand involvement of the firm's president with the local institutions, as well as his credentials in higher education (Appendix C) would enable applicants to have confidence in the services. These are major strengths.

Another strength would be the ability to assess clients' work experience relative to college credit using accepted standards such as those of the American Council on Education, to offer proficiency and CLEP examinations enabling the client to accelerate his or her program and to offer the client several options for completing desired programs utilizing a variety of educational resources.

Among the weaknesses for the success of the plan would be the fact that each of the local institutions offers its own service, the distance between them is minimal, and cooperation is commendable. The administrative staffs are readily available and quite willing to give individual and personalized attention to inquirers and applicants.

A second weakness is that the academic programs are sufficiently differentiated to make selections of course and programs easy.

Northwest College of Art focuses on the visual and commercial arts and appeals primarily to immediate post-high school graduates. (Appendix D)

Southern Illinois University provides a program for persons interested in teaching in vocational and technical fields in high schools and colleges. It appeals basically to military personnel, especially to those nearing retirement or separation from service and who wish to prepare themselves for a second career. (Appendix E)

Olympic College provides the bulk of lower level (freshman and sophomore) courses for the other institutions in Kitsap County. It is working to expand its scope with 2 + 2 baccalaureate degree programs in 1994 and beyond.

City University's strength is as a graduate institution offering MBA and other master's degree programs. It offers a limited number of undergraduate courses such as History of Business in America but at a greater cost than its main competitor. (Appendix F)

Chapman University reaches more students, offers more courses, and costs less than the other private institutions. It is not limited to military personnel but its location at Naval Submarine Base Bangor gives it an advantage with naval personnel. (Appendix G)

A third weakness is that Navy Campus, located at Subbase Bangor provides a similar service for military personnel to that proposed here. It has experienced significant growth in services within the past year. All areas including testing, assessment, liaison with local institutions, and providing information for external degree programs, particularly DANTES (Defense Activity for Non-traditional Education Support) and SOC (Service Members Opportunity Colleges) rose 30% to 100% in fiscal year 1995 first quarter over the comparable quarter in fiscal year 1994. (Appendix H)

The opportunities for expansion of adult involvement in higher education in Kitsap County are enormous. With the County's projected rate of growth, expanded presence of a more technically oriented military, concerted efforts to diversify the economy, and need for increased managerial and leadership personnel in current and anticipated product and service areas Kitsap County can and no doubt will make higher education for adults more of a priority. This is, at least in part, the impetus for Olympic College's aggressive pursuit of a 2 + 2 or 4 year degree program as well as the Economic Development Council of Kitsap County's very recent publication of "A Guide to Evening and Weekend Degree Options for Residents of Kitsap County" (1995)

There is also the opportunity to take advantage of a growing national awareness of the role of adult higher education especially in degree completion programs. (Spencer 1995)

The desire of consumers to find ways to simplify administrative and financial processes in most areas of their lives as for instance in the use of travel agents, real estate, financial and mortgage brokers, indicates an opportunity for an education broker.

The threat is primarily from a positive side of the contemporary situation. The directors of the three major private academic institutions (Chapman, City, and SIU) know each other and work well together in a cooperative spirit. They have a reputation for putting the student first thereby being customer oriented. Their reliance on Olympic College to provide lower level courses enables them to economize and diversity offerings and restrain costs.

The threat also would be from the reasonable question, "Why should I pay for a service which I can get free?" The College Connection would need to focus on marketing a service which encourages return to college for those who have given it little thought, considered themselves too old to learn, or were simply not sure how to go about continuing their higher education. It would help to simplify what for many persons is a complicated, confusing and sometimes frustrating experience.

Product Objectives

Basic objectives for the next 12 months are:

1. To increase awareness of adults 25 years of age or over of the availability of opportunities for higher education in Kitsap County.

2. To amass resources necessary for providing clients with essential comparative information for making an appropriate choice.

3. To work with local institutions as they further define and clarify their various niches

4. To gain credibility as an educational consultant who is fair and honest to the academic institutions providing educational experiences for clients

5. To gain a reputation as an educational broker who encourages clients to determine their own educational goals, establish the resources in time and money which they wish to devote to these and ascertain the desired type of learning experience the client seeks.

6. To establish relationships with education brokers in other geographic areas to learn with and from them how to improve the service.

7. To find the most efficient and effective software to enable the firm to provide timely responses to essential operations such as testing, e.g. the immediate feedback on GRE computerization.

8. To establish personal and computer connections with academic institutions so as to eliminate all but the most essential paperwork for the client.

9. To eliminate the necessity of the client completing separate and different forms for each institution.

10. To assist a minimum of 30 clients per month to begin or resume their college education.

As the service grows a couple of other product extensions would be in order:

1. Work with high school students and their families to provide the type service real estate agents sometimes provide for clients relocating to distant areas through relevant visual resources. The advantage is the one-stop nature of this service reducing need for numerous individual contacts and requests for catalogues, information, etc.

2. Provide a broker service for prospective adjunct faculty. Kitsap County has an increasing number of retired persons, not all of them in their 60s or 70s, many of whom are qualified to teach college courses. A single resume or curriculum vitae would be compiled with sufficient information to enable The College Connection to customize it. Transcripts would be requested and verified. Work experience would be evaluated and validated. Teaching aptitude and qualifications would be assessed. This one-stop service would eliminate the necessity of prospective teachers working their way through the mazes of the separate institutions in the area while assisting the applicant in getting an interview for prospective employment.

The Marketing Mix

The College Connection would be a new concept for Kitsap County beyond the military community. Consequently, its acceptance would be based on how well it was perceived as contributing to the growth and well-being of the community as a whole as well as the quality of services to individual clients.

It would be essential to have carefully thought-out the mission statement or strategy, developed interpersonal relationships with community leaders, amassed the requisite resources to effectively accomplish the firm's objectives in meeting clients' needs, and provided the kind of service which would assure word-of-mouth endorsement.

The marketing approaches currently being used by the institutions are sound and would be utilized also by the College Connection. These include:

1. Involvement in the Chamber of Commerce, Economic Development Council, and similar opportunities for networking and interacting with community leaders concerned with higher education in Kitsap County.

2. Enthusiastic cooperation with academic directors and staffs to establish positive impressions of the service and diminish perceived threats.

3. Full use of newspaper advertising in the general daily/Sunday newspaper *The Bremerton Sun* and in specialized newspapers such as *Community Style, Trident Tides, Kitsap Business Journal,* etc.

4. Bus, bill-board, and poster advertisements on Kitsap County Transit buses.

5. Listing in the educational section of business directories as well as in the area telephone directories.

6. Television spots offering specific tips to adults on getting on with their higher education. These are quite inexpensive in the local market.

7. Direct mailings of the type and style seen in the example given in Appendix I to targeted adults in Kitsap County.

8. Booths at community service events such as Job Fairs at the Fairgrounds and in retail malls etc.

9. Presentations at civic organization, adult interest groups, etc.

10 Encouraging present clients to pass the word of the service on to others and providing them with attractive and informative business cards and brochures.

The desired image of The College Connection would be of an educational broker expert in its field and committed to providing premiere personal service to the client at a reasonable cost. Promotional discounts and rebates are not contemplated. To keep the priority of the relationship on the client remuneration from academic institutions is not anticipated. The College Connection would be financed by the fees charged clients. Business and professional organizations would be encouraged to provide this service to their employees as part of their educational benefits package. A single fee is desired, including all elements of assessment, testing, interviewing, counseling, and application preparation. However, it may be that in some cases a prorated fee would be acceptable when some of these services are not needed.

The median household income in Kitsap County is $32,043 (Appendix A). Persons 35-54, i.e. 28,557 of the 69,488 households, are in the $35K-$49.9K% bracket. The 25-34 and 55-64 year olds (23,669) are in the $25K-34.9K category. The initial primary target age would be the 35-54 year old population who are looking toward improving their opportunities for advancement with their present employer or who are preparing to embark on another career.

The market niche would be primarily those who have some college but no degree, i.e. 33,913 persons or 29% of persons over 25. No finer breakdown for specific age categories beyond 25 was available. An important second element of this primary market would be those with associate degrees, i.e. 9, 648 or 8.2%. The market for undergraduate baccalaureate degrees would thus be 37.2% or 43,561 persons. The service could be provided and maintained if it reached and served 1%-5% of these. It should enhance services and show a profit at 6%-10% and become a profitable venture requiring expansion with additional staff and equipment with 10%-20% of the potential market.

The secondary market would be for those who were interested in pursuing graduate degrees: 16,212 or 13.9% who hold bachelor's degrees. Only a small percentage of those with graduate or professional degrees, 7,000 or 6.0% could be expected to enroll in further graduate degree programs though many of them would be involved in or interested in continuing education thus constituting another smaller segment of the market. Service to graduate oriented clients would be more costly therefore the fee would reflect this. The potential customer base in this market is considerably smaller than that for undergraduate degrees.

Conclusion

Kitsap County offers tremendous opportunities for growth in higher education for adults. The College Connection could be a valuable and viable part of that growth. I do not intend to pursue this idea commercially but have found it exciting to consider and develop it. A good bit of encouragement was given as I gathered information for the plan. I am aware that there is much more which would have to be done before an actual implementation but I believe that what has been presented in this paper shows its feasibility.

[Since there is not room for the appendices let me simply point out that the statistical data in the paper came basically from the Puget Sound Regional Council's "1990 Census of Population and Housing" for Kitsap County. Each of the institutional profiles includes program, curriculum, schedule, students, admissions, tuition, financial aid, primary market and marketing. References included printed resources, personal interviews, and telephone interviews] #

c. *"Baldridge Quality Award for Spiritual Services Unit of The Hospice of the Florida Suncoast"* QM500, City University of Seattle, October 29, 1995.

This next paper bridged the academic world I was involved in and my personal life. When I wrote it I had been retired from Navy Chaplaincy three years and was deeply involved as a Hospice volunteer. I was serving my first term as a Board of Trustees member when I wrote the paper. Five years later while serving my second term on the Board as its President Hospice of Kitsap County had taken up a very special place in my life. As I often said when speaking on Hospice's behalf, "next to my family, Hospice is my greatest love." I continued that relationship for almost 20 years.

The full title of the paper was "Application of Baldrige Quality Award Criterion 5.0 to Spiritual Services Unit of The Hospice of the Florida Suncoast," The paper has been edited for inclusion here with most of the statistical supporting data omitted.

Introduction

One of the most important changes in American
Business over the past decade has been the growing
Recognition of the strategic importance of quality or
Total Quality Management (TQM).

(Hart and Schlesinger, Page 433)

Total Quality Management is no longer restricted to American business narrowly conceived as manufacturing or the production of

193

durable goods. It has permeated American business in its widest manifestations including education (Del Valle), the military (Chief of Naval Education and Training), and countless organizations providing services as their products including numerous non-profit or not-for-profit agencies.

The preeminence of a quest for quality in American business may be noted in the eleven year series of a section on Quality appearing annually in Fortune magazine (Bowles, 1994, Pages 157-202; Bowles, 1995, Pages 198-228)

The Baldrige Quality System

A prominent impetus to wider recognition of and growth in the quest for quality has been the Malcolm Baldrige National Quality Award signed into law in 1987. Not all recipients have fared well and much has been made of those failures. However, the preponderance of evidence is that application of the Baldrige criteria, regardless of whether or not a firm applies for the prize, is a venture yielding incalculable rewards.

As Christopher Hart and Leonard Schlesinger maintain, "Once a quality system is in place, it inevitably helps a company prioritize and manage its many functions more efficiently." (Page 435) Using the Baldrige criteria conscientiously cannot but help improve the quality of performance since, "Baldrige is neither more nor less than a performance model." (Hart and Schlesinger, Page 436)

The Baldrige system provides a quality model which helps the user to do several things. Among them are assess what in the organization is already being done well and what needs improvement, set strategic priorities for all of the organization's quality improvement needs, develop quality action plans that integrate the Human Resource functions with the Total Quality Management function, and monitor the result of TQM activities on an on-going basis for continuous improvement and later action planning. (Hart and Schlesinger, Pages 435-436)

Hart and Schlesinger summarize the major strategies underlying all the Baldrige categories in this manner: develop a vision, define quality from the customer's point of view, continually improve, measure – gather objective data on performance—and tie approach to results, benchmark, integrate all effort making quality strategic, involve everyone in the organization by building teams and empowering employees, take charge.

It is no accident that "Leadership" stands at the forefront of the award's criteria. Top management commitment to TQM and mangers' positions as quality role models are universally accepted as the sine qua non for quality improvement. (Pages 441-442)

Anyone wishing to get from theory to application can follow Stephen George's "do-it-yourself way to transform your business" using the Baldrige Quality system.

The Spiritual Care Unit of the Hospice of the Florida Suncoast

In this brief paper we are going to look at the application of the TQM approach to one segment of an organization and assess that application using the Baldrige criteria found in the works of Stephen George and Bruce and Suzanne Brocka.

The segment chosen is the Spiritual Care Unit of the Hospice of the Florida Suncoast. The data on which this assessment is based appears as an appendix to this paper [not included here]. It is the sketchy outline of a presentation to the First National Conference Series on Spiritual/Bereavement/Psycho-Social Aspects of Hospice Care conducted by the National Hospice Organization and the Council of Hospice Professionals in San Francisco, August 17-23, 1995.

The criterion selected for assessment purposes is 5.0 (Management of Process Quality). Other criteria, particularly 6.0 (Quality and Operational Results) and 7.0 (Customer Focus and Satisfaction) though applicable were not assessed.

The available material begins with a presentation on "Concern for Quality: the Soul of Spiritual Care". A ten step Quality Improvement model is given in the form of a worksheet. The Scope of Services/Care/Functions follows keyed to the "important aspects of care" from the worksheet. A sample "Quality Improvement – Records Review Worksheet" is followed by four sheets for documentation of performances using differentiated indicators.

I found this information an impressive program which measures well on Baldrige criterion 5.0. As a member of the Board of Trustees of

Hospice of Kitsap County I have served for two years on the Practice Committee where issues of Quality Control and Assurance are regularly discussed and monitored. I am now Convener of the Spiritual Care Advisory Council an interfaith body working with the staff, primarily the Spiritual Counselor/Chaplain, providing training for voluntary spiritual care givers. The Council is also serving as interim Board of Directors for a Robert Wood Johnson grant to inaugurate an Adopt-a-Patient program for local spiritual/faith communities.

I have chosen to look at the Florida case rather than Hospice of Kitsap County for two reasons: first, I believe I can treat it more objectively, and second, I am confident I can learn a great deal from this study which will benefit Hospice of Kitsap County.

The Florida Suncoast presentation in its introduction seeks to establish receptivity to the goal of measuring quality as an urgent opportunity which works with but is not synonymous with management goals.

The outline of the presentation on Quality Process is in line with basic TQM teachings including the gathering of information must have a purpose beyond simply measuring information, commitment and widespread support is vital to the process, the purpose of research must be understood before the techniques or tools can be formulated and applied, the whole program must develop from within rather than being imposed from above or from the outside, communicating quality must be an affirmation of the organization's commitment to quality and the resources essential to continuously improving it.

The actual "Application of Quality Program Components" follows guidelines presented in Brocka and Brocka and George. While there must be unity in spiritual care this does not mean uniformity, individual differences must be recognized and respected, responsibilities must be clearly delineated and accepted for when everyone is in charge no one is responsible, the scope of care/service must be clearly articulated or defined, various aspects of care must be prioritized in terms of their importance, quality indicators must be identified so as to be manageable or useful, the need for establishing thresholds for evaluation must be accepted and planned for, relevant data must be gathered, organized, and made useable, education within the unit and beyond of what the data means about the current situation and the areas requiring attention must take place, identified problems must be approached and actions taken to resolve them, the plan, do, check, act (PDCA) paradigm must be employed in the assessment of actions documenting improvement and setting out further actions to be taken, and the findings of the quality process as enacted must be communicated for future growth to take place.

The presentation also included lessons learned including "if I had to do it over again" and "common barriers to implementing a quality program".

The Scope of Services/Care/Functions is explored using symbols indicating high volume activities, high risk activities, and problem prone areas. Twenty-two specific items are examined and marked.

A sample "Records Review Worksheet" identifies four components/criteria and provides for documenting the sources of information. A place is provided in each incident for "comments/exceptions".

Completed forms for three indicators are provided: 1) a Care Assessment and Care Plan Documentation, 2) Access to Services Documentation, and 3) Patient Care Documentation.

Assessment

Using this information, how does the Spiritual Care Unit measure up on Baldrige Criterion 5.0 Management of Process Quality in which the highest score would be 140 points. Approach, Deployment, and Results have been combined for a single assessment.

5.1	Design and Introduction of Quality Products and Services (40 points)	90%	36.0
5.2	Process Management: Product and Service Production and Delivery Processes (35 points)	90%	31.5
5.3	Process Management: Business Processes and Support Services	85%	25.5

	(30 points)		
5.4	Supplier Quality (20 points)	75%	15.0
5.5	Quality Assessment (15 points)	90%	13.5
	Totals	84%	121.5

Conclusion

Perhaps this assessment has been a bit severe. It is quite possible that an on-site evaluation with opportunity to 1) examine more relevant data, 2) explore in greater depth the documentation provided. 3) discuss the actual application of the quality process, and 4) personally observe the process at work would have yielded a higher score.

As a former examiner for the Southern Association of Colleges and Schools I am aware that limited data, such as that used in this project, gives only inadequate resources for making an accurate assessment.

However, even a score of 121.5 out of a possible 140 points or 84% is commendable and should serve as encouragement to the organization that it is moving in the right direction toward continuous quality improvement.

Annotated Bibliography

Berrey, Cayl, Amy Avergun, and Darlene Russ-Eft. "Highly Responsive Teams and Your Competitive Advantage," *Journal for Quality and Participation*. September 1993. Pages 72-76. Offers practical guidance for establishing and maintaining effective teams including tables as key factors for "sustaining team initiatives," "leading teams," and "evolution of team leadership," as well as, "requisites for highly responsible teams."

Bowles, Jerry, "Quality Happens Through People," (Advertisement) *Fortune*, September 18, 1995. Pages 198-228. The eleventh annual presentation of *Fortune's* special "advertisement" section on quality. This one centers on persons in the process. Succinctly, it states TQM's present focus: "Today's managers and workers alike have to practice cooperation and collaboration with everybody, inside and outside the firm, from colleagues and subordinates to customers and suppliers. They must be team players and lifelong learners." Page S3.

Bowles, Jerry, "Quality 2000: The Next Decade of Progress," (Advertisement) *Fortune,* September 19, 1994. Pages 157-202. An extended 45 page "advertisement" section celebrating the tenth year of National Quality month and *Fortune's* special coverage. This issue focuses on four points: 1) reinventing the corporation and globalization (core competencies), 2) customerization and the smart machine (information sharing), 3) quality through people (teamwork), and 4) the new frontiers of quality (learning organizations). It also highlights the Quality Forum X – Quality 2000: the Next Decade of Progress sponsored by ATT&T, Ford Motor Company, *Fortune* magazine, and ASQC.

Brocka, Bruce and M. Suzanne Brocka. *Quality Management: Implementing the Best Ideas of the Masters.* Irwin, 1992. A full-length treatment of Quality Management including fundamental issues, masters of the movement, dynamics, tools and techniques, and resources.

Chief of Naval Education and Training. *Introduction to Total Quality Leadership. Student Guide.* [No publication information is given]. An elemental guide for students in the Department of the Navy's mandated training. It deals primarily with Deming's 14 points and his red-bead experiment and with a few of the essential statistical tools.

Del Valle, Christina, "TQM: Now, it's a Class Act," *Business Week,* October 31, 1994. Pages 72-73. Shows the application of TQM to George Westinghouse Vocational and Technical High School in Brooklyn, New York. "Westinghouse is one of a small but growing number of schools that are turning to TQM in hopes of achieving educational reform."

George, Stephen. *The Baldrige Quality System: The Do-It—Yourself Way to Transform Your Business.* John Wiley & Sons, 1992. A comprehensive treatment of the Baldrige System and Categories and a guide to self-assessment using the Baldrige criteria. Part Four offers a plan for applying for the prestigious award.

Harrar, George, "Baldrige Notwithstanding," *Forbes ASAP,* February 28, 1994. Pages 44-46, 48, 57. AT&T's Universal Card Services Division used its receipt of a Malcolm Baldrige Award as a stimulus to an even more radical and intensive reinvention of itself. It's agreed upon values are a litany of TQM: "mutual respect, teamwork, continuous improvement, sense of urgency, and customer delight." Page 57.

Hart, Christopher W.L., "The Power of Internal Guarantees," *Harvard Business Review*, January-February 1995. Pages 64-73. Hart, a former Baldrige examiner and trainer and author of several important articles on TQM concentrates on one small practical approach to improve quality which is applicable to almost any type and size organization.

Hart, Christopher W. L. and Leonard Schlesinger, "Total Quality Management and the Human Resource Professional: Applying the Baldrige Framework to Human Resources," *Human Resources Management,* Winter 1991. Pages 433-454. An important article not only for Human Resource professionals but for anyone wanting better understanding of TQM's value and especially the positive effects of knowledge and application of the Baldrige Award criteria.

The Hospice of the Florida Suncoast, "Concern for Quality: the Soul of Spiritual Care," [publication information not available] An outline of a presentation given at the First National Conference Series on spiritual/Bereavement/Psycho-Social Aspects of Hospice Care presented by National Hospice Organizations and the Council of Hospice Professionals. San Francisco, California, August 17-23, 1995. #

d. *"Steinway & Sons"*, MB580, City University of Seattle, December 1999/

For personal reasons I enjoyed writing, an analysis of Steinway & Sons. When Marilyn and I, with our four children, moved into our dream house on Romany Road in Lexington we were fortunate to have the gracious gift of interior decorating by Lexington's premier interior designer, Rebecca Van Meter who was Marilyn's personal friend and had audited some courses with me at Transylvania. Both Marilyn and John, our son, were accomplished pianists. We had opportunity to purchase a completely rebuilt Steinway baby grand piano. The local piano technician had taken a Steinway with a 1918 sound board and completely restrung the strings, putting in new felt pads as appropriate. It was a beautiful piece of furniture but even more was a rare and remarkable piano to play and listen to. This personal involvement with Steinway & Sons made the writing of the paper for the course an extraordinary pleasure. I have edited the paper leaving out the financial data and analysis, the bibliography, and other parts not necessary for presenting the essence of the paper.

Introduction

We are proud to lead a company with a heritage like Steinway's. But it's not all history. We have a bright future ahead of us. By combining our strategies for growth with the deep-rooted traditions that have made Steinway great, we will strengthened our position as a market leader well into the 21st century.

(1998 Annual Report, Page 7)

The Letter to Shareholders in the 1998 Annual Report of Steinway Musical Instruments, Inc., concludes with this visionary statement signed by Kyle R. Kirkland, Chairman of the Board and Dana D. Messina, President and Chief Executive Officer. The Company is almost 150 years old; the primary management officers are both in their mid-thirties, the youngest members of the Board of Directors. Steinway has a rich past, an enviable present, and a promising future under such vigorously capable leaders.

This case analysis of Steinway & Sons looks at the Steinway mystique before examining the history of the venerable firm. It then considers the case as presented in the textbook by Charles Hill and Garth Jones. This is followed by consideration of developments since the case was written. Following the guidelines of the Course Syllabus, the analysis focuses on the question, or issue, of whether Steinway should have a greater presence in China, and if so, what that presence should be. A brief conclusion completes the study.

The Steinway Mystique

There is no greater name in classical musical instruments than Steinway, with the possible exception of Stradivarius for violins. At least, there is no name as readily recognized as the standard of excellence in its field. Steinway & Sons is as universally acclaimed in the arts as Mercedes Benz in the automotive field. Over 900 of the world's greatest musical artists endorse by their personal ownership and concert use, without remuneration from the Company, the Steinway grand piano. In fact, it is even maintained, "Today more than 90% of all classical music concerts featuring a piano are performed on a Steinway concert grand piano." (Hill and Jones, C182)

Owning a Steinway is a symbol of status and prestige besides being a sound investment. Its nearest competitors, Yamaha and Baldwin, may be able to provide full rich and powerful tones and often at only half the price, but they do not have the immediate attribution of highest quality and general acceptance as the best.

Almost from the beginning, Steinway was the top of the class. When Henry E. Steinway and his sons opened their factory in New York and produced piano number 483, the first to be labeled a Steinway & Sons, they were the pace setters in a growing industry. Henry had made 482 pianos in his native Germany and then in his newly adopted home, America. Number 483 was sold in 1853 for $500 to a New York family and is now on display at the Metropolitan Museum of Art. (www.gungl.com) Through extraordinary innovation, insistant devotion to quality, and adroit marketing, Steinway found its niche as a cultural icon.

Steinway has been so well known and highly respected that it has been treated favorably in countless articles and several full-length books. The articles have appeared not only in respected business journals, but in such high profile media as the *Smithsonian* and *The New York Times.* Among the books are Miles Chapin and Rodica Prato's, *88 Keys – the Making of a Steinway Piano* (1997), Susan Goldberg's, *Steinway from Glory to Controversy* (1996) and *The House of Steinway* (1988), Richard K. Lieberman's, *Steinway and Sons* (1995), D.W. Fostle's, *The Steinway Saga* (1995), and R.V. Ratcliffe's. *Steinway and Sons* (1989). Steinway has been the subject of case studies in numerous graduate schools of business including those at Harvard, Vanderbilt, and the University of Washington.

There is no disputing the claim that Steinway & Sons builds the finest pianos in the world. This is due in part to the almost legendary acknowledgement of the belief that, "Steinway and Sons pianos are built to a single exacting standard: build each instrument to be the finest ever created and then make the next one even better if possible."

(www.Steinway.com). The three guiding principles: 1) building to an exacting standard, (2) allowing no compromise in quality, and (3) striving to continuously improve have been the Company's most consistently sustained strategic commitment.

Steinway Musical Instruments, Inc. of which Steinway & Sons is a wholly owned subsidiary presents itself tastefully and modestly in its 1998 Annual Report which artfully combines graphics and text to convey a positive, coordinated, and convincing message and image. The cover picture is of a concert orchestra on the stage of Steinway Hall in 1890. Steinway Hall was America's leading concert hall before the opening of Carnegie Hall in 1891. A highlight of the firm's activity in 1998 was repurchase of the Hall by Steinway Musical Instruments, Inc... It had been sold in 1971; the bottom two floors were then leased as a showroom and sales office. This repurchase is not just a symbolic gesture; it becomes once more a landmark of the cultural prominence of Steinway in the arts in America and around the world. It is a reminder that the firm has continued not only to build the finest pianos in the world but has been a leader in the cultural and artistic education of Americans.

Steinway History

Steinway's history is so well known from having been told so often and so well that it is only necessary to point to some of the more salient aspects.

After immigrating to America from Germany, Henrich E. Steinweg Americanized his name to Henry E. Steinway and continued his craft. In a short time, he and his equally talented sons began crafting highest quality pianos of rare distinction:

> In a remarkably short period of time between March 5, 1853,
> when they went into business, and April 1, 1860, when they
> opened their new factory, the Steinway family had triumphed
> in America. (www.osc.cuny.edu)

From 1855 on every major award and gold medal in their field was theirs. Along with the accolades came recognition that the Steinway family had revolutionized the piano industry. The immediate success which Henry Steinway and his sons enjoyed continued unabated as they kept leading their industry in patents and innovations. Today, Steinway holds over 100 patents relating to the piano. They are recognized as the originators and perfecters of the manufacturing process which was to be adopted throughout the piano industry.

A Steinway & Sons piano is an almost perfect blend of science and art, craftsmanship and technology. Highly skilled craftsmen take about a year to build a Steinway grand piano using only the finest available materials in assembling the 12,000 parts, exclusive of the 28,000 screws, needed for the process.

Steinway & Sons is not only the acknowledged leader in the process of piano manufacturing but is also considered the developer of the modern piano through their leadership and innovation.

Innovation has been, however, only one of the two major keys to Steinway's success through the years. The other has been marketing. As April Gasbarre observes, "While technological considerations as well as impeccable craftsmanship formed the core of Steinway's success, promotion also contributed greatly to the company's prosperity." (Page 427)

The fortuitous combination of technological creativity and marketing genius was not accidental. As D.W. Fostle observed it was a deliberate part of Steinway's corporate strategy to build an innovative product which won the treasured prizes, was played by the best performers, was seen as a mark of excellence and achievement, and would consequently bring a premium price. (Noted in Gasbarre, Page 427)

The product's high quality and price may be seen in this succinct mission statement by the firm's founder:

> We provide customers with the highest quality instrument
> and services, consistent with Steinway's reputation for
> excellence, by building the finest piano in the world and
> selling it at a reasonable profit. (Hill and Jones, C177)

Yet, the course of excellence has not always been smooth. In the late 1860s one of the brothers (Theodore) wanted to change the direction of the firm away from this mission statement to gain a greater market share by building instruments of lesser quality for a lower price. He was overruled by his brother William and the insistence on highest possible quality prevailed.

Steinway's choice to dominate the high-end of the market has depended, for success, on a profitable American economy. When recessions and depressions have come Steinway's profits have accordingly declined. The great depression of the 1930s was followed by five war years when pianos were not the firm's products. Those years, for the most part, Steinway operated at a loss. Gasbarre says it clearly, "Steinway only recorded profits in four of the 16 years from 1930 to 1945." (Page 428)

A formidable challenge to Steinway's profitability came in the 1960s when Asian firms such as Yamaha, Kawai, and Young Chang introduced into America pianos of good quality at much lower costs. Their pianos were selling at roughly half the price of a Steinway thereby gaining an increasingly larger share of the domestic market.

In 1972 the Steinway family decided to sell the firm to Columbia Broadcasting System, Musical Instruments Division. CBS retained Henry Z. Steinway as president until his retirement in 1980. However, Steinway did not prosper under CBS: "Steinway was plagued by bureaucratic confusion, changing strategies, and parades of efficiency experts.... Quality control slipped." (Hill and Jones, C178)

After ten unprofitable and frustrating years CBS sold Steinway to John and Robert Birmingham of Boston in 1985 for less than $50 million. In the decade in which they owned Steinway Bruce Stevens became president. He continues today to provide creative and profitable leadership as president of Steinway & Sons. The Birmingham brothers affirmed their commitment to Steinway's traditional values: "Our guiding principle has been to guard and nurture the quality and integrity of the Steinway piano." (Hill and Jones, C178). During this time numerous changes for the better were instituted including modernization, a three year strategic planning process, and in 1991 introduction of a new line of pianos. Boston pianos have from the beginning been manufactured for Steinway by Kawai in Japan and have sold for about $10,000. These were considered by the Company to be entry level pianos for persons aspiring to someday own a Steinway.

In 1995 the Birminghams sold Steinway to the Selmer Company for $100 million, more than double the price they had paid for it ten years before. In August 1996 the new owners made the IPO to raise $60 million.

[The Textbook Case Presentaton follows and is omitted.
The section Steinway Today contains detailed financial
information and analysis but is also omitted as is the
section The Analysis since it is more Germaine to the
course than an example of writing on this topic]

Conclusion

There is only one Steinway & Sons. Its history is fascinating, but its present and future are even more intriguing. Under the leadership of Kyle Kirkland and Dana Messina, Steinway Musical Instruments, Inc. with its two primary subsidiaries Selmer Company and Steinway and Sons, is at the top of its form. It is the world music industry's largest company and by many marks its most successful.

With incomparable brand image and recognition, solid financial condition, exceptionally capable leadership, commitment to quality, sound strategic planning and implementation, reasoned policies for integration through acquisition and expansion, Steinway Musical Instruments, Inc. is in an inviable position to take advantage of opportunities for an increased presence in China.

As the Pacific Rim becomes the economic center of the 21st century Steinway stands ready to be a leader in high-end musical instruments in Asia, both traditional pianos and contemporary electronic audio luxury equipment, including a digital piano. #

e. "Goodyear: the Gault years, 1991-1996," MB580, City University of Seattle, December 1999.

This paper on a brief period in Goodyear's history is illustrative of the power and influence of a particular individual in a multinational company. It starts with didactic questions which set the stage then proceeds to analyze the case as presented in the textbook. Certain sections are omitted since they contain material not essential for illustrating my basic concern of the role of an exceptional executive in leading a company at a given time in its history.

Introduction

What do you do when you come in second in the race for CEO of General Electric and the winner is Jack Welch? If you are Stanley C. Gault, Senior Vice President of General Electric, you go back home to Wooster, Ohio and become head of Rubbermaid, a company your father founded as Wooster Rubber Company when you were a youth.

What do you do when you have performed strategic miracles and brought moribund Rubbermaid back to life and made it a business entity to be reckoned with? At 54 you retire, if you are Stanley C. Gault and in a matter of weeks you accept the challenge of the Goodyear Tire & Rubber Company to pull another rabbit out of the management hat.

What do you do when you have, as Zachary Schiller says, "been a miracle worker at Goodyear Tire & Rubber Company." and have "cut costs, pushed new products, sold off non-tire assets, issued new stock, and slashed the choking debt"? If you are Stanley C. Gault you continue living in Wooster, where you were born and educated and to which you chose to return as a generous and gracious citizen benefactor of the community.

This paper, containing a brief analysis of the Goodyear Tire & Rubber Company during the Gault years, 1991-1996 proceeds by examining the case study as presented in the textbook. It then highlights some of the more significant points in Goodyear's history focusing on three specific aspects – labor, financial, and global involvement. The requisite analysis of the case is then given followed by a concluding section. These elements are treated within the parameters of the Case Study. An Afterword is given calling attention to a few developments since Gault left Goodyear.

The Case: Goodyear – the Gault Years

When Stanley C. Gault accepted the Goodyear challenge, he said to the Board:

I am very pleased to be joining the team at Goodyear,
which is the greatest name in the rubber industry.

It has a superior brand franchise, high-quality products,

state-of-the-art technology and manufacturing facilities,

broad distribution, and very promising new products

scheduled to be introduced later this year. Although

the rubber business is experiencing industry-wide problems,

I am confident that Goodyear shareholders can look forward

to a bright future. As a strong believer in hands-on management

and open communication between corporate managers and

the investment community, I intend to keep our leaders and

shareholders fully informed about the company's progress.

(Hill and Jones C426)

Gault was the first outsider to be elected CEO since 1921, almost three quarters of a century. Most of his predecessors had come up through the ranks. Gault came from the Boardroom. His success at both General Electric and Rubbermaid had made him a well-known and highly respected leader renowned for his indefatigable commitment to whatever he involved himself in and his impeccable integrity, insight, and ability to inspire others.

As Peter Nulty pointed out when Gault was elected to the National Business Hall of Fame while CEO at Goodyear, "Stan Gault has a curriculum vitae as distinguished as anyone in corporate life." (Page 119) When he was chosen one of three CEOs of the Year by the *Financial World* it was said of him and the other two "admirals of industry":

Their achievements go far beyond survival and resurrection,

to global preeminence as exemplars of the American

business ethic of service to customers, work force, community,

shareholders and ultimately to country." (Rappleye)

When Gault became CEO the tire and rubber industry, along with other major industries was changing rapidly. Gault was well aware of that, as he made presciently clear in a remarkable address delivered about a year after his retirement from Goodyear. In that address, "Economic Renaissance Through Education Reform", he spoke eloquently of what had made America great: natural resources, capital, technology, and a skilled and educated work force as he pleaded for educational reform. The

208

speech is laced with appreciative references to Goodyear and uses the tire and rubber industry to illustrate the dramatic changes in business brought about by "the tradition-shattering impact of global competition." As he succinctly stated, "In almost the bat of an eye, Goodyear's prime competitors were no longer the cross-town rivals such as Firestone, Goodrich, and General.... They suddenly were cross-world rivals Michelin, Bridgestone, and Continental."

Another challenge, in addition to globalization and the growing prominence of world-class competition, was the changing domestic tire market and distribution system. Goodyear had marketed its tires through its own distribution system of company owned and franchised stores. But, discount and warehouse club stores such as K Mart, Walmart, and Costco were now marketing tires along with other household products. Sears and other major retailers also were merchandising name brands in addition to their own. Gault believed Goodyear would have to find a way to expand its distribution system to take advantage of this drastic change in marketing.

Still another challenge was the financial state of Goodyear. In 1986 Sir James Goldsmith had led a hostile takeover charge which the Company repelled at great cost. The long-term debt incurred in repelling that charge in 1986-87 was $3.7 billion. Diversification outside the rubber industry had not proven profitable and morale had suffered. Goodyear was in need of reducing its 80% dependency on original equipment tire sales. Research and development had been scaled back and jobs had been reduced by 6,786. Restructuring had brought about consolidation of the business into two major divisions: (1) tire, and (2) non-tire products.

In characteristic fashion, Stanley Gault was convinced that piecemeal measures could not bring about the changes necessary for success. The turnaround of Goodyear would, as he remarked in the address noted above, require "a return to basics". This meant putting into practice on a corporate scale the personal values so dear to Stan Gault – – trust, openness, dedication, hard work, honesty, integrity, and putting the company's and others welfare above one's personal gain. His basic business concepts included a clearly articulated mission statement, an awareness of environmental and contextual factors, cognizance of the strengths and weaknesses of Goodyear's major competitors, devotion to long-term objectives and strategies to achieve them, sufficient resources to accomplish both those present and future objectives, and a realistic contingency plan to deal with the exigencies of both business and the industry. (Hill and Jones table 1, C429)

Gault's principles were the driving force behind his dynamic leadership:

> These are a simple set of business principles that I have honored throughout my career....They are low-cost, high-quality, and customer satisfaction. They are new product development, aggressive merchandising and new customer and new business development. Undeniably, they are the prudent management of assets entrusted to us; good communications and sound human relationships with all associates; and a commitment to a total quality culture which by itself will be the single most important force for success in the 1990s and beyond. (Hill and Jones C 429)

These principles had brought him widespread recognition and numerous awards in the business world and the wider human community and he was confident they would make a difference for the better at Goodyear.

For any possible critic who might see these as unsubstantial or Idealistic, Gault translated them into the language of management as expressed in his twelve objectives for the 1990s:

> 1. Achieving significant debt reduction
> 2. Increasing the company's financial performance
> 3. Holding a quality leadership position
> 4. Striving to be a low-cost producer
> 5. Providing superior satisfaction in meeting customer's expectation
> 6. Increasing market share
> 7. Introducing new, exciting customer-oriented products

8. Strengthening merchandising, advertising, and distribution programs

9. Enhancing shareholder value

10. Expanding the company's global presence

11 Being a socially responsible corporation

12 Maximizing the company's human resource capability

(Hill and Jones, table 3, C431)

Gault's values, principles, and objectives coalesced into a rich lore of "teachable moments" in which his actions were embodied. Incidents of his exemplifying trust, energy, enthusiasm, dedication, company and community above self, clear expectations of excellence, and treating others as associates, not as employees or hired hands became legendary, the very stuff out of which corporate cultures are made. Gault closed the above mentioned address with a story that perfectly expressed his own beliefs as he guided Goodyear as its CEO:

> Earlier in my career with General Electric. I was invited
> into the office of the legendary retailer, J.C. Penney.
> I was running the Hotpoint Division of General Electric
> and we produced major appliances for Penneys.
> Mr. Penney had known and remembered my father,
> who almost 50 years earlier had sold him toy balloons.
> He told me he was anxious to meet Clyde Gault's son.
> On the day of my visit, he was celebrating his
> 90th birthday. Obviously he was no longer the vigorous
> young man of his youth. But the spirit of that young man
> rang true in his voice. He enjoyed sharing some of his
> experiences with me and concluded by saying, "Young man,
> at my age, my eyesight may be failing, but my vision
> continues to improve."

("Economic Renaissance Trough Education Reform")

Stanley Gault's own vision for Goodyear could not have been sharper. He intended to bring about greater productivity through strategic partnerships and alliances, restructuring the business so that it had one focus ("We are a tire company), three primary areas (tires, general products, and oil transportation), and eight strategic business units (North American Tire, Goodyear Europe, Goodyear Latin America, Goodyear Asia, Engineered Products, Chemicals, Celeron, and Kelly Springfield).

Goodyear had been involved in automobile racing in a big way almost from its beginning and though this was not a SBU it was a major player. The workforce was trimmed from 108,000 in 1991 to 85,000 in 1995. Billions of dollars of non-core assets were sold and millions of dollars were spent in capital expenditures expanding and modernizing Goodyear's facilities worldwide. An impressive list of debt reduction measures may be seen in table 5 C433 of the textbook. The debt, which in 1990 had been $3.7 billion was by 1992 down to $1.9 billion. A year later another one half billion had been taken away lowering it to $1.4 billion. A concise summary of the state of financial affairs may be seen in what follows:

> In a slack economy, 1991 Goodyear sales were $10.9 billion,
> slightly below its sales record of 11.3 billion the prior year.
> Earnings per share for 1991 were $1.61 compared with
> $.66 during 1990. Operating margin was 7.2 percent in 1991
> compared, with 5.4 percent in 1990. The debt-to-debt-plus-equity
> ratio dropped significantly to 49.2 percent at year end from 63.3
> percent in 1990. Improved results reflected the benefits of
> personnel reductions, cost reduction programs, productivity
> improvements, price increases, and lower material costs.
>
> (Hill and Jones C434)

By 1993 Goodyear was outpacing the industry and had validated its commitments to greater profitability, debt reduction, industry leadership, growth, serving customer needs, and greater performance. Gault expressed these gains in goals for 1994 he called Performance Plans Plus (PPP):

> 1. Sales increase of between 4.5 and 5 percent per year
> ("twice the industry growth rate")
> 2. Operating margin to reach 12 percent from 6 percent in 1990.

212

3. Increase capital expenditures to between $500 and $700 million annually.

4. Lower sales, administrative, and general expenses to below 15 percent of sales from over 18 percent.

5. Bring debt-to-debt-plus-equity ratio down to 25 to 30 percent from 63 percent in 1991

6. Pay out 20 to 25 percent dividends on prior year earnings.   (Hill and Jones, table 6, C435)

In 1994 in Gault's "quest to be the best tire and rubber Company in the world" Goodyear broke every performance record in its history (Hill and Jones C435)

Gault turned his attention as vigorously to marketing as he had to debt reduction. He was convinced that the "success formula" which had served him so well throughout his career was equally applicable here: "create value for shareholders by generating consistent earnings growth and delivering high value-added products to the customer." (Hill and Jones C439). To render value to the customer two things were necessary – – the customer's needs must be satisfied and products must be available where the customer will buy them. Distribution was extended beyond company-owned and franchised stores into mass-market channels and a new type company store (Just Tires) was opened in order to get the product to the customer. Judicious use continued to be made of the seemingly ubiquitous Goodyear blimp extolling, at Gault's direction Goodyear's position as "#1 tires". Goodyear's marketing, including its advertising, led to the attribution, "Goodyear owns one of the best managed and most valuable brand names in the world" (Hill and Jones C443)

In his own indirect way Gault had insisted Goodyear's Research and Development abandon its conservative procedure and introduce new and profitable products in a timely fashion. Aquatred quickly became Goodyear's most award-winning product. Its run flat or extended mobility tires also garnered attention and sales. Multifunctional teams were formed not simply to meet the customer's needs but to anticipate them. This new model for business was part of Goodyear's commitment to total quality culture which would live up to Gault's expectation – "I expect our products to be the best in the industry" (Hill and Jones C445) Under Gault there was a vibrant emphasis on new product development imbued with quality. The Goodyear Quality Principles and Continuous Quality Improvement Program may be seen in tables 20 and 21 on C446 in the textbook.

During the Gault years Goodyear kept moving more and more toward an ever greater global presence with Latin America and Asia playing increasing roles. There were new trade agreements in Latin America, joint ventures in China and India, and further acquisitions in Europe.

As the Gault years were coming to an end with the completion of his five-year plan and leadership commitment, the Board of Directors elected Samir F. Gibara as Gault's successor. For the first time the four offices of president, chairman, CEO, and COO were given to one person. Formally, they had been divided between two persons.

Gault said of his successor:

Sam brings to the chairman's office more than 30 years of
international business experience in management, finance,
strategic planning, marketing and operations. His background
in virtually all areas of global operations already has been
an invaluable asset in Goodyear's drive to increase its
international presence in the world's long-term,
high-growth regions.   (Gamboa)

Samir G. "Sam" Gibara had been president and chief operating officer since 1995. Before that he had been executive vice president, vice president of strategic planning and business development, acting vice president of finance and served in numerous high level management positions all over the world for Goodyear. He holds a bachelor's degree in business administration from the University of Cairo, Egypt being his native country, and a master's degree in international business and finance from Harvard University. He appeared to be a worthy successor to the inimitable Stanley C. Gault who by all indications had achieved his clearly stated goals and restored Goodyear to a position of competitive

214

advantage. As Hill and Jones concluded: "What altered its [Goodyear's] fortunes was a combination of a new CEO, who restored the company's competitive advantage and a change in the nature of competition within the industry." (242)   #

f. *Weyerhaeuser Company: a strategic management research project.* MB 580: City University of Seattle, February 5, 2000.

This paper, on the Weyerhaeuser Company, is the longest I Wrote., It was almost 100 pages, 99 to be exact. It would have been the equivalent of a master's thesis in many graduate schools. This was the capstone project for my MBA. I have edited it including here only the abstract, table of contents,   introduction, overview, and conclusion.

Table of Contents:

Abstract	i
Preface	ii
Introduction	1
Overview	2
History of Weyerhaeuser Company	5
Weyerhaeuser's corporate culture	23
Corporate structure	32
Company mission, strategy, policies, and Objectives	42
Marketing by Weyerhaeuser	50
Corporate finance	56
Weyerhaeuser in the forest products industry	64
Weyerhaeuser's future	76
Conclusion: strengths, weaknesses, and strategic recommendations	80

Appendices:

I. Presidents, Chairmen of the Board, and General Managers of Weyerhaeuser Timber Company and Weyerhaeuser Company — 86
II. Senior Management Team, 1999 — 87
III. Subsidiaries of Weyerhaeuser Company — 88
IV. Brief historical time-table — 90
V. Some business rankings for Weyerhaeuser

Company   91
       Annotated bibliography   94
                    Abstract:

Weyerhaeuser's strategic vision is to be the world's best forest products company. That goal is put into perspective in an overview before examining the company's history from its beginnings in 1900 to its centennial celebration on January 18, 2000. The heart of the company and the key to its successful longevity and productivity is its sense of values embodied in its corporate culture. The company's structure, mission, strategy, financial situation, marketing approach, and international scope are all considered. Weyerhaeuser's prominent place in the wood products and paper and allied products industries is treated before facing Weyerhaeuser's future. In conclusion the company's strengths and weaknesses are noted in order to arrive at strategic recommendations. The paper provides Appendices on Corporate Leaders, Senior Management Team, Subsidiaries, Historical Milestones, and Business Rankings. An Annotated Bibliography concludes the research project.

                  Introduction:

Weyerhaeuser Company celebrated its first century on January 18, 2000. Some of the richness of that century of continuous operating success is explored in this paper. Weyerhaeuser began with an impeccable reputation for integrity which it has maintained as its strategic polar star up to the present. Its situation as a leader in the forest products industry and as a well-integrated firm using timber to its fullest is marked by technological and marketing innovations that match its social responsibility.

Weyerhaeuser Company rapidly moved beyond its origin in the Pacific Northwest to become a nationally recognized symbol of quality in its industry. As Ralph Hidy, Frank Hill, and Allan Nevins observed, "The Weyerhaeuser Company has become almost a national symbol of quality products and of long-range planning in the forest products industry." (*Timber and Men*, 575). As it begins its second century, Weyerhaeuser's operations move further and further beyond the place of its beginnings into the global marketplace.

Weyerhaeuser Company is the world's largest private owner of timber and the world's largest pulp and paper company, owning 5.1 million acres of forestland in the United States and managing 27 million acres under long-term agreement in Canada. Its forests are strategically managed for sustained yield in perpetuity. Manufacturing plants are located conveniently near the company's forestlands. Though Weyerhaeuser has expanded through the years to integrate its business operations and at times even diversified into non-core businesses, it has been from the start, what it continues to be today, a firm committed to leadership in the forest products industry.

This paper begins with an overview of the company before exploring Weyerhaeuser's rich history. Since values are unabashedly extolled and adhered to by Weyerhaeuser Company it is important to next consider Weyerhaeuser's corporate culture. Corporate structure and leadership then provide a basis for examining the company's mission, strategy, policies, and objectives. Weyerhaeuser's financial situation plays a vital role in the firm's strategic management and is looked at from a variety of sources. Market strategy, the area where innovation has been most evident is then dealt with because of its contributions to the company's success. As Weyerhaeuser moves into its second century it reaffirms its commitment to international involvement and accepts responsibility as a leader in the wood products and paper and allied products industries. In conclusion, the company's strengths and weaknesses are noted before strategic management recommendations are offered.

Overview:

By their own account, Weyerhaeuser's primary businesses include: Growing and harvesting trees, the manufacture, distribution and sale of wood products including logs, wood chips and building products, the manufacture, distribution and sale of pulp, paper and packaging products as well as paper recycling, real estate construction and development (*Weyerhaeuser in Action*)

A number of factors should be balanced in treating the Weyerhaeuser Company. First, the name Weyerhaeuser is often used as if

217

it were applicable to a single, simple, unified business entity. However, Weyerhaeuser stands for a remarkable array of properties and in recent times an equally remarkable range of undertakings..... They possess separate boards of directors, have separate managements and separate planning, and exercise complete independence in establishing policy and conducting operations. *(Timber and Men, 553)*

Second is the fact of the intricacies of family involvements in these related but non-unified businesses. Weyerhaeuser is not the only name that is projected forward through the century. Many of the original investor families, such as the Ingrams, Nortons, and Mussers, have also continued their involvement through several generations. Frederick W. Weyerhaeuser the founder was first involved in a partnership with his wife's sister's husband, F.C.A Denkmann. His wife's maiden name was Bloedel, a name to become famous in both the United States and Canada in the forest products industry and associated with the recent major merger on November 1, 1999 of Weyerhaeuser and MacMillan Bloedel.

There has been a steady stream of sons, daughters, sons-in-law, grandsons and granddaughters, and now great grandsons and great granddaughters and their spouses who have continued the heritage of the founding fathers.

Members of the Weyerhaeuser family were heavily involved in the timber and forest products industry well before 1900 and the incorporation of Weyerhaeuser Timber Company. Frederick was himself involved in over 50 companies and subsidiaries. *(Tradition through the Trees, 26)* Weyerhaeuser Timber Company, itself, held shares in twenty-seven corporations in 1914. *(Timber and Men, 588)*

The forest products industry has been fertile ground for disparate, rather than unified, operations and companies. As Hidy, Hill, and Nevins point out, "The wonder is that so large an institution as the Weyerhaeuser Company finally developed and survived. *(Timber and Men, 554)*

A third factor is the incredible survival and success of Weyerhaeuser because of the extremely capable corporate executives it has been fortunate enough to have had throughout its history. Men such as the Weyerhaeusers George S. Long, and Charles Ingram would have been standouts in any industry.

Robert Ficken reflected, "More than anything else, Weyerhaeuser hoped to pass on a thriving business to his four sons." (92) Those sons not only received an incredible heritage from their father but received it as their responsibility as leaders to pass on to their descendants and their descendants' descendants after enriching it by their own contributions.

Several descriptions of Weyerhaeuser provide an overview of the business/businesses. Perhaps, the most succinct is the following from *Disclosure Corporate Snapshots:*

Acquires, owns and leases private commercial forestland and sawmills;

Manufactures, distributes and sells forest products including pulp, paper and paperboard products, container and packaging products, corrugated packaging, coated and uncoated fine papers, industrial and agricultural packaging and bleached paperboard used for production of liquid containers;

Produces and sells softwood   lumber, plywood and veneer, hardwood lumber and plywood, doors, logs, chips, timber and building materials;

Manufactures newsprint;

Operates extensive wastepaper collection system;

Develops real estate properties including single-family housing, residential lots and master-planned communities and formerly provided mortgage related services.

As it begins its second century, Weyerhaeuser is:

The world's largest owner of softwood timber and the world's largest producer of market pulp and softwood lumber.

One of the largest producers of containerboard packaging and fine paper.

The world's largest producer and distributor of engineered wood products.

Among the world's largest producers of hardwood lumber.

A company that serves customers in more than 60 countries. *(Weyerhaeuser in Action)*

[The body of the paper containing crucial substantive, financial, and analytical material indicated in the Table of Contents is omitted due to length]

Conclusion:

Weyerhaeuser is well on its way to fulfilling its vision of being the world's best forest products company as it begins its second century. Joni Sensel quotes Bruce Zobel, an international forestry consultant who said based on his experience with dozens of forest products companies around the world, "Weyerhaeuser is clearly the best, most innovative, and progressive of the group. Every where I work, Weyerhaeuser is looked upon as the world leader in forestry." *(Traditions through the Trees, 190)*

In its first century it has demonstrated an impressive array of strengths and a remarkably small number of weaknesses. Among its greatest strengths are:

A basic strategy of long-term growth and profitability seen first and continuing through strategic purchase of timberlands at low-cost.

Longevity – sustained performance for 100 years in an industry where survival over the long haul is a rarity.

Development and convincing use of sustained high yield forestry not only for its own benefit but for the benefit of its industry and society as a whole. It is worth noting that Steve Anderson, President of the Forest Historical Society, considers that sustained yield forestry may have been the company's single greatest contribution to society. *(Traditions through the Trees, 124)*

Innovativeness in finding ways to use 100% of its raw resource, timber: making effective use of research and development for itself and for the industry as a whole.

Vertical integration of its business which has contributed to fullest use of resources.

Commitment to being an ethical business founded on recognized, actualized values.

Stewardship of resources including the environment through significant contributions to nature conservation.

Prudent use of the financial resources entrusted to it by its shareholders.

Wise use of capital expenditures and long-term debt in keeping its facilities modernized and improving efficiency and effectiveness.

Steady, reliable dividend growth through most of its history.

A Conservative financial strategy that values long-term growth over short-term profitability.

Dedication to eliminating waste as far as possible including ever greater productive use of recycling.

The extreme good fortune of having had exceptionally capable persons as leaders and managers throughout its long history.

A stellar reputation dating back to its founder and continuing unbroken up to the present, resulting in extraordinary brand equity for the company.

It choice to be the proactive leader in the industry rather than a reactive follower.

Ability to flexibly implement its strategy by responding to the contemporary situation. When construction of mills was the most appropriate way that was the path chosen. When diversification appeared to be the way to guard against the cyclical dangers of the economy which negatively impacted the industry, this was tried. Today growth through acquisition of businesses which meet the criteria of the company's core business is the order of the day. Joint ventures and partnerships are providing greater opportunities in the global forest products arena.

Ability to refocus, reengineer, reorganize, restructure in a humane way.

A corporate culture which values human dignity, respect for persons, and partnerships.

Use of technology in a timely and productive fashion. For example, Weyerhaeuser was the industry leader in the use of trucks, tractors, power saws,,etc. in logging. It was also the leader in its industry of creative applications of computer technology. Its realization of the cruciality of technological awareness is accentuated by the fact that its involvement in this area is headed by George Weyerhaeuser, Jr. as Senior Vice President, Technology who said recently: "How our society gets its materials is going to change, and we want to be part of it." (*The Sun,* January 18, 2000, B4). He noted that the impact of electronic technology on business is not yet known, particularly regarding the use of paper and paper products.

Program of giving back to the communities in which it lives and works funds through the Weyerhaeuser Foundation whereby life is enriched.

Continual recognition of the importance of safety in all its operations.

Acceptance of the challenge of cultural diversity by making it a strategic objective.

A practical Roadmap to Success with a leader committed to its fullest implementation which should result in the goal of a greater than 19% Return on Net Assets for the company.

Creative use of advertising to enhance the value of the company and the industry in the public eye.

Awareness of the need to take the lead in global orientation of the forest products industry.

A few weaknesses may also be noted:

Slowness of the decision-making process in a world of phenomenally rapid change.

A sometimes too casual or informal way of doing business long after high mobility and transiency of the population necessitated impersonal formal structures and procedures to complement the personal dimension so vital to Weyerhaeuser.

Danger of becoming in-grown because of the close and continuing ties of the families of the original investors.

Insecurity caused by restructuring, though Weyerhaeuser has done better than most large corporations in working with persons and communities directly negatively impacted by their actions.

It is obvious that Weyerhaeuser is fully aware of the value of strategic planning and practice. It is equally obvious that the company is cognizant and justifiably proud of its great number of strengths even as it works to correct its small number of weaknesses. Recommendations for such a firm as this are extremely difficult. Nevertheless, a few recommendations follow:

Keep focused on the core competencies which have in the past and will in the future contribute to Weyerhaeuser's competitive advantage.

Continue efforts already underway to improve efficiency through simplifying and consolidating where this is the appropriate course to pursue.

Intensify dedication to quality – a value which has been Weyerhaeuser's hallmark throughout its first century – by critical appraisal and use of total quality management.

Move boldly forward in innovation and technological advance consistent with the company's strategic objectives.

Make sure the programs it has instituted for customer responsiveness are taken seriously throughout the organization so as to bring about improvements in anticipating customer needs with products they want, when they want them, at a price they are willing to pay.

Expand partnerships, joint ventures, and strategic alliances to play an ever larger role in the global forest products industry's contributions to the growth of the world's economy.

Settle as quickly, and as judiciously as possible the law suits that have been pending for almost twenty years regarding the alleged defectiveness of hardboard siding manufactured by the company.

Continue to advance conservation of the environment both on its own and in collaboration and dialogue with others committed to the same cause.

Separate the offices of President and CEO from that of the Chairman of the Board. The Board should have a degree of autonomy to act fairly and responsibly in the long-term interest of the firm should there ever be a conflict with the company's operating leader. It is difficult to exercise this function effectively if the chair of that body charged with advising and instructing senior leadership is the one who is being advised and instructed. This is a structural recommendation having nothing to do with personality or confidence in the person chosen by the Board to lead the company in fulfilling its vision, strategic goals, and objectives.

Weyerhaeuser is a remarkable firm. There is every reason to believe from what has been presented in this paper that "the future is growing" is more than a slogan or tagline. It is a way of life reflecting Weyerhaeuser's exciting past. But, even more important it is the key to projecting the company forward into the future as one of America's most admired companies in any industry. #

4. Book Reviews

I have enjoyed writing book reviews though I have written far fewer than I would like to have written. Most of those written while I was a full time college professor were for books on some aspect of religion. Those written since my retirement have a broader scope. I have selected some of those which illustrate the diversity of my interests and concerns. They appear in chronological order.

a. *What Christians Believe* by Georgia Harkness. Abingdon Press, 1965. 72 pages. *The Christian*, February 2, 1966.

This is a splendid little book (only 72 pages). The author has succeeded in showing that "theology is not for the experts only; it is for everybody." The language is clear and simple with no excess verbal baggage. Attention is focused on some of the more important Christian beliefs: God, the Bible, Jesus Christ, the Holy Spirit, the Church, and the Christian life. The skill of a great teacher and the knowledge of a competent scholar are happily blended in presenting insights and information about beliefs to sustain action. It deserves wide use. #

b. *The Church in the Racially Changing Community*, by R.L. Wilson and J.H. Davis. Abingdon Press, 1966. 159 pages. *The Christian, 1967*

It is rare to find a book dealing with so crucial a concern which is not only honest, forthright, and sound but at the same time deliberately practical. Any group of persons wanting to understand the options of the white church in a neighborhood undergoing racial change would do well to read and discuss this small book. It is based on studies of more than 60 churches in 22 cities, but at no point is it reduced to a statistical resume.

The authors have succeeded in keeping us aware that these churches are composed of people who lead many roles in their lives including home-owner, businessman, parent, and church member. A basic belief of the book is clear: "While the Gospel is not determined by the social and cultural context, its presentation is done within such a framework." (p. 139). When this framework is a racially changing community a church has three options: 1) sell and relocate, 2) remain and isolate, or 3) minister to whoever lives in the community. Each of these options is examined with fairness and discussed in terms of positive and negative factors in its acceptance. Some startling conclusions about who effects change and how this occurs are put forth. Here is analysis without preachment, help without condescension, and hope for a sense of mission in being the church in the world. It should be a must for ministers, board chairmen, and others concerned with facing contemporary issues in the church squarely and wisely. #

c. *Strangers and Exiles: a History of Religious Refugees,* by Frederick A. Norwood. Abingdon Press, 1969. Vol 1, 496 pages; Vol 2, 527 pages. *Growth and Change,* January 1971. Pages 48-49.

Why should a review of a history of religious refugees appear in a journal of regional development? A number of reasons might be given such as religion is an indispensable factor in social change; religion is a cultural phenomenon affecting the economic and political views and practices of its adherents; or religion is the concrete manifestation of a person's ultimate dedication, loyalty, or concern and either supports or conflicts with social involvement. Also, because refugees are wandering, uprooted, driven people who pose problems – economic, political, sociological, psychological, and religious – they become prime factors in growth and change, sometimes stimulating, sometimes retarding.

None of these reasons fit the first two chapters of *Strangers and Exiles*. Rather than emphasizing the condition of the Israelites as refugees, Chapter 1 primarily discussed Norwood's orthodox presupposition that "all refugees live in 'Nod, the land of wandering because they are human and therefore sinners." The second chapter, instead of opening up the situation of refugees for conscience' sake during the formation of the New Testament, labored the use of a few selected scriptural passages as rationale for the church's defense of and against persecution for a thousand years. Norwood reiterated the well-known fact that the persecuted Christians became avid persecutors of heretics, schismatics, and other disaffected members. Little was said, however, of the equally well-known condition of legalistically established western Christendom persecuting the outsider.

Perhaps the question is better answered by examining the organization of this lengthy and tedious work. Part 1 covers roughly 1500 B.C. to about A.D. 1500. Time is capsulated in Part 2 (1517-1685) as Norwood follows the medieval penchant for persecution and religious intolerance in its Protestant as well as its Roman Catholic expression. The focus narrows in Part 3 (1685-1914) where concentration is given to Jews, Huguenots, and Mennonites, including a case study of the "Alexanderwohl Mennonite Migration," with lesser attention to such matters as refugee movements into the New World. Almost as if it were a separate work, Part 4 deals with the twentieth century "homelsss man," reflective of the modern blurring of the distinction between sacred and secular. Statistics become preponderant as our war-torn and mobile world is the arena not only for extraordinary numbers or religious refugees but for unprecedented agencies for relief and resettlement.

In spite of Norwood's apparently deliberate attempt to find a style of writing to relieve the tedium, the clichés, slang, and colloquialisms are only distractions. The work is from first to last what is acknowledged in the beginning – the resuscitated and amplified publishing of a doctoral dissertation. In fact much of the material has appeared elsewhere.

While a scholar like Karl Barth or F.C. Copelston may leave large blocks of material in the original language complimenting the reader as well as enhancing his own reputation for erudition, Norwood's persistent utilization not only of French, German, and Latin but even of a little Greek and some Dutch is pseudo-scholarly. Such matters cause us to ask for whom the book was written. If for the specialist in the problem of religious refugees then the exhaustive bibliography, annotated footnotes, and full index will prove of immense worth, and the extensive use of non-English references will be no major detraction. This archival resource provides data in geographic redistribution and causes for movement as well as plans, preparation, and reaction by the refugees and those who set them to flight as well as those who receive them. However, if one looks for vibrancy in making real the fears, frustrations, hopes, dreams, and real life experiences of refugees as suffering human being, he will have to look elsewhere.

By the time the reader reaches the end, if he perseveres, at least one lesson is clear: sophistication and technological advancement have not solved some of the most acute human problems, one of which is the religious refugee. Norwood sets this problem in a new context near the conclusion: "Unless some factors of control are forthcoming, the increasingly volatile migratory movements and pressures of population will grow until there is no room left for refugees anywhere."#

d. *The Literature of Theology: a Guide for Students and Pastors*, by John A. Bollier. Westminster, 1979. 208 pages. *The Military Chaplain*, 1980

This work is about as exciting as a motorcycle parts catalog. But, then if you are either a motorcycle aficionado or mechanic such a catalog is indispensable.

The work was written first for the author's students in bibliographic instruction at Yale Divinity School. It is an excellent and valued guide for such a purpose. To someone new to and unfamiliar with the fields or perplexed by theological libraries it offers a basic starting point in research. To pastors, including chaplains, who feel at ease with their basic knowledge of standard reference works in religion it is of less import.

A more useful guide in a wider context is Robert Rogers's *The Humanities: A Selective Guide to Information Sources*, Libraries Unlimited, 1974. 400 pages, which has a creditable section on religion. As well as the religion section there are others on philosophy, visual arts, performing arts, and language and literature. Each section has three sub-sections: trends, accessing information, and principle information sources. Rogers's style is more engaging and less pedantic than Bollier's.

Bollier, Acting Divinity Librarian at Yale, has held to his intent to include only "reference tools such as bibliographies, encyclopedias, dictionaries, indexes, abstracts, handbooks, guides, manuals, catalogs, and commentaries." Monographic works are not referenced. This largely accounts for the unevenness of the sections. The bulk of material deals with resources in biblical studies due to the abundance of such material. Theological literature per se is treated in only five pages. A paucity of materials in practical theology including such staples as homiletics and counseling is comparably thin.

With few exceptions the 540 works annotated are in English though a few essential sources in German and French are included. The annotations are descriptive and obvious with little evaluative or comparative comment.

The title itself poses a quandary. As a theologian I came to the book expecting a review of basic resources and assistance in dealing with the diversity of theological literature of recent years. Theological, however, is used here in its wider context to refer to the literature of the curriculum of theological seminaries. There is no simple solution to clarity on this matter. Perhaps, however, a transposition would be appropriate and less misleading: "A Guide to Professional Literature for Theological Students and Pastors."

One positive contribution of Bollier's work for me was a look at my own library with the realization that were I just beginning my acquisitions more of the investment would be in reference works. While they are more expensive, if well chosen, they are more useful for a longer period of time than the quickly dated literature we read in an attempt to keep current. Most of these latter works could be borrowed from theological libraries or purchased only after consulting reliable reviews such as those in *Religious Studies Review*.

Some reference works may be read for the fun of it as well as the knowledge contained therein. This is not one of them. It is a bibliographic guide and as such offers a handy, reliable reference guide for research for theological students and scholarly oriented pastors. Most military chaplains will find the work of little relevance unless they are engaged in research and have convenient access to a seminary or major university library.

e. A single review of three books in the *Journal of the Society of Christian Ethics,* vol. 30, no. 2, Fall/Winter 2010. Pages 199-202. *Being Consumed: Economics and Christian Desire,* by William T. Cavanaugh. William B. Eerdmans, 2008, 103 pages. *Religious Perspectives on Business Ethics: an Anthology,* by Thomas O'Brien and Scott Paeth, editors. With a Foreword by Patricia Werhane. Rowman & Littlefield, 2007. 359 pages. *Just Business Practices in a Diverse and Developing World: Essays on International Business and Global Responsibilities,* by Frederick Bird and Manuel Velasquez, editors. Palgrave Macmillan, 2006. 301 pages.

Economic events of the past six months have changed the way books on business ethics will be received. The certainties and assumptions of the past have been profoundly shaken and questions only hinted at before have taken center stage. The three books reviewed here were all published before the economic collapse of late 2008, yet each anticipated, in its own way, some of the threats, dangers, and challenges which could be seen in the building crisis.

Being Consumed will resonate with those from an avowedly spiritually disciplined life, particularly from the Roman Catholic perspective, have seen and felt the coming destructiveness of an economy built on greed and the lust for acquisition, and the inordinate desire to consume. "In the four brief chapters of this book, I deal with these basic matters of economic life: the free market, consumerism, globalization, and scarcity" (page vii) This is true of the other two works reviewed as well but in an increasingly more extensive and difficult level. This work is deliberately theological and will especially appeal to those who find convincing and helpful the insights of Augustine and the experiences of the practices of the Church, particularly the Eucharist. It will have only limited appeal, or understanding, to persons less well versed in Christian doctrine and practice.

It is Cavanaugh's conviction that, "the Church is called to be a different kind of economic space and to foster such spaces in the world." (page ix) It is not, however entirely clear how and what shape that space takes place. His hope, nevertheless, is clear that this book will "provide inspiration for the Christian imagination to envision and enact new kinds of practices." (page xii)

In examining the vital place of consumers in a free market economy Cavanaugh sees as basic, "its ability to turn virtually anything into a commodity, that is, into something that can be bought and sold." (page 34) This is characterized not by attachment to things but instead to detachment rendering their valuation difficult if not impossible, leading to an endless round of buying and selling. A similar conclusion is reached in reference to globalization where, "Everything is available, but nothing matters." (page 69) A decidedly Christian approach is presented as the alternative.

Religious Perspectives on Business Ethics addresses a broader audience and does so without presuming active involvement in a practicing Christian community. It makes an excellent resource for persons, whether as individual readers or classroom participants, who want to grapple with the issues of Religious Ethics and Normative Theories (Part I), Religious Approaches to Economic Life (Part II), and Religion and Questions of Contemporary Business (Part III). The editors provide solid pedagogical guidance for using the book in a classroom setting, superb introductory treatment of ethical theory, and an excellent foray into how religious ethics affects the practice of business. These three initial chapters would be worth the price of the book. It should be no surprise that the editors have wisely gathered together in this anthology incredibly insightful contributions from some of the luminaries of business ethics such as Paul Camenisch, Ronald Duska, Robert Solomon, Kenneth Goodpaster, Laura Nash, Dennis MaCann, and Daryl Koehn to name but some among many other notables. The book is well organized to include a vast spectrum of issues and topics from the expanse of business ethics today such as the nature of business ethics itself, the challenges for business ethics by the contemporary situation, Zen and Confucian contributions, the place of covenants, and global capitalism in the new context of Christian social ethics. There is little doubt but that this work will become a basic resource in business ethics courses that take into account the significance of religious perspectives.

The reader will find here much of what he or she would expect to find in such an anthology but with new and exciting expressions. But, to many readers' delight they will find unexpected treasures along the way. One would hardly have expected to find "six economic myths heard from the pulpit," or a treatment of the way Zen can play itself out in mindful management, or how Confucian ethics' focus on trust can strengthen that vital element in contemporary business, or a circumspect treatment of Jewish ethics relative to environmental issues. The marvelous theoretical insights of the anthology are put to good use in the practically oriented chapters in the last section in which strengths and weaknesses of ecclesiastical proclamations on economic issues are candidly explored, feminist and traditional treatments of 'wage justice" are harmonized, and global capitalism is seen as forcing anyone who takes Christian social ethics seriously to expand their horizons.

This is a rich anthology in which every chapter is supported by appropriate documentation and has a helpful section of "Questions for Discussion." Most of the chapters will be read with eagerness and excitement and none will be seen as not worth the effort. The editors are to be commended for their editorial work in conceptualizing, securing the right authors for the issues, bringing style and content into pleasant agreement, and binding it all together by their exceptional introductions.

Just Business Practices in a Diverse and Developing World is edited by two of the most prolific scholars in the field of business ethics and will make a worthy contribution to graduate students and other scholars in the field. The print is quite small so that the book packs an enormous amount of provocative material into its pages. Its focus is primarily the theoretical underpinning of justice and international business and it holds to that throughout. The preponderance of the material is written by Frederick Bird with his characteristic painstaking thoroughness in which he precisely delineates at the beginning of each chapter not only what he intends to be about but how he intends to develop it. That form carries over in his editorial work of the other chapters as well. For those who like the challenges of struggling in depth with such issues as a political ethic for international business or the role of ethical auditing or perspectives on global poverty this work provides sufficient content to demand persistent concentration. While most of the content is theoretical, there are relevant treatments of the application of theory to specific areas of business endeavor such as mining, textile manufacturing, and economic developments in South Korea.

The book's three parts center round distinct challenges to the ability of international businesses making a constructive difference in developing economic areas. First is the challenge of "balancing the need to respond to and respect local customs and moral conventions while still operating with a common perspective about the responsible ways of engaging in business." (page xvii) The second challenge is "to find ways of balancing their social responsibilities with their business interests." (page xviii) The third challenge is in the "clashes between idealists who demand that international business in developing areas should give priority to social responsibility and the realists who are conscious of the larger obstacles, difficulties, and constraints which these businesses face." (page xix)

These three challenges "correspond to three perennial challenges that any viable ethic must address." (page xix) "First, it must be able to articulate moral standards that allow people to act responsively to contextual and historically contingent circumstances while maintaining a basic common moral perspective that remains authoritative for all." (page xix) "Second, a viable ethic must find ways of balancing categorical moral

232

claims (i.e. that people ought to act in certain ways pre-eminently out of respect for such claims) with the ulterior benefits of acting morally." (page xix) "Third, a viable ethic must also find ways of making it seem credible that moral programmes they favour can work to transform the world as it is." (page xix) In other words, "Any viable ethic must find ways of connecting the world as we find it to the world as we hope it to become." (page xix)

Meeting these challenges is the formidable task the editors set for themselves. It remains for the reader, after painstaking consideration of their closely reasoned arguments, to decide how well they have met those challenges and given insight into how just business practices can take place in a diverse and developing world.

These three books are illustrative of the wide range of options available to those who are interested in expanding their knowledge and understanding of the role of religious perspectives in knowing and doing business ethics today. #

f. *Destiny in the Pacific* by John Schork. Jupiter-Pixel, 2008. 382 pages. *Naval History Book Review*, Issue 39, May 2014, online.

I was utterly surprised by this novel of naval aviation in the Pacific during World War II because it was a radical departure from the way I knew the author to approach any task. Its creativity astounded me. It presented an imaginative approach I had never seen in him when we were shipmates. Its author, Retired Navy Captain John Schork, was Executive Officer of USS Midway (CV41) during Desert Storm; I was Command Chaplain at the time. John was meticulous and thorough in everything he undertook. He would accept nothing less than the best from himself or anyone else. In writing this novel he was characteristically thorough and meticulous in the research necessary for giving the book authenticity. He is a master of accurate and vivid description. The surprise for me was in his insightful portrayal of human, particularly romantic, relationships.

Captain Schork retired from the Navy after serving as Commanding Officer of Naval Air Station, Whidbey Island, WA and settled in the beautiful Pacific Northwest where he became a successful stock broker/financial advisor. My knowledge of and experience with him aboard the MIDWAY had not prepared me for this incredible work of creative writing.

This is the most gripping novel about World War II I have read. It is hard to believe that it is a work of fiction. The characters are vividly portrayed. The situations are graphically intense. The information needed to give it plausibility is well-grounded in fact. If taken all together it appears over the top but that does not detract from the thrill and excitement of following the exploits of Bryan Michaels, from an inauspicious start to a well-deserved ending with all the plaudits and honors of a marvelously admirable hero.

Destiny in the Pacific packs so much heroic action into one naval aviator's life that it strains the bounds of credulity. It is hard to imagine one young daring pilot disgraced and disqualified from flying then later restored by no less a towering figure than Admiral Chester Nimitz. He then fights valiantly at the Battle of Coral Sea and lives to distinguish himself for his service at the Battle of Midway. When an injury to his eye, sustained in that battle, disqualifies him from further service as a pilot he becomes the heroic skipper of a PT Boat leading a small group of men in a daring rescue of a Navy cryptologist lest the top secret information he has fall into the hands of the enemy. It so happens that the Navy nurse, Liz, whom Bryan loves was also on the downed plane. They had gone down in a PBY off a small South Pacific Island and were held by the Japanese. After their rescue Bryan is taken to Australia where none other than General Douglas McArthur has a chat with him about his exploits and assigns him to a joint Australian-American clandestine operation.

Now for the fourth time, he comes out the hero personally decorated with a Silver Star and Navy Cross by General McArthur while Liz and Bryan's father, Rear Admiral Chuck Michaels look proudly on. At the end of the book RADM Bryan Michaels looks back with deep gratitude at the friends he has known and lost.

Destiny in the Pacific is a remarkably well-crafted story dedicated "to the greatest generation" particularly those who turned appalling defeat at Pearl Harbor into overwhelming victory. The author devotes particular attention to expressing appreciation for the role Australian military forces played in achieving that victory over Japan.

The horrors, brutality, and cruelty of war are viscerally depicted. Death of shipmates is poignantly portrayed and remembered. There are character developments and sub-plots which keep a reader anticipating their further treatment. Personal relationships and romantic involvements are genuinely, honestly, and tenderly expressed. As they used to say, "he completely blew my socks off" with his handling of these. I had not seen that dimension of him before.

Anyone wanting a captivating story of an All-American hero need look no further than *Destiny in the Pacific*. I am thoroughly in awe of John Schork's creative genius and look forward to further works from this exceptionally gifted (and disciplined) author. #

g. *Ready Sea-power: a History of the U.S. Seventh Fleet,* by Edward J. Marolda. Naval History & Heritage Command, Department of the Navy, 2012. 216 pages. *Naval History Book Review,* Issue 42, Sep 2014 online.

Ready Sea-power is an attractive book. The format and design make it an appealing coffee table pleasure for guests to flip through and comment on, as guests in our home have done. The large selection of well-chosen pictures and other illustrations fit well with the text. Each chapter has a special inset usually highlighting a ship, often an aircraft carrier or the flagship of the Seventh Fleet, which can very easily stand alone. Persons who have played prominent roles in Seventh Fleet history and operations are treated with respect and admiration. The author worthily acknowledges the contributions of that distinguished core of naval historians to which he belongs. All-in-all it is a pleasure to hold in one's hands and read.

The author, Edward Marolda, is noted for his extensive knowledge and writing on the role of the United States Navy in Asia and the Pacific. While other historians could also have done well with the task, he has the background and insights to make this an engrossing story of one of the Navy's most vital elements.

Each chapter begins with a concise statement of what will follow in the chapter and ends with an equally concise summary conclusion. Persons, events, places are all woven together in a seamless story. The author is at pains to vividly demonstrate the vital role the Seventh Fleet has played in times of war including World War II, the Korean Conflict, the war in Vietnam and the Gulf War but also in lesser conflicts particularly in the Far East such as Operation Paul Bunyan in Korea and the difficult engagements against terrorism and piracy.

He is just as committed to portraying the essential role the Seventh Fleet has played in maintaining the peace through serving as a type of ambassador of American goodwill not only in extensive far-flung humanitarian efforts, but in overt diplomatic missions particularly with China, as well. Seventh Fleet units participate in more than a hundred exercises a year, many of them with other nations such as Japan, Australia, New Zealand, South Korea, the Philippines, Thailand and more recently India thus giving evidence of the place of the Seventh Fleet in multinational cooperation and commitment to maintaining open sea-lanes for commerce and protecting America's national interests as well as the safety and security of its allies. The delicate dance with China is carefully set forth showing how Seventh Fleet has often been the lead partner in that experience. Histories can be written in many ways. If the author had been writing for other historians or naval scholars he would have provided the documentation requisite to that task. This is not, however, a book for that audience. Therefore, the citations are general rather than specific. An author is acknowledged as the source of a quoted statement but the actual work in which that citation appears is not given. While this is adequate for its purpose I would have liked the citations as endnotes.

The authenticity of the work is enhanced by the fact that Dr. Marolda was able to spend some time in face-to-face interviews with key players in the Seventh Fleet in the couple of years before publication of the book. He therefore drew not only on his accomplished skill as a historian familiar with the records essential for writing such a history but has brought those to life with personal acquaintance with the persons making that history in its latter stages.

The book encompasses the life and work of the Seventh Fleet from its inception in World War II (1943) up to its involvement in peace and war from its home port in Yokosuka, Japan through 2010.

A list of Commanders of the Seventh Fleet is provided. Several of those went on to Command the Pacific Fleet or become Commander in Chief United States Pacific Command. The author does not make that connection in a linear fashion but access to the internet enables anyone interested to see that nine Commanders of Seventh Fleet went on to become Commanders of Pacific Fleet, two became Command in Chief United States Pacific Command, and five of them became the Chief of Naval Operations. The latter were Admirals Thomas Moorer, James Holloway, Thomas Hayward, Carlisle Trost and Jonathan Greenert. This, in itself, should give some indication of how significant a role the Seventh Fleet has played in leadership of the United States Navy.

Since most of my naval career was spent on Seventh Fleet ships I found the book especially meaningful. I began active duty with Destroyer Squadron Fifteen and was on the USS LOCKWOOD (FF1064) for Operation Paul Bunyan. I was back in Japan years later on the MIDWAY when we deployed to the Indian Ocean and then back again when the MIDWAY set sail for Operations Desert Shield and Desert Storm. The faces and places the author presents are among my most cherished memories of naval life.

There is one minor caveat I have. The Index which I expect was done by a research assistant (or software program) rather than the author omits a reference to USS MIDWAY (CV41) though I counted seventeen citations including the marvelous inset highlighting the MIDWAY on page 85. Otherwise, the book does what it sets out to do in commendable fashion making knowledge of the Seventh Fleet available to a wide and hopefully more appreciative readership.#

h. *At The Center*, by Dorothy Van Soest. Apprentice House, Loyola University Maryland, 2015. 305 pages. Amazon.com online

The title, *At the Center*, does not appear until late in the book. This oft used literary device has been used quite effectively by the author. By the time the reader reaches that point he or she has already discerned multiple possibilities including personal, sociological, psychological, cultural, ethnic, geographic, and philosophical among them.

This riveting story of tensions between personal moral principles and practices and adherence to bureaucratic policies and procedures continually opens new possibilities of resolution. The book's basic plot is subdivided from the start into two powerful parallel sub-plots which ultimately coalesce in the dramatic climax of the story. Hints of resolution are given along the way as characters are marvelously fleshed out. Just as it is a magnificent indictment of good intentions gone awry it is at the same time a startling affirmation of the power of growth, perception, and redemption.

While it is a work of fiction in which the clash of cultures/ethnicities – Native American and White – has devastating effect, it also portrays how personalities that initially mistrust or misread one another are able to work together for a higher good than their own evolving identities in an uncomfortable, but compelling cause.

The author is careful to maintain that *At The Center* is a novel, a work of fiction in which persons, places, or incidents are not coincident with historically verifiable information from newspaper archives or even court documents. Yet, the author's background which has led her to now being Dean Emeritus of the School of School Work of the University of Washington has provided the seminal knowledge from which the story grows. She does not want the reader to see in it isolated incidents in which the innocent are victimized by those they trusted. However, her gripping story cannot help but grasp the reader's mind and conscience making the story and the people in it as real as any one might meet in an office of human services or in some foster homes.

There is, in the end, a triumphant declaration of the persistence of virtue and duly rewarded integrity but on the way there are times of weeping and wondering. There is nothing gratuitous about this exceptional novel. Everything has its clearly expressed purpose even the little joys and sorrows of everyday experiences along the way.

238

The reader may not remember the names of the well-wrought characters once the journey has ended, but he or she can never put away the unforgettable situations they both confront and create.

At The Center is a five star read for anyone who loves a compelling story masterfully told!

5. Correspondence

Correspondence is a time-honored form of writing. It may be seen in two basic forms though the terms may be different depending on the emphases: informal and formal, personal and impersonal, private and public. It may be as simple as a thank you note or as extensive as a multipage letter between friends. Every business or secretarial school, when those were popular, had a course in Business Correspondence. Many organizations such as the United States Navy publish Manuals of Correspondence. Most large firms have published policies and procedures, or at least guidelines, for correspondence representing the firm. At the rarified level of correspondence between nations definite protocols are observed and a breach in these is considered an egregious error.

In our day correspondence has gone through radical changes. In my earliest years all personal correspondence was to be handwritten. A typewritten note was considered improper. In time type written letters became acceptable and even preferred, especially if one's penmanship was not the best. The typewriter gave way to the computer keyboard and emails replaced postal correspondence. In the more recent evolution even emails are being replaced with social media "tweets".

The joy of holding a personal letter from a friend in one's hands and being able to read it over and over again as often as desired has almost completely gone away.

I have labored over this section of the book as much as any, for a number of reasons. Not the least of which is that I would have to gain permission of correspondents for including their works in print. Also some of the more cherished letters were quite personal and not meant for a public audience. Others, such as correspondence with my wives, children and grandchildren would be redundant or of little interest to anyone else. I think of correspondence I had with my grandson Jackson Stansell when he was in elementary school and wrote me asking about life when I was a child about his age – 6 or 7. But, that ground has already been covered.

Letters between me and Marilyn move all the way from the love letters of our college romance on through times I was away from home such as doing two or more weeks of Naval Reserve duty on up through the less than cordial correspondence when we were going through our divorce.

Letters between me and Namiko were often from a lonesome sailor away from home for an extended period of time on up through our life together which ended when she developed Alzheimers and returned to Japan and lived with her family. Through the years we talked as much as we could whenever the ship was in port or we were separated and living in two continents. Ships in those days did not have email capabilities so there was always a long line of sailors (officers and enlisted) queued up waiting their turns with great anticipation.

Since Blossom and I have not been apart for more than a very few days in our relatively short marriage there are no letters here exchanged by us. .

Among my most cherished correspondence are letters from David Blakeslee, my closest friend for over half a century, who died far too young. He was a master letter writer as he was so accomplished at everything else he did. I wish I could share with you his marvelously descriptive and often funny accounts of his personal, family, and professional life. Letters from other friends through the years are cherished but reached neither the volume nor the depth of those from David.

I was often called upon to write letters of recommendation for former students, friends, and shipmates. Again it would be a breach of confidentiality to include those. Many of them were in support of an application for a position with a firm or institution. Some were in support of a person's nomination for an award or honor such as Volunteer of the Year.

Similar, though somewhat different were letters of advocacy in which I pleaded someone's case either in a judicial or a professional situation where there was need for clarification and pointing out the strengths and potential of that person. I am pleased that those usually met with success. A special type of advocacy letter was to support a Navy colleague's appeal to the Board of Corrections of Naval Records for what to them, and to me, was an unjustified negative assessment in an adverse fitness report. The opposite of these letters were those in support of an applicant for commissioning or reinstatement in rank .

Under Status of Forces agreements, naval personnel stationed overseas must submit application with supporting documents to gain command approval for marriage to "a foreign national." I wrote numerous letters for navy personnel in the Commands to which I was attached.

Some of my letters were especially joyous as in the case of letters attesting to the good character of a person or persons seeking adoption of an infant through one of the recognized adoption agencies making Asian children available to American parents.

There has been such a great number of letters of gratitude I have received over the years. A few of those were printed in the previous volume.

Another whole classification of correspondence is that of letters of condolence, encouragement, and sympathy. These are far too numerous to even begin to express how much each one of those persons meant to me and my concern for the family and friends they left behind.

There was correspondence which I will simply call circumstantial or situational such as letters to boat people USS PELELIU (LHA5) rescued or letters to chaplains of the Navies of other nations with whom I had become acquainted.

I am as aware as you that this barely touches the edges of types of correspondence. But, at least it gives some idea of the range and scope.

6. Poems

These should probably not be dignified with the appellation Poems; more like doggerel. Oh well, as one of Blossom's son would say, "They are what they are."

a. "On Seeing a Cob-web moved by Debussy", A poem written in The Fine Arts Humanities classroom at Transylvania while listening to a piece by Debussy: Spring 1967.

Warm-waved turbulence distressing delicate strain.
Light orbed recess sheltering strands spun firm
　　　　for losing in obscure moments.
Music motioning minds meant for meaning and
　　　　meeting eyes tasting graceful modulations.
Swirls, sways, stays attached in surging dances of
　　　　freedom.
Firm as the gossamer bonds that give it delicacy.
A clamor of light-heat-sound-waves wanting
　　　　dominance.
Beautiful for flowing freely; meaningful for serenely
　　　　holding.

b. "On hearing Paul Tillich lecture at Transylvania" Spring 1965

There was a young theologian from Deutsch
Who fleeing Hitler's fiery red torch
Came to Union to teach and Harvard to preach
And Chicago to sit on the porch.

Essays, articles, lectures and such
He delivered for fees that were much
And at every new turn was Ultimate Concern
For God beyond human touch.
To Transylvania he came to relate
How absolutes and relatives mate
In a morality sans authorities, but one
When he said it, it was great.
One thing further remains to see

How accepting the self that is me
And receiving grace for the whole human race
I can live with the Courage to Be
c. A mystique, Winter 1969
A mystique more mysterious than moral
        dilemmas justify.
Grasping desperately at every fleeting
        glance or chance approach.
Fantasies fill working hours and waiting
        waking wonders why.
        d. "The Watchman's Report" (written in my office at Transylvania during an all- night writing session when the campus watchman stopped by. Winter 1975
Frantic glances in wrong places
Seeking thrills from too radiant faces
Mystifying games played with scrawled lines
        from late nights solitarily together.
Cryptic messages running tortuous traces of
        unerasable words saying what may not be said.
An evening's pious intent shattered by a Watchman's lament
Of light-run speeders fleeing themselves;
Of keys punched in orderly round properly found;
Of slack-down girls too heated to wince at winter's
        freezing fingers
Too wet to weep at Watchman's watching.
Tomorrow comes before today has left so
        Unceremoniously .#

III. What Might have been – a flight into fancy

I consider myself fortunate to have grown up in the age of radio. Some even call the 1930s and 40s "the golden age of radio". Just as reading provides vicarious resources for different life experiences than one is actually able to have, so radio provides rich imagination and vivid imagery. It was an everyday ritual to lie on the floor in front of the radio and listen to The Lone Ranger, Sky King, or Jack Armstrong, the All-American boy. So it was a weekly delight to listen as a child snuggled in my grandmother's feather bed in the dark to the scary sounds of Inner Sanctum or the Green Hornet.

One could be transported in one's mind's eye to the baseball field where the play-by-play commentary was so enthusiastic and you could even hear the vendors in the background pitching their wares – cold beer, peanuts, popcorn, cracker jacks. In the evenings we would often sit as a family in the living room listening to such favorites as Lux Radio Theater, the Jack Benny Show, Ozzie and Harriet, The Great Gildersleeve, Fibber McGee and Molly, and so many more. But it is one particular Saturday morning program that fits this book well: Let's Pretend with Nila Mack. The listener was invited to join the cast and pretend we were there to see, not just hear familiar fairy tales and some original children's broadcasts.

Television, rich and powerful as it is, could not have formed my imagination as did radio. My generation was the last to grow up with radio rather than television. In fact, I was 28 years old before we had a 19" black and white television set in our home. That was a gift from my dad and mom to their grandchildren while we were living in Eureka. Theirs was the television generation and their children's has become the electronic generation with smart phones, I Pads, laptop computers and wizardry beyond my comprehension. I try to avail myself of the advantages of these as I am able and am especially grateful for the time saving capabilities of computers for word-processing even if there are times when glitches occur and valuable time has to be spent in resolving issues. Add to this great advantage the incredible resource of instantaneous research via Google or other search engines. Those many

245

hours I have spent going to the library to look something up if my home reference resources were insufficient have been transformed into seconds of inputting an identifying word and finding myself with a plethora of sites from which to choose.

When Wikipedia first appeared, like most other college professors, I cautioned students against its use and recommended they have other more substantial research tools in play with documentation of papers. As time went on two things happened. Wikipedia got better and better, that is, more and more reliable and I overcame my "paper print" bias. Now I find it almost indispensable when used judiciously.

Let's leave this little historical excursus and go back to "let's pretend". I want to indulge myself and you in a fanciful flight of what might have been.

We'll leave the big issues of my birth to Jim and Margaret Murphey in Augusta, Georgia in 1932 as a point of mystery and gratitude. What if I had been born to a different father and mother on a different continent at a different time? What if instead of a loving family I had known only rejection and put down and defeat? What if it had been a world without a Depression, the Second World War, the prosperity that followed and all that came after?

As I say, let's leave these big issues alone and take a fanciful flight into actual decision points in my life over which I had at least some control and even pivot points which were beyond my control. I am not as bold as Paul Anka who wrote the song or Frank Sinatra who made it almost ubiquitous, but, the life I have lived was truly "my way". Just an interesting aside here. When I first went to Japan in 1976 every bar I went into was playing "My Way" and the Karioke singers threw themselves into it – this in the country where the motto "the nail that sticks up gets hammered down." was firmly implanted from birth.

Anyway, I do not engage in this flight of fancy with regret or remorse. I have come to the belief that I would not be who I am and where I am today if each of the decisions and turns in the road were not taken as they were. I shall leave to someone else to judge whether I would have lived a better, perhaps more exemplary life, if I had made different decisions. At least it would have been another life than the one I have actually lived. I am going to be discreet about what I choose for these flights and very selective. Anyway, here are a few.

Let's go back to high school. What if I had chosen to go to Bob Jones University in Greenville, South Carolina, or the Christian College of Georgia at the University of Georgia? Add to that, what if I had married Caroline Fowler my high school sweetheart and we had gone on to seminary at Emory in Atlanta or Lexington Theological Seminary in Kentucky. I think we would have returned to Georgia when the academic preparation was over and I would have served a series of churches, maybe even becoming Senior Minister of Peachtree Christian Church, Atlanta. Even my dreams have been grandiose why not my flights into fancy. We would have had several children who would have been very dear to both sets of grandparents' hearts and who saw them often..

What if Marilyn and I had waited until we graduated from TCU before we got married and went on to Yale Divinity School for the Bachelor of Divinity degree and to Edinburgh, Scotland for the Ph.D. in New Testament studies? What if we had waited at least until we were in New Haven before we had children and had not had the number that we did as soon as we did? I would perhaps have taught biblical studies in a college or seminary related to my denomination but perhaps in an interdenominational graduate school.

What if I had gotten anyone of the teaching positions I applied for unsuccessfully? Or what if I had been chosen as an academic dean or vice president or even a college president? As the list in the appendix shows I had some chances at that but only one of them resulted in an actual offer which Marilyn and I decided not to accept – Academic Vice President of Alaska Methodist University. It was as simple as Marilyn saying and meaning, "I'm not going to Alaska." After that the benefactors who had gotten me the interviews said they would not recommend me for other positions since it appeared I would not accept them. I remember the conversation I had with the renowned past College President who had arranged the Alaska interview in which he said. "I will not recommend you again. I wanted you to go to Alaska for two or three years then I would have gotten you an interview for an Academic Vice-Presidency or College Presidency in the South." Ah, that lament so often spoken, "the saddest words of tongue or pen, what might have been." If that had been the trajectory I probably would never have become a Navy Chaplain,

What if Marilyn and I had not divorced after 27 years of marriage? What if we had remained faithful to one another for all the ensuing years? We would have celebrated our 66th wedding anniversary this year. What impact would that have had on our children's lives? I am so proud of each one of them but wonder what turns their lives would have taken if their mother and I had lived "happily ever after".

What if I had not decided to become a Naval Reserve Chaplain and become as involved as I did in Navy life? What if I had not chosen to pursue active duty and stayed a Reserve Chaplain? I am confident as one person in the Chief of Chaplains Office said "you would surely have retired as a Captain". Again I do not regret the choices and their consequences. As I often said, active duty in the Navy took me as Willie Nelson would have it "to places I had never been, seeing things I might never see again." This was a liberal education in itself which no amount of schooling could have possibly provided.

What if I had been promoted to Commander the first time I was eligible? My record was exemplary with 4.0 ratings, letters of commendation and appreciation, and a Navy Commendation medal. There were those on the selection board who had their own agenda and biases which got in the way. If that had not been the case I possibly would still have been detailed, i.e. sent to Naval Submarine Base Bangor. What if then I had been selected for Captain while at Bangor. I probably would not have been sent to Yokosuka as Command Chaplain of USS MIDWAY (CV41). That would have meant I would not have been at the Chapel of Hope, Yokosuka before returning to the MIDWAY for Desert Shield/Desert Storm. I am so glad everything worked out as it did though the considerable increase in retirement pay would have been good.

What if Namiko Yabuki Kawai and I had not married? What if she had been anything less than a perfect Navy wife? What if she had not developed dementia then Alzheimers which had claimed her mother before her? What if I had insisted that she stay in America and I had cared for her as best I could until she had to be cared for elsewhere and we had moved to a Japanese-speaking care center in Seattle and I had stayed there with her beyond the 29 years of our marriage?

One last fanciful flight? What if Blossom Tibbits and I had not married and shared our lives for the past 9 years? What if we had been able to keep the incredible grounds of her beautiful home on Liberty Bay and had been able to keep up with the housework in her spacious home which she and her husband Chuck had built and lived in until his death in 1999? What if we had not moved to Country Meadows in December 2010 and quickly become involved in the life of this vital retirement community?

I think this is enough of this fancilful flight. As I have tried to say before I would not be who I am today if following Robert Frost's advice I had taken the road less traveled. I do not have much confidence in my ability to discern God's will in the future – enough to say that wherever I go and whoever I am, I am God's and He is with me and I with Him here and hereafter. I have a strong belief that God has been active in my life all along the way. I do not adhere to the Flip Wilson "school of theology" which avows, "the devil made me do it," nor for that matter, "God made me do it." I am as I have often said, a firm believer in Nicholas Berdyaev's insights that "life is both a gift and an achievement," and that "we are co-creators with God of our destiny." It is with that conviction that I can sing I did it my way, but not **just** my way. As St. Augustine a long time ago concluded whatever good has come about in my life is a gift from God, whatever not so good has been a part of it is a result of my choices along the way. Thanks be to God for this incredible journey called life.

Conclusion

I think it is time to wrap this up. I have both looked forward to this conclusion and dreaded it. I looked forward to it because it will have fulfilled my desire to write thoughts along the way for my family. I dread concluding it because I am sure there are things I shall remember later and wonder why those escaped me as I reflected along the way and did not include them.

As I conclude, I realize that I have really said precious little about either speaking or writing that would help anyone grappling with the challenges and opportunities each presents. What I have done is express some of my own basic viewpoints and then used those as a frame for the verbal pictures the examples of my speaking and writing present.

Readers will judge them differently. To some they will be well worth their while and they will keep dipping into them until they have at least glanced at them all. Others will not find a point of connection and wonder why it was so important to me to include them here. As I look back over what I have included I am pleased with the range and often the depth of the presentations. To me some of them are not bad, some are actually good, and a few deserve the delighted response, "WOW". I hope I have not deceived myself regarding their worth. Only, you the reader, can assess their importance for you.

I regret that my record keeping was not complete and that amidst all the travels and moving some of the documents I would most loved to have included in this series could not be found. I am nevertheless grateful to God that He has "kept my memory green" and enabled me to remember as much as I have. I hope I have neither distorted nor glorified it too much.

Appendices
Appendix I: Biographical Listings and Treatments
1. Listings (in alphabetical order)

American Philosophical Association. *Proceedings and Addresses,* November 2011, Volume 85, Issue 2. Membership List, page 301.

Association for Practical and Professional Ethics, *Twentieth Anniversary, Member Directory.* February 18, 2011. Page 49.

Christian Church (Disciples of Christ). *Yearbook & Directory 2008.* Published by the Office of the General Minister and President, 2008. Page 728.

City University of Seattle, 40th Anniversary. *Alumni Today, 2013,* Harris Connect, 2013. Page A274.

Dictionary of International Biography, 1975,

Eureka College Bulletin, 1965-1966. Faculty, Page 90.

Outstanding Educators of America, 1974. Page 340.

Personalities of the South. American Biographical Institute, 1974. Page 455.

The Society for Business Ethics, *Membership Directory, 2007,* Page 29

The Society of Christian Ethics. *Membership Directory.* Society of Christian Ethics, 1996. Page 83; 2009 (50th Anniversary Directory), Page 65.

Texas Christian University Alumni Directory 1992 Edition. Publishing Concepts, 1992. Page 255.

Transylvania University Bulletin, September 1975. The Faculty, Page 77.

Transylvania University Catalog, 1968-69. The Faculty, Page 140.

Transylvania University Faculty Handbook, 1975-76. Pages D1, D2.

United States Navy Chaplains, 1972-1981. Volume VIII in the History of the Chaplain Corps. NavPers 15507. Page 118.

University of Kentucky, 130th Anniversary, *Alumni Directory, 1996.* Harris Publishing, 1996. Page 474.

Vanderbilt Alumni Directory 1991-92, Moore Data Management Services, 1992. Page 521.

Vanderbilt University, Abstracts of Theses, 1963-1964 (Master' only. Doctoral Dissertations are simply listed). Page 9.

Vanderbilt University, the 89ᵗʰ Commencement Program. Doctor of Philosophy, Page 37.

Who's Who in America 2012. 66ᵗʰ Edition. Marquis Who's Who, 2012. Page 3181 (volume 2)

Who's Who in Religion, 1ˢᵗ Edition, 1975-76. Marquis Who's Who, 1976. Page 402

The Wonder of Woodmont, by Bess White Cochran. Written for the 25ᵗʰ Birthday, July 18, 1968. Privately printed. 57 pages. Pages 27, 30, 31.

2. Treatments/references to (in chronological order)

1971, June 14, "Diploma No Success Bid, Transy Grads are told," *The Lexington Leader,* Pages 1 and 6.

2000, November 20, "Unsung Hero: Always there in time of need," *Bremerton Sun,* Page A2

2002, November 6, "*Adventure of life key for professor,*" by Brianne Herron. *Olympian,* Page 10.

2004, January 6, "Olympic College: First day of school for new campus in Poulsbo." Pages A1 & A4

2005, March 30, "*Silverdale Rotary honors Chapman students,*" by Kassie Korich. *Central Kitsap Reporter.* Page A6.

2006, June 14, Picture by Gary Bowlby with caption. "*Paul and Namiko Murphey celebrated a family reunion…*" *Central Kitsap Reporter.* Page A6.

2007, March 26, "*Putting a Face on Ethics in Business,*" By Brynn Grimley. *Kitsap Sun,* Pages A1 and A2.

2014, August 8, "*Life as a Navy Chaplain: serving on board 24/7*". By Leslie Kelly. *Central Kitsap Reporter.* Page A10.

3. Yearbooks

Academy of Richmond County, *The Rainbow, 1948.* Augusta, GA. Pages not numbered:. Class of 1949, The Richmond Academy Band, Order of DeMolay, Cadet Hi-Y, Academy of Richmond County, *The Rainbow, 1949.* Augusta, GA. Pages not numbered: Seniors, [caption under Jack Murphy; mine under his picture]

Texas Christian University, *The Horned Frog, 1950*. Fort Worth, TX. Pages 65, 236, 297.

Texas Christian University, *The Horned Frog, 1953*. Fort Worth, TX. Page 292.

Eureka College, *Prism* 1961, Eureka, IL Page 126.

Eureka College, *Prism* 1964, Eureka, IL, pages 30, 57.

Transylvania University, *Crimson '68*, Lexington, KY, Pages 10, 20, 77, 92, 93.

Transylvania University, *Crimson '69*, Lexington, KY, Page 45.

Transylvania University, *Crimson .70*, Lexington, KY, Pages 139.

4. Cruise books/Commissioning books

USS PELELIU (LHA5) Commissioning book, 1980 Un-numbered pages.

USS MIDWAY (CV41), "The Magic Touch" 85-87, Chaplain, four unnumbered pages.

USS MIDWAY (CV41), "Desert Magic", 1990-1991, Chaplain, four unnumbered pages.

Appendix II: Bibliography
1. Books: (in alphabetical order)

The Concept of Death in the Theology of Nicholas Berdyaev, Paul Tillich, and Helmut Thielicke. Original typewritten copy. (typed by Marilyn S. Murphey). 394 pages.

The Concept of Death in the Theology of Nicholas Berdyaev, Paul Tillich, and Helmut Thielicke. University Microfilms, 1974. 394 pages. (Ph.D. Dissertation, Vanderbilt University, 1964)

Death and Dying: Bibliographic Resources. Create Space, 2013. 247 pages.

Decide-Act! Christian Board of Publication, 1970. 192 pages.

Decide-Act! Teacher's Guide. Christian Board of Publication, 1969. 160 pages.

Evening Prayers at Sea, by Chaplain Paul W. Murphey, LCDR, CHC, USNR. Publisher not identified. Pages unnumbered [170]. Typed by Lt. Richard James, USS PELELIU (LHA 5), Ship's Secretary. Spiral buckram binding. All these prayers are included in *Sacred Moments, Prayers of a Navy Chaplain at Sea and Ashore, Volume 1 Prayers at Sea: Destroyer Squadron Fifteen (CDS 15) and USS PELELIU (LHA5).*

Living Life, Facing Death: a Better Way of Living and Dying. Lucas Park Books, 2011. 161 pages.

Sacred Moments, Prayers of a Navy Chaplain at Sea and Ashore. Volume I Prayers at Sea: Destroyer Squadron Fifteen (CDS15) and USS PELELIU (LHA 5). Create Space, 2013. 235 pages.

Sacred Moments, Prayers of a Navy Chaplain at Sea and Ashore, Volume II Prayers at Sea: USS MIDWAY (CV41). Create Space, 2013. 229 pages.

Sacred Moments, Prayers of a Navy Chaplain at Sea and Ashore, Volume III Prayers Ashore. Create Space, 2013. 188 pages.

Sacred Moments, Prayers of a Navy Chaplain at Sea and Ashore. Volume IV. Index. Create Space, 2013. 76 pages.

Thoughts along the way. Volume 1: To be a Preacher, Create Space, 2016. 231 pages.

Thoughts along the way, Volume 2: Ministering is caring. Create Space, 2017. 275 pages.

Thoughts along the way. Volume 3: To Teach is to learn. Create Space. 2017. 232 pages.

Thoughts along the way. Volume 4: I have something to say. Create Space, 2017. 280 pages.

2. Articles: (in alphabetical order)

"The Board of Trustees of Hospice of Kitsap County," *The Sojourner*, HKC, January 26, 2000.

"Campus and Church in Common Commitment," *Liberal Education*, October 1966. Pages 303-307.

"The Chaplain as Ethicist," written for *Military Chaplain's Review* but not published due to not submitting in time for deadline. 1982.

"College is a Family Affair," *Hearthstone*, October 1961. Pages 22-23, 30.

"The Community Breaker," *The Catalyst*, August 1971. Pages 2-7.

"Conflict within Community," *Eureka College Bulletin*, December 1964. [5 pages]

"Crisis during Rush Week," *Stories from 'neath the Elms: Eureka College, 1940-1970*, edited by Loren Logsdon. Eureka Printing, 2011. Pages 285-286.

"Death of God". Two feature articles in the *Crimson Rambler* (Transylvania University campus newspaper), 1) *"Few surprised to learn that God is Dead"*, February 18, 1966, page 3. 2) *"In absence of God, Jesus seen as Father image"*). February 25, pages 3-4.

"FOCUS Established at EC," *Stories from 'neath the Elms: Eureka College, 1940-1970*, edited by Loren Logsdon. Eureka Printing, 2011. Pages 378-380.

"The meaning of the holidays—forward with hope," *MIDWAY Multiplex*, December 24, 1986. Pages 5-6.

"The Ministry of the Church," *The Christian*, November 14, 1965. Pages 4-5.

"Murphey Pans *Transylvanian:* a critical review." *The Rambler*, April 21, 1967. Page 4

"No Dream, No Destiny". *The Christian*, March 28, 1971. Pages 4-5.

"Role of the Chaplain on Eureka Campus," *The Illinois Christian*, December 1960. Pages 11-13.

"Some random reflections on my five wonderful years at Eureka College," *Stories from 'neath the Elms: Eureka College, 1940-1970*, edited by Loren Logsdon. Eureka Printing, 2011. Pages 254-257.

'Suggestions for Effective Teaching and Learning." *Bethany Guide*, April 1972. Pages 29-33.

"Technods and Methiques for Teachers of Youth", *Bethany Guide*, April 1971. Pages 32-35.

"Think and Act, Act and Think," *Bethany Guide*, May 1971. Pages 21-23.

"To Hell with Sin," *The Catalyst*, October 1969. Pages 4-5, 35-37.

"What did you bring to college?" *The Pegasus*, Eureka College, IL, September 14, 1962.

Co-authored with Jim Kendall, CEO, Telebyte Northwest:: (in chronological order)

"Yes, but is it right? Ethics in Business." *Kitsap Business Journal*, July 2003. Pages 42-43.

"Business Ethics, Part 1: Contract? What's a contract?" Kitsap Business Journal, August 2003. Page 11.

"*Business Ethics, Part 2: Contract? What's a contract?" Kitsap Business Journal*, September 2003.

"Business Ethics: I'm not getting sentimental over you … I'm in business!" Kitsap Business Journal, October 2003. Page 11.

"Business + Ethics: Not an option," Kitsap Business Journal, November 2003, Page 11.

"The Business-Ethics Plan: Where to Start," Kitsap Business Journal, February 2004. Page 6.

3. Book Reviews: (listed alphabetically by title)

At the Center, by Dorothy Van Soest. Apprentice House, Loyola University Maryland, 2015. 305 pages. Amazon.com online.

Being Consumed: Economics and Christian Desire, by W.T. Cavanaugh. Eerdman's, 2008. *Religious Perspectives on Business Ethics: An Anthology.* By Thomas O'Brien and Scott Paeth, editors. Rowman and Littlefield, 2007.

Just Business Practices in a Diverse and Developing World: Essays on International Business and Global Responsibilities. . By Fredrick Bird and Manuel Velasquez, editors. Palgrave/Macmillan, 2006. *Journal of the Society of Christian Ethics.* Fall/Winter 2010. pages 199-202.

Blackrobe in Blue: The Navy Chaplaincy of John P. Foley, S.J., 1942-46, by Steve O'Brien. iUniverse, 2002. 348 pages. *Naval History Book Review,* Issue 35, Nov 2013, online.

But for the Grace of God: Divine Initiative and Human Need. (Christian Foundation Series) by Philip E. Hughes. Westminster Press, 1967. 94 pages. *The Christian,* October 15, 1967. Page 28.

The Church in the Racially Changing Community, by R.L. Wilson and J.H. Davis. Abingdon, 1966. 159 pages. *The Christian,* October 15, 1967

Destiny in the Pacific, by John Schork. Jupiter-Pixel, 2008. 382 pages. *Naval History Book Review,* Issue 39, May 2014 online.

Faith to Act: An Essay on the Meaning of Christian Existence, by Jack Boozer and William A. Beardslee. Abingdon. 272 pages. *The Christian,* March 17, 1968. Page 28.

"Globaldoodle": a play by William Thompson. Review in *The Rambler* of performance at Mitchell Fine Arts Center, Transylvania. November 17, 1967.

The Gospel of our Suffering, by Soren Kierkegaard. Eerdman's, 1964. 150 pages. *The Christian* ?

Immortality and Resurrection: four essays by Oscar Cullmann, Harry A. Wolfson, Werner Jaeger, and Henry J. Cadbury, edited with an introduction by Krister Stendahl. Macmillan, 1967. 149 pages. *The Christian,* September 17, 1967. Page 26.

The Literature of Theology: a Guide for Students and Pastors, by John A. Bollier. Westminster, 1979. 208 pages. *The Military Chaplain,* 1980.

Memory and Hope: an Inquiry Concerning the Presence of Christ, by Dietrich Ritschl. Macmillan, 1968. 237 pages. *The Christian,* October 13, 1968. Page 28.

"Murphey pans Transylvanian", *The Rambler,* April 21, 1967.

The Nature of Faith, by Gerhard Ebeling. Fortress, 1968. 191 pages. *The Christian* ?

Philosophical Resources for Christian Thought, edited with an introductory essay by Perry LeFevre. Abingdon Press, 1968. 142 pages. *The Christian,* April 19, 1968.

Preface to Bonhoeffer: the man and two of his shorter writings, by John D. Godsey.. Fortress Press, 1965. 73 pages. *The Christian ?*

Ready Sea-power: a History of the U.S. Seventh Fleet, by Edward J. Marolda. Naval History and Heritage Command, Department of the Navy, 2012. 216 pages. *Naval History Book Review,* Issue 42, Sep 2014 online.

Saving Big Ben: the USS Franklin and Father Joseph T. O'Callahan, by John R. Satterfield, Naval Institute Press, 2011. 175 pages. *Naval History Book Review,* Issue 19, May 2012 online.

Strangers and Exiles: A History of Religious Refugees, by Frederick A. Norwood. Nashville, Abngdon Press, 1969. Vol. 1 400 pages and Vol. 2 527 pages. *Growth and Change: a Journal of Regional Development.* Vol. 2, No. 1, January 1971. Pages 48-49.

To Know God Better, by Winfred Rhodes, Harper, 1958. *The Christian ?*

What can I Believe? Talks to Youth on the Christian Faith, by Walter L. Cook. Abingdon, 1965. 112 pages. *The Christian,* Jan 5, 1966.

What Christians Believe, by Georgia Harkness. Abingdon, 1965. 72 pages. *The Christian,* Feb 2, 1966.

White Protestantism and the Negro, by David M. Reimers. Oxford University Press, 1965. 236 pages. *The Christian ?*

4. Addresses, Speeches, Meditations, Devotionals -- in chronological order.

Religion in Life Week, Iowa State University, Ames, Iowa, denominational representative and panel participant, January 1962

Participant in Conference on Pre-seminary education, Drake University, Des Moines, Iowa, 1964

"To one of the least of these," Meditation at Faculty Workshop, Eureka College, September 2, 1964

Devotional for Southern Junior High School Parent Teacher Association, Lexington, Kentucky, November 14, 1966.

"The Limits of Christian Ethics in a Pluralistic Society," Dean's Seminar, Transylvania University, Lexington, March 1967

"A Covenant with the Past, the Future, and the Present," United Ministries in Higher Education Conference, Montreat, North Carolina, August 1967

"Old language in a New Age," Conference on Theology and Ethics, Christmount, North Carolina, August 1967

Devotional for Tates Creek Senior High PTA, Lexington, October 10, 1967.

"Absolutes and Relatives in Christian Ethics," Central Kentucky Ministers Association, Lexington, March 1968.

"Luther and Erasmus," Transylvania University, Lexington, 1968.

"Religion and the Arts, or the Dramatic and the Theatrical"

"What in hell is the church doing?" Greater St. Louis Council of Christian Churches, Hamilton Christian Church, Missouri, September 15, 1968.

College age group at Park United Methodist Church, Lexington, October 6, 1968

Chapel, Lexington Theological Seminary, February 12, 1969.

Morning Meditations, Far East Network (FEN), Japan, October 17-21, 1977.

Devotional, Ombudsman Council, Naval Submarine Base, Bangor, Washington, March 15, 1985.

Prayers in *Occasional Ministries* published by U.S. Navy Chaplain Corps, 1985.

Morning Meditations, Far East Network (FEN), Japan, March 10-14, 1986.

Morning Meditations, Far East Network (FEN), Japan, Summer, 1988

Morning Meditations, Far East Network (FEN), October 1989.

KMID-TV Meditations, USS MIDWAY (CV41), February 1991.

KMID-TV Meditations, USS MIDWAY (CV41), March 1991.

5. Unpublished papers: (in alphabetical order)

"Academic libraries in the South, 1850-1900", 1976

"Art of dying," 1974

"Democracy, Local Autonomy and Cooperation," March 1994.

"Embryo of a college," 1965

"Luther and Erasmus," 1968

"Standards for College Libraries applied to the Frances Carrick Thomas Library, Transylvania University, Lexington, Kentucky, February 1975

"Violence and the Christian Faith," April 1971

"Why Naval Aviation Must be Strong," Spring 1949.

6. Papers prepared for classes in chronological order.

a. Vanderbilt Divinity School (1953-56) or Vanderbilt Graduate School (1956-59) – incomplete list.

"The Christological Controversy: reading reports," November 22, 1955.

"The Holy Spirit in the theology of Nels F.S. Ferre," Seminar in contemporary theology, 1957. 31 pages.

"American Democratic Culture and Locally Autonomous Church Polity," Seminar in Christianity and American Culture. 1958. 54 pages.

"Calvin's concept of the Holy Spirit," Seminar in historical theology. 1958. 24 pages.

"The Evangelical Alliance in the Nineteenth Century," Seminar in modern church history. 1958. 64 pages.

"Revelational and philosophical formulations of the Self," Seminar in philosophical theology. 1959. 48 pages.

b. University of Kentucky (1973-75) School of Library Science – incomplete list

"Academic libraries in the South, 1850-1900", 1975

"Contract and covenant: an approach to Library management," 1974.

"Death is not dead yet: a bibliographic essay" 1975

c. Naval War College

"Elements of Napoleon's Military Genius," correspondence course with Naval War College, 1977. 16 pages.

"The mythic reality of Athenian Naval Superiority," 1976.

"Thucydides on the causes of the Peloponnesian War" 1976.

d. City University of Seattle—incomplete list

"A critical analysis of Chris Argyris's, "Good Communication that blocks learning," *Harvard Business Review*, July-August 1994. Managerial Communication, 1994

"A critical analysis of Peter F. Drucker's, The Information Executives Truly Need," *Harvard Business Review*, January-February, 1995. Management Accounting, 1995

"Marketing plan for an educational broker for adult learners to operate as The College Connection," Marketing Management, 1995.

"Application of Baldridge Quality Award Criterion 5.0 to Spiritual Sercies Unit of the Hospice of the Florida Suncoast," Quality Management Theory. 1995

"A critical analysis of John P. Kotter's 'Leading change: why transformation efforts fail'," *Harvard Business Review*, November-December 1994. Quality Management Theory. 1995

"A critical analysis of Rajon R. Kamath and Jeffrey K. Liker's, 'A second look at Japanese Product Development'," *Harvard Business Review*, November-December, 1994. Quality Management Theory, 1995

"A critical analysis of C. Fred Bergsten's, Globalizing Free Trade," *Foreign Affairs*, May-June, 1996. Legal Systems in a Global Economy, 1996

"A critical analysis of Clifford J. Shultz II and Bill Saporito's "Protecting Intellectual Property: strategies and recommendations to deter counterfeiting and brand-piracy in global markets," *Columbia Journal of World Business*, Spring 1966. Legal Systems in a Global Economy, 1996

"Balance of payments," International Business, 1999. A case analysis of "Ford and Mazda share the driver's seat," International Business, 1999

"A critical analysis of Hal B. Gregersen, Allen J. Morrison, and J. Stewart Black's, 'Developing Leaders for the Global Frontier," *Sloan Management Review*, Fall, 1998. International Business, 1999

"A critical analysis of Michael E. Porter and Hirotaka Takeuchi's,

'Fixing what really ails Japan," Foreign Affairs, May-June 1999. International Business, 1999

Digicomp Computer Corporation: a case study," Operational Management, 1999

"Nonanalytical approaches to Operational Management: a critical analysis." Operational Management, 1999

"Shenandoah Valley Region Trauma Care: a case study" Operational Management, 1999

"Steinway and Sons," Business Policy, 1999.

"Goodyear: the Gault Years, 1991-1996," Business Policy, 1999

"Weyerhaeuser Company: a strategic management research project", Business Policy, 2000. 99 pages.

7. Manuscripts prepared for publication but not published

"Academic Libraries in the South, 1850-1900," 87 pages. Rejected by *Journal of Library History*, 1979. "too little use of primary sources and too much reliance on secondary sources."

"Democracy, Local Autonomy and Cooperation," 36 pages. 1992. rejected by Disciples of Christ Historical Society. "does not fit with our current publishing plans."

"The Chaplain as ethicist" 1982. 26 pages, written for *Military Chaplain's Review* but arrived too late for intended issue's scheduled publication.

"The Mythic reality of Athenian Naval Superiority," 14 pages. 1977. "does not fit our publication plans"

8. Bibliographies

A Bibliography on Business and Professional Ethics, Revised 2008. 18 pages.

A Bibliography on Death. Part I: Basic/General. August 1975. 16 pages.

A Bibliography on Death. Part II: For Medical Personnel. August 1975. 16 pages.

A Bibliography on Death. Part III: Ministerial. August 1975. 10 pages.

Death is not dead yet: a bibliographic essay. Prepared for Chaplains and Medical Staff at Camp LeJeune, North Carolina, August 1975. 20 pages.

Death – denial no more: literature on death, 1950-1975. Outline, 2 pages.

Appendix III: Speaking engagements and Presentations.

(Does not include sermons delivered and most presentations in churches, or while on active duty as a Navy Chaplain. In chronological order).

Disciples of Christ representative for Religious Emphasis Week, Iowa State University, Ames, Iowa, 1963.

"The Limits of Christian Ethics in a Pluralistic Society," Dean's Seminar to Faculty of Transylvania University, April 24, 1967.

"What's new in theology?" Lay School of Theology, Christmount Christian Assembly, Black Mountain, North Carolina, July 23-28, 1967

"Old Language in a New Age," an address at Conversations on Theology and Ethics, Christmount Christian Assembly, Black Mountain,, North Carolina, August 21-25, 1967.

"The Nature of the Covenant," three lectures given to the Southeastern United Campus Ministries Conference, Montreat, North Carolina, August 31-September 2, 1967

College youth retreat, resource person, First Christian Church, Knoxville, Tennessee, January 11-12, 1969.

Chapel address at Lexington Theological Seminary, February 12, 1969

"Basics for teaching," Crestwood Christian Church, Lexington, Kentucky, April 1969.

"Keynote on *Purpose*," Religious Week, Midway Junior College, Midway, Kentucky. March 28, 1970

"The Self Study," Transylvania Banquet at Tennessee Assembly of Christian Churches, Memphis, Tennessee, April 1970

"Hegel and religion", Hegel festival, Transylvania University, May 22, 1970

Played the role of Deputy Governor Danforth in Arthur Miller's play, *The Crucible* at Transylvania University, March 3, 6, 1971

"Making moral decisions today," Christian Youth Fellowship, Lafayette Christian Church, Lexington, September 12, 1971

Presentation to theological forum, Georgetown College, Georgetown, Kentucky, September 21, 1971

"The Church and Education," District 8 Annual Convention, .Midway College, Midway, Kentucky, September 26, 1971

"The new Humanities Program at Transylvania and a Report on the Self-Study", presented at East Tennessee Transylvania Society, Oak Ridge, Tennessee, November 4, 1971

"Israel, it's history and contemporary situation," Frankfort Episcopal Men, Holiday Inn, Frankfort, Kentucky, November ??

"What is a liberal arts education?" Student Orientation, Transylvania University, Lexington, September 11, 1972

"The Literary Arts and Theology," Central Kentucky Christian Ministers Association, Lexington Theological Seminary, March 1973

Consultant in the Humanities for Midway College, Kentucky, Spring-Fall, 1973.

"The theological implications of Copernicus," Holleian Society Symposium, Transylvania, April 18, 1973

"Transylvania, the Liberal Arts, and you and me," College Life Seminar, Transylvania, September 10, 1973

Member of the Southern Association visitation team to Shenandoah College and Conservatory of Music, Winchester, Virginia, September 23-25, 1973

"The Christian family faces death," Lafayette Christian Church, Lexington, June 10, 1974

"Talking with children and parents about death," Faculty of United Child Development Center, Lexington, February 1975

"A Christian Perspective on Death," Lenten Forum, Lakewood Christian Church, Lakewood, Ohio, March 1975

"The value of the Liberal Arts in Career Education," Midway College, annual career day. April 1, 1975

"A relevant approach to teaching the Bible," Cooperative Protestant Churches, Richmond, Kentucky, April 6, 1975

"Education in the 21st century," Lion's Club, Augusta, Georgia, 1975

"A Faculty member's expectations on periodicals," Workshop for librarians of small colleges in Kentucky, 1975

"The Physician and Death." Presentation to Navy Doctors at the Navy Regional Medical Center, Camp Lejeune, North Carolina, August 14, 1975..

"Meeting Death," Parents Weekend, Transylvania, October 1975

"The challenge of educational innovation," Board of Curators, Transylvania, October 20, 1975

"Ministry at sea," Religious Leaders Friendship Day (Japanese/American), Chapel of Hope, Commander Fleet Activities, Yokosuka, Japan, April 23, 1986

"Ministry to ships at sea," Religious Leaders Friendship Day (Japanese/American), Chapel of Hope, 1987

"Highlights of a Navy Chaplain's Career," Crista Shores Vespers for Veteran's Day, Silverdale, Washington, November 11, 1998.

Trainer of volunteers for Hospice of Kitsap County, 1998, 2002-2005.

Facilitated "Embracing our Future" a workshop for Hospice of Kitsap County, Community Center, Silverdale, Washington, September 22, 1999.

"Multicultural Awareness", Olympic College, Bremerton Campus, April 10, 2000.

Panel member on "End of Life" coalition, Central Kitsap Presbyterian Church, Bremerton, Washington, June 1, 2000.

"A Tribute to Dr. Bob Rozendal upon his retirement", Silverdale, Washington, August 25, 2000.

"When doing the right thing isn't easy," Leadership Forum on Ethics. Naval Hospital, Bremerton, Washington, March 27, 2003

"Business Ethics is essential" Silverdale Sunrise Rotary Club, 2003

"Why is business ethics essential?" Port Orchard Rotary Club, 2003

A dialogue on ethics with Jim Kendall, West Puget Sound Chapter of Washington State Professional Engineers, Port Orchard, Washington, September 18, 2003

While attending the Advanced Chaplains Course at the Navy Chaplains School, Newport, Rhode Island, Spring1975 visited with LCDR and Mrs. Tom Watson (Dot Couch) Faculty of Navy Justice School. We would be together again while I was at Chapel of Hope and Tom, then a Captain, was Officer in Charge of the Naval Judge Advocate General Office, Commander Fleet Activities Yokosuka. Dot had been a high school student in Summer Youth camp while I was Minister of Education at Woodmont Christian Church. Also visited Touro Synagogue, America's oldest Jewish synagogue. Visited three surviving Shakers at Sabbathday Lake, Maine. Spoke with Sister Mildred and Brother Ted about recent developments in Shaker historiography and courses I was teaching on the Shakers.#

Appendix IV: What might have been

(Listed here are some of the job opportunities which came my way. Some were simply inquiries about interest and availability. Others were genuine offers or involvement in a selection process. These are listed in chronological order.)

1953 Finalist for William H. Danforth Fellowship for graduate education. Would have paid all expenses for a Ph.D. Not selected.

1970 Inquiry from Dr. William Reed about my interest in applying for the Deanship of Add Ran College of Arts and Sciences at Texas Christian University.

1970 Consideration by Search Committee of Drury College, MO for position of President. Not selected. Considered then for Dean of the Faculty. Not selected.

1970 Nominated by Dean John Bryden, Transylvania for National Endowment for the Humanities Summer Fellowship. Not selected.

1971 Nominated by Dean Bryden for Fulbright Fellowship. Not selected.

1972 Offered the position of Academic Vice President at Alaska Methodist University. Did not accept.

1972 Considered for Dean of the College of Arts and Science, Miami University, Ohio. Not selected

1972. Recommended by Mr. Ted Broida, Board of Curators, Transylvania University for administrative positions at University of North Carolina, Charlotte and William and Mary. Not chosen.

1973 Met with Pulpit Committee of Woodmont Christian Church, Nashville, Tennessee for position of Senior Minister upon Dr. Frank Drowota's retirement. Honored, but decided that since I had prepared for a ministry of teaching by obtaining the Ph..D. degree I would continue college teaching rather than assume responsibilities for pastoral ministry.

1973 One of five finalists (150 applicants) for Presidency of Culver-Stockton College, Missouri. Not selected.

1973 One of five finalists for Academic Vice President and Dean of the Faculty, Bethany College, West Virginia. Not selected.

1974 Inquiry from Phillips University for position of Dean of the Graduate Seminary, Enid, Oklahoma

1974 Inquiry from University Christian Church, Austin, Texas for position of Senior Minister.

1975 Inquiry from Phillips University, Enid for position of President. Declined to submit application.

1975 Offered a teaching position in the College of Library Science at the University of Kentucky. Had already committed to active duty as Navy Chaplain.

1978 Adverse fitness report 1978 from Commodore Destroyer Squadron 15 due to disapproval of my decision to divorce Marilyn. Removed by order of Board of Correction of Naval Records, 1979.

1981, 82, 83 Failure to select for promotion to Commander,

1989. 90, 91 Failure to select for Captain

(These "Passovers' were in spite of 4.0 fitness reports and numerous awards and commendations including 3 Navy Commendation Medals and a Meritorious Service Medal. Failure to promote to Commander because of divorce and subsequent marriage to a "foreign national"; to Captain because of age and requirement as a USNR rather than USN to leave active duty at age 60)

2010 Rejection letters from publishers: Abingdon Press, Augsburg Press, Bethany Press, McGraw-Hill, Oxford University Press, Westminster Press for manuscript *Living Life – Facing Death*

2011 Had to give up college teaching at age 79 since the full-time philosophy faculty member decided Olympic College would offer only three courses per term which he would teach in Humanities (Eastern Religions and Western Religions) and Philosophy instead of the 9-12 per term which were being offered. #

Books by the Author

Living Life, Facing Death, Lucas Park Books, 2011.

Death and Dying: Bibliographic Resources, Create Space, 2013

Sacred Moments, Prayers of a Navy Chaplain at Sea and Ashore
Volume I: *Prayers at Sea: Destroyer Squadron Fifteen (CDS15) and USS PELELIU (LHA5).* Create Space, 2013

Sacred Moments, Prayers of a Navy Chaplain at Sea and Ashore.
Volume II: *Prayers at Sea: USS MIDWAY (CV41).*
Create Space, 2013.

Sacred Moments, Prayers of a Navy Chaplain at Sea and Ashore.
Volume III: *Prayers Ashore.* Create Space, 2013.

Sacred Moments, Prayers of a Navy Chaplain at Sea and Ashore.
Volume IV: *Index.* Create Space, 2013

To be a Preacher, Create Space, 2016. (volume 1 of
Thoughts along the way)

Ministering is Caring, Create Space, 2017 (volume 2 of
Thoughts along the way)

To teach is to learn, Create Space, 2017 (volume 3 of
Thoughts along the way)

To teach is to learn, Revised edition, Create Space, 2017

I have something to say, Create Space, 2017. (volume 4 of
Thoughts along the way)

Author may be contacted at pwmurphey@wavecable.com,
360-930-4120 or at 12162 Country Meadows LN NW,
Silverdale, WA 98383.